GLOBAL SECURITY WATCH
SYRIA

GLOBAL SECURITY WATCH
SYRIA

Fred H. Lawson

 PRAEGER

AN IMPRINT OF ABC-CLIO, LLC
Santa Barbara, California • Denver, Colorado • Oxford, England

Library of Congress Cataloging-in-Publication Data

Lawson, Fred Haley, 1952–
    Global security watch—Syria / Fred H. Lawson.
        p. cm. — (Global security watch)
    Includes bibliographical references and index.
    ISBN 978–0–313–35957–6 (hardback) — ISBN 978–0–313–35958–3 (ebook)
1. Syria—Strategic aspects. 2. Syria—Foreign relations—1971– 3. Syria—Politics and government—2000– I. Title. II. Title: Syria.
DS98.6.L39   2013
956.9104′2—dc23   2012035439

ISBN: 978–0–313–35957–6
EISBN: 978–0–313–35958–3

17 16 15 14 13   1 2 3 4 5

This book is also available on the World Wide Web as an eBook.
Visit www.abc-clio.com for details.

Praeger
An Imprint of ABC-CLIO, LLC

ABC-CLIO, LLC
130 Cremona Drive, P.O. Box 1911
Santa Barbara, California 93116-1911

This book is printed on acid-free paper ∞

Manufactured in the United States of America

Contents

Acknowledgments

Geoffrey Schad drew up an initial version of the Chronology for a projected reference volume on Syria that I had hoped the Syrian Studies Association would put together. Mary Ann Wight wrestled the map into shape. I am grateful to both for providing readers with important information in readily accessible ways.

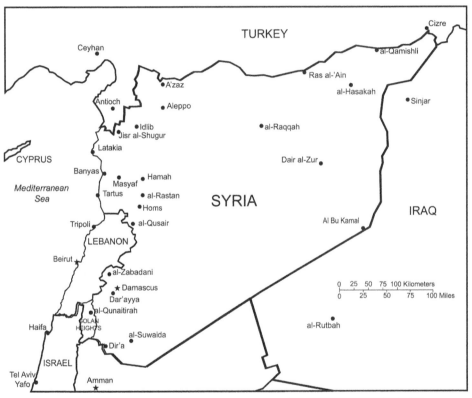

Bruce Jones Design Inc. adapted by Mary Ann Wight

Introduction

During the first week of July 2012, the Syrian navy carried out large-scale exercises involving warships, attack helicopters, and land-based missiles. The purpose of the maneuvers, according to Syrian state television, was to "defend Syria's shores against any possible aggression."[1] At the same time, Iraq's foreign minister warned that cadres of the global terrorist network al-Qa'idah were crossing the border into Syria to spread violence throughout the Middle East.[2] News that a high-ranking commander in the elite Republican Guard had defected and fled to France coincided with reports that delegates to a congress of opposition groups meeting in Cairo had descended into fistfights and chair throwing when the closing communiqué was read aloud.[3] After the congress broke up, one of the two major opposition coalitions, the National Coordinating Committee of the Forces for Democratic Change, issued a statement that praised Syrian soldiers who had refused to shoot at protesters and denounced the militarization of the struggle against the Ba'th Party–led regime, particularly the tactics employed by the Free Syrian Army.[4] Meanwhile, Syria's minister of internal commerce and the protection of consumption admonished citizens to deal with the ongoing shortage of household fuel by "adapting to the crisis" and "organizing themselves to defend their interests."[5]

Taken together, these snapshots illustrate the broad range of threats that confronted Syria during the summer of 2012. Some of these threats came from outside the country's borders, as Syrian officials never missed an opportunity to point out. President Bashshar al-Asad told German television on July 8, for instance, that the violence that had engulfed Syria was the work of "gangs, different kinds of gangs," whose activities were sponsored and funded by Turkey, Saudi Arabia, Qatar, and the United States.[6] The likelihood of an armed clash with Turkey did indeed seem high at that particular moment, barely a week after the

Syrian armed forces had shot down a Turkish reconnaissance aircraft that was fly-ing just outside Syrian airspace.

Other threats facing the country were largely internal. A severe and persistent drought had decimated agricultural production in the years after 2008 and had driven thousands of rural laborers to shantytowns on the outskirts of the cities in search of work and sustenance. An influx of imported manufactured goods from Turkey, and increasingly from the People's Republic of China as well, had ruined local industry and left large numbers of workers, especially in the ineffi-cient state-run companies, with little hope of secure employment. As in other countries of the Arab world, policies that deregulated the market and encouraged the expansion of private enterprise severely disrupted long-established patterns of production and accumulation without generating sustained growth in their place.

Strategic and economic threats paled in comparison with the popular discon-tent that exploded into violence in the spring of 2011. Unlike Tunisia and Egypt, where the military and security forces for the most part restrained themselves in the face of widespread public disorder, Syria exhibited a more familiar and pre-dictable pattern in which troops and proregime thugs almost immediately resorted to force to disperse and punish the protesters. Scattered groups of sol-diers who refused to comply with orders to shoot at unarmed civilians formed popular militias and turned their meager weapons against the authorities. By the eighth month of the uprising, Syria had descended into civil war.

Students of security studies have suggested two different ways to make sense of all this. One way is to explore the connections between foreign and domestic threats. The most influential example of this kind of analysis is Steven David's dis-cussion of external and internal balancing. David argues that highly vulnerable leaderships can be expected to be equally worried about foreign and domestic threats and will take steps that can counteract both kinds of threats simultaneously. Specifically, leaders do their best to break up the coalition of external and internal forces that challenges their position, most often doing so by "split[ting] the align-ment against them and focus[ing] their energies on their most dangerous (domes-tic) opponents. To do this," David continues, "they appease the international allies of their domestic opponents." David labels this strategy "omnibalancing."[7]

Students of Middle East politics have found David's concept of omnibalancing to be highly attractive. Most leaderships across the region confront serious threats from foreign and domestic challengers, usually at the same time; great powers have often formed close partnerships with local actors to carry out their global objec-tives; states in the region are widely believed to be recent creations that lack funda-mental legitimacy as political entities; and the very term *omnibalancing* has connotations that resonate with the complex alliance behaviors that can be observed in this part of the world. The notion has therefore been applied to countries as diverse as Saudi Arabia,[8] Iraq,[9] Oman,[10] Turkey,[11] Uzbekistan,[12] and Iran and Syria.[13] Gerd Nonneman suggests that omnibalancing provides the key to understanding foreign-policy behavior throughout the Middle East.[14]

Applications to Middle Eastern cases tend, however, to use the concept of omnibalancing in ways that drain it of most of its explanatory power. On one hand, the concept has been extended far beyond its original theoretical domain and has been applied to all kinds of foreign and domestic outcomes, not just to why states sometimes change strategic partners. Hillel Frisch, for example, uses omnibalancing to explain why so many monarchies continue to exist in the Arab world.[15] On the other hand, the precise argument that David advances—that vulnerable leaderships forge alliances with the foreign partners of their most threatening domestic rivals—routinely gets watered down to the broad, almost vacuous claim that policy makers "not only balance different elements (threats and opportunities) in the different parts of the external environment (the traditional view), they also need to balance these with the variable pressures at home." Consequently, "the precise 'package' that results will depend on the importance and location of these threats and opportunities."[16] Omnibalancing has become little more than a description of attempts to "integrate domestic and systemic factors in the explanation of changes in international alliances."[17]

An alternative way to comprehend the multiple threats that confront contemporary Syria is to differentiate between state security and regime security. This analytical distinction inspired a substantial academic literature during the early 1990s but failed to generate a sustained research program. Early proponents of the concept of regime security hypothesized that leaders exert greater effort to retain power than they do to defend or further the interests of the country as a whole. As domestic challenges gain momentum, the incentives for a beleaguered leadership to put its own political survival above those of the nation become too strong to resist. This line of argument, like the concept of omnibalancing, was developed with special reference to comparatively weak, poor states and was quickly adopted by scholars concerned with the Middle East.[18]

Those who have tried to disentangle state security from regime security usually claim that comprehensive national interests are more likely to diverge from leaders' parochial interests in autocracies than they do in democracies. It is easy to imagine ways in which autocratic rulers might pursue objectives that jeopardize the security of the country as a whole. In democracies, by contrast, one would expect that leaders who put the survival of the present government ahead of the national interest would soon get removed from office. Yet it would clearly be a mistake to assume that democratic rulers always prioritize the common good above the desire to retain power. Any research program that investigates the circumstances under which regime security trumps state security will need to include all types of political systems.

Like omnibalancing, regime security is generally considered to be more salient in weak, poor countries than it is in strong, rich ones. But even in the former, regimes may either be fragile and vulnerable or well-articulated and resilient. Furthermore, regime building and state building take place at different rates and produce variable outcomes. Studies of security dynamics in the Middle East, or indeed in any region of the world, would do well to chart the trajectories of regime consolidation and state formation, and then explore whatever connections might be present between these two analytically distinct processes.

Security policy in Syria is often assumed to be driven by the interests of a narrow political elite, and more precisely by a handful of powerful individuals who share sectarian, ideological, and even familial affinities. Since 1970, the president, senior commanders of the armed forces, heads of the paramilitary security services, key government ministers, and the inner circle of the ruling party have all been drawn from the minority 'Alawi community. How this came about is a complicated and often poorly understood story.[19] During the late 1960s and early 1970s, the 'Alawi-dominated political elite carried out economic and social programs that gave disproportionate benefits to 'Alawis.[20] After 2000, however, large parts of the 'Alawi community have been marginalized and neglected by state agencies. If it were ever true to say that Syria's political elite and 'Alawi citizenry harbored common interests and acted as a unified bloc, such an assertion has not been warranted for the past decade.

It is equally misleading to claim that the civil war that has gripped Syria since late 2011 constitutes a contest between heterodox 'Alawi rulers and orthodox Sunni challengers. There can be little question that the Syrian Muslim Brothers, a Sunni Islamist movement, quickly gained the ascendency among opposition forces and eclipsed the liberal civil rights activists who drew up the Damascus Declaration in October 2005. Influential 'Alawis have nevertheless played a significant role in the opposition, both inside and outside the country, from the start of the uprising. Escalating violence may well have generated more pronounced polarization along sectarian lines as the months have gone by, but such mutual homogenization of the two contending camps is more a consequence than a cause of the conflict.

Much stands uncertain as of October 2012. The regime survived the initial shock of the popular disorders but defended the existing system with such brutality and indiscriminateness that the revolt escalated rather than diminished as time passed. Opposition forces found themselves unable to draw up a compelling platform and often unable to work with one another. Syria's regional partners have engaged in actions that provoked rising hostility from its primary regional and global adversaries and that threaten to entrap Damascus in conflicts in Lebanon, the Palestinian territories, and the Gulf. All one can do at this point is lay out the major trends that brought things to a crisis. This is not the first time that Syria has confronted a maelstrom of external and internal forces, and it will almost certainly not be the last.

NOTES

1. Reuters, July 8, 2012.
2. Associated Press, July 5, 2012.
3. Reuters, July 3, 2012; *al-Watan* (Damascus), July 4, 2012.
4. Angry Arab News Service, July 8, 2012.
5. *al-Ba'th*, July 8, 2012.
6. British Broadcasting Corporation, July 8, 2012.
7. Steven R. David, "Explaining Third World Alignment," *World Politics* 43 (January 1991): 236.
8. Gerd Nonneman, "Determinants and Patterns of Saudi Foreign Policy," in *Saudi Arabia in the Balance*, eds. Gerd Nonneman and Paul Aarts (London: Hurst, 2005); Baron Reinhold, "Omnibalancing and the House of Sa'ud," unpublished master's thesis, Naval Postgraduate School, Monterey, CA, 2001.
9. Jason E. Strakes, "The 'Omnibalancing' Proposition and Baghdad's Foreign Policy," *Mediterranean Quarterly* 22 (Summer 2011).
10. Marc J. O'Reilly, "Omanibalancing: Oman Confronts an Uncertain Future," *Middle East Journal* 52 (Winter 1998).
11. Robert Olson, "Turkey-Iran Relations, 1997 to 2000," *Third World Quarterly* 21 (October 2000).
12. Matteo Fumagalli, "Alignments and Realignments in Central Asia: The Rationale and Implications of Uzbekistan's Rapprochement with Russia," *International Political Science Review* 28 (June 2007).
13. Anoushiravan Ehteshami and Raymond A. Hinnebusch, *Iran and Syria* (London: Routledge, 1997); Christopher Bergen, "Omnibalancing in Syria: Prospects for Foreign Policy," unpublished master's thesis, Naval Postgraduate School, Monterey, CA, 2000.
14. Gerd Nonneman, "Analyzing the Foreign Policies of the Middle East and North Africa: A Conceptual Framework," in *Analyzing Middle East Foreign Policies and the Relationship with Europe*, ed. Gerd Nonneman (London: Routledge, 2005).
15. Hillel Frisch, "Why Monarchies Persist: Balancing between Internal and External Vulnerability," *Review of International Studies* 37 (January 2011).
16. Nonneman, "Analyzing the Foreign Policies," 13.
17. Fumagalli, "Alignments and Realignments in Central Asia," 254. See also Michael Barnett and Jack S. Levy, "Domestic Sources of Alliances and Alignments: The Case of Egypt, 1962–1973," *International Organization* 45 (Summer 1991). A more nuanced argument, one closer to David's original proposition, can be found in F. Gregory Gause III, "Balancing What? Threat Perception and Alliance Choice in the Gulf," *Security Studies* 13 (Winter 2003–2004).
18. Mark J. Gasiorowski, "Regime Legitimacy and National Security: The Case of Pahlavi Iran," in *National Security in the Third World*, eds. Edward E. Azar and Chung-In Moon (Aldershot: Edward Elgar, 1988); Yezid Sayigh, *Confronting the 1990s: Security in the Developing Countries*, Adelphi Papers 251 (London: International Institute of Strategic Studies, Summer 1990); Bahgat Korany, Paul Noble, and Rex Brynen, eds., *The Many Faces of National Security in the Arab World* (London: Macmillan, 1993); Mohammed Ayoob, *The Third World Security Predicament* (Boulder, CO: Lynne Rienner, 1995).
19. Alasdair Drysdale, "The Syrian Armed Forces in National Politics: The Role of the Geographic and Ethnic Periphery," in *Soldiers, Peasants and Bureaucrats*, eds. Roman

Kolkowicz and Andrzej Korbonski (London: George Allen and Unwin, 1982); Nikolaos van Dam, "Middle Eastern Political Cliches: 'Takriti' and 'Sunni Rule' in Iraq; 'Alawi Rule' in Syria—A Critical Appraisal," *Orient* 21 (January 1980); Nikolaos van Dam, *The Struggle for Power in Syria*, 4th ed. (London: I. B. Tauris, 2011); Hanna Batatu, "Some Observations on the Social Roots of Syria's Ruling, Military Group and the Causes for Its Dominance," *Middle East Journal* 35 (Summer 1981); Hanna Batatu, *Syria's Peasantry, the Descendants of Its Lesser Rural Notables and Their Politics* (Princeton, NJ: Princeton University Press, 1999).

20. Alasdair Drysdale, "The Regional Equalization of Health Care and Education in Syria since the Ba'thi Revolution," *International Journal of Middle East Studies* 13 (February 1981); Batatu, *Syria's Peasantry*, chap. 3; Fabrice Balanche, *La Region Alaouite et le Pouvoir Syrien* (Paris: Editions Karthala, 2006).

CHAPTER 1

Political-Economic Transformation in Ba'thi Syria

For the past half century, Syria has been ruled by a coalition of political actors that includes military commanders, heads of paramilitary security forces, government officials, and senior members of the Socialist Arab Renaissance Party (*Hizb al-Ba'th al-'Arabi al-Ishtiraki*, or Ba'th). These four components of the regime have at various times been joined by industrial workers and farm laborers, by entrepreneurial businesspeople with close personal connections to the military and security forces, and by small-scale private manufacturers and tradespeople. Shifts in the configuration of the dominant political coalition have been associated with different packages of economic and social policy and have provided the foundation for important changes in the country's foreign policy as well. So even though it is correct to say that Syria has had a Ba'thi regime since 1963, the complexion and orientation of the country's leadership have varied profoundly over time.

1963–1965: REVOLUTIONARY AMBIVALENCE

During the first months after the coup d'état of March 1963, the diverse assortment of military commanders who took charge of Syria set out to establish a less exploitative—and therefore nominally "socialist"—order in the financial, industrial, and agricultural sectors of the local economy. State officials seized control of banks and insurance companies in May and announced an Agrarian Reform Law in mid-June. The latter imposed severely reduced ceilings on private landholdings while easing the terms under which farm laborers could purchase agricultural land for their own use. Such measures reflected the program of the radical cadres of the Ba'th Party, whose primary allies were the industrial workers of Aleppo and Damascus and poor farmers and landless laborers who toiled in the central plains around Hamah, the impoverished valleys of the mountainous western coast, and the hardscrabble southern highlands of Dir'a and al-Suwaida.

At the same time, more moderate components of the ruling coalition made an effort to reassure private businesspeople that nationalization would not be carried out against "productive industrial sectors, which sincerely serve the interests of the people."[1] The minister of the economy justified the seizure of the banks in terms of the inordinate degree of influence they exercised over the politicians of the old regime, as well as their reluctance to invest in local projects. By taking steps to pacify propertied interests, especially the industrialists and rich merchants of the cities, state officials managed to retain the acquiescence, if not the active support, of small-scale manufacturers and tradespeople, who harbored deep misgivings about the redistributive inclinations of the Ba'this, proponents of Egyptian-style Arab socialism (Nasirists), and independent socialists who constituted the vanguard of the new order.

Radical delegates to the Ba'th Party congress that took place in Damascus in October 1963 pushed through a resolution that directed the government to set up collective farms on the lands that had been expropriated under the terms of the Agrarian Reform Law. Meanwhile, moderates inside the party managed to postpone the nationalization of Syria's largest industrial companies until a comprehensive study of the manufacturing sector could be undertaken.[2] Toward the end of the year, the moderates relaxed the strict controls on foreign exchange that had been put in place immediately after the coup and began to allow banks to sell foreign currency on the open market.

Tensions between radicals and moderates opened an opportunity for opponents of the Ba'th Party's nominally socialist program to challenge the new regime. Small-scale manufacturers and shopkeepers launched a series of protests and strikes in the north-central cities of Aleppo, Hamah, and Homs from February to April 1964, prompting the authorities to deploy regular army units to suppress the disorders. When popular unrest started to take shape in Damascus, the authorities sanctioned the formation of armed workers' battalions composed of militant union activists from the larger cities. The workers' militia was ordered to break up strikes by shopkeepers and patrol the streets of unruly neighborhoods.[3] These actions were backed up by units of the Ba'th Party's own militia, the National Guard.

Moderates in the ruling coalition responded to the rebellions of early 1964 by relaxing the state's grip on the local economy. The newly appointed prime minister, the Ba'th Party's Salah al-Din Bitar, announced in late May that private enterprise would continue to play a crucial role in the early stages of the country's transition to socialism. In an attempt to combine the public and private sectors with a minimum of conflict, the Council of Ministers proposed to set up a "common sector," in which the state would purchase 25 percent of particular companies and assist in managing them in partnership with private owners. Furthermore, the authorities effectively abandoned the plan to set up collective farms and instead consolidated expropriated land into a collection of more-or-less autonomous agrarian cooperatives.

Such comparatively liberal measures were challenged as early as May 1964 by radicals based in provincial branches of the Ba'th Party. Labor activists seized control of several large factories in the north-central cities and installed a loose form of self-management in these enterprises. By mid-summer, radical Ba'this had succeeded in pressuring the regime to authorize the creation of a countrywide trade union federation and adopt a revised labor law that augmented the government's role in protecting workers' rights.[4] The growing strength of the radical wing of the Ba'th Party became evident later that fall when the party's Regional (Syrian) Command replaced Prime Minister Bitar with General Amin al-Hafiz and then appointed the hardline socialist 'Abd al-Karim Jundi as minister of agrarian reform. The new Council of Ministers supervised the formation of a General Farm Laborers' Union and mandated a pronounced acceleration in the confiscation and redistribution of agricultural land, particularly in the central plains. In mid-December, the Council of Ministers issued a decree that reserved for the state all future revenues from the production of hydrocarbons, a move that, in Itamar Rabinovich's apt phrase, "nationalized in advance" the country's oil and gas sector.[5] Such measures buttressed the position of the radical wing of the Ba'th Party even as they alienated private businesspeople and their allies inside the party.

1965–1969: RADICAL RESTRUCTURING

During the first week of January 1965, state officials issued a package of directives—known collectively as the Ramadan Socialist Decrees—designed to impose state control over the most important economic enterprises in Syria. The decrees nationalized more than 100 of the country's largest industrial and commercial companies and substantially increased state participation in 15 major companies that made up the common sector.[6] Additional steps to enhance the role of the public sector were taken in February. State officials set up the Public Consumption Institution to regulate the distribution of foodstuffs and other essential staples and then created the Import-Export Society to manage the importation of coffee, tea, rice, paper, unrefined sugar, canned meat and fish, iron and steel products, and agricultural machinery.

Small-scale manufacturers and shopkeepers in Aleppo and Damascus reacted to the January decrees by shutting down their businesses and organizing antigovernment demonstrations. The protests were broken up by the police and the workers' militia, who arrested striking tradespeople and confiscated their properties. A special military court went so far as to sentence to death 11 men associated with the wave of strikes on the grounds that they had conspired to return the country to the hands of "reactionary elements."[7] Such draconian measures failed to end resistance to nationalization; sporadic strikes and demonstrations persisted into the spring in Aleppo, Hamah, and Homs. As a result, the authorities curtailed the nationalization program and offered modest compensation to those whose properties had already been sequestered. The government also announced that the construction sector would be left in private hands.

In early May 1965, state officials nationalized 55 large cotton-ginning mills and took charge of the exportation of cotton, wheat, and barley. By the middle of the year, the central administration had seized control of the country's foreign and locally owned electricity companies, petroleum distribution companies, and wholesale trading houses.[8] The government then announced plans to establish a state-run foreign trade organization and a network of public-sector marketing cooperatives to handle the distribution and sale of imported and domestically produced consumer goods.[9] The cornerstone of this complex, the cotton marketing organization, started operations during the first week of June.

Early 1965 thus marks a crucial turning point for Syria's Ba'th Party–led regime. Prior to this time, state officials and party activists had been able to carry out policies that were intended to improve the lives of industrial workers, small farmers, and agricultural laborers without jeopardizing the interests of small-scale manufacturers and tradespeople, whose activities were largely confined to the domestic market. But beginning that January, state officials tightened their grip on key sectors of the local economy, generating a good deal of discontent among the petite bourgeoisie of the north-central cities. This trend led moderate forces inside the ruling coalition to criticize the "inordinate" expansion of the public sector and make overtures to Western governments for economic assistance. Disagreements between the radical and moderate wings of the Ba'th Party over how to handle rising economic tensions and political disorder led to heightened jockeying among disparate factions of the party's Military Committee. This jockeying set the stage for the coup d'état of February 1966, in which allies of Generals Salah Jadid and Hafiz al-Asad displaced the government headed by President Amin al-Hafiz.

Immediately after the February coup, the reconfigured Council of Ministers led by Prime Minister Yusuf Zu'ayyin issued a public statement, which informed foreign governments that they need not reassess their relations with Syria as the country's domestic and foreign policies were going to remain unchanged. Nevertheless, by the first week of March the party newspaper *al-Ba'th* reported that the "mission" of the new Ba'thi leadership would be to improve the Syrian economy through "developing and deepening [its] Socialist experience."[10] The resolutions that were passed at an Extraordinary Regional (Syrian) Congress of the party that took place in mid-March "essentially reaffirmed" the nationalization and centralization programs that had been carried out during the preceding year.[11]

In early March, the government proclaimed the end of the first stage of Syria's agricultural reform program, in which excessive holdings of farmland had been confiscated from large landowners; it announced that a second phase was set to begin, in which expropriated properties would be distributed to small farmers and agricultural laborers. The total area of land seized by the state during 1966 amounted to some 46,000 hectares, down significantly from the 220,800 hectares that had been seized the year before. But almost 70,400 hectares of productive farm land were actually distributed to new owners in 1966, up from the 20,500 that had been passed out in 1965.[12] By the end of the year, local committees consisting of representatives of the Ba'th Party and the farm laborers' union had coalesced to supervise the distribution of land. In addition, state officials boosted the degree of central administrative control over the agrarian cooperatives. Fifty-nine cooperatives were put under the purview of the Ministry of Agriculture and Agrarian Reform in 1966; a further 162 were incorporated by the end of 1967.[13] Through the rural cooperatives, government agencies supervised crop selection, regulated the allocation of such inputs as seeds and fertilizer, and coordinated marketing of the most important cash crops. At the same time, the authorities initiated a number of large, state-run agricultural projects on reclaimed land in the northeastern provinces, where centrally planned irrigation systems were being constructed with the assistance of Soviet advisers.[14]

Industrial policy during the first year or so following the February 1966 coup reflected a concerted effort on the part of state officials to build up large-scale public-sector enterprises in key sectors of the local economy. The largest single project envisaged in the Second Five-Year Plan (1966–1970) was the construction of a high dam across the Euphrates River at Tabqa in al-Raqqah province. This project had been mapped out with help from the Federal Republic of Germany in 1963–1964 but was taken over by Soviet engineers in January 1966 as diplomatic relations between Damascus and Bonn deteriorated. By the end of 1966, the project had been augmented to include a cluster of irrigation works and an ambitious land-reclamation scheme in areas adjacent to the dam.[15] Major investments were also made in pipeline building, railway extension, and port expansion. More important, the government signed contracts with Soviet and Czech companies to build a state-of-the-art fertilizer factory at Homs, with the People's Republic of China to construct a large-scale cotton spinning mill at Hamah, and with a Polish engineering company to outfit a steel rolling plant at Hamah.[16] These projects signaled a sharp rise in heavy industrial investment. During the years 1961 through 1965, annual investment in Syrian industry had averaged some 113 million Syrian pounds; for 1966 through 1967, the figure jumped to around 181 million, reaching more than 252 million in 1968 through 1969.[17]

In an effort to protect infant public-sector enterprises, state officials increasingly restricted the flow of imports coming into the Syrian market.

The government announced in early April 1966 that it would start to levy higher duties on European and Arab products that were reexported into the country from Lebanon. In early June, the Ministry of Finance revised the exchange rate for the Syrian pound, effectively raising the cost of imports.[18] The following January, a ban was imposed on the importation of a broad range of luxury items. Furthermore, state officials made more extensive use of bilateral barter arrangements with the governments of Eastern Europe. These arrangements, like the one signed with Hungary in September, channeled vital imports through public-sector enterprises rather than through private companies.[19] By late October, a joint Syrian-Soviet economic committee had been formed to discuss the implementation of trade and economic assistance agreements between the two countries. As a result of these discussions, Syria's Import-Export Society became the sole agent for Soviet machinery, fertilizers, motorcycles, bicycles, newsprint, and other manufactured goods.[20]

During the fall of 1966, the government came under pressure from workers' unions, whose leaders demanded higher pay and better working conditions in public-sector enterprises. These complaints led to the establishment of a more generous profit-sharing scheme, along with a program run by the newly created General Federation of Women to operate day-care centers for working mothers and training institutes to provide women with industrial and clerical skills. Outlays to fund these policies kept the public sector operating at the edge of solvency and thus enhanced the competitiveness of smaller-scale private manufacturers relative to the large state-run enterprises.

Policies designed to entrench public-sector enterprises in Syria's industrial and agricultural sectors were by early 1967 running up against severe shortages of investment capital. The Second Five-Year Plan called for 60 percent of investment in public utilities to come from the private sector; a virtually identical proportion of total agricultural investment was expected to derive from the same source. Private enterprise was also projected to provide 100 million Syrian pounds to cover the cost of the public debt and other services during 1966 through 1970, along with 125 million for new transportation and communication schemes.[21] One indicator of the importance that the government attached to private capital for the success of the Second Five-Year Plan lies in the promulgation of the Economic Sanctions Law. This statute mandated up to 15 years' imprisonment for anyone convicted of "economic sabotage," an offense that included the transfer of foreign currency and other financial assets outside the country.[22]

Government officials tried to solve the central administration's growing fiscal difficulties by expanding state control over industry and trade. On January 1, 1967, the five largest banks that had been nationalized in 1963 were merged into a single institution, the Commercial Bank of Syria. This move accompanied the consolidation of the financial sector into five sector-specific institutions: the Industrial Bank, the Agricultural Cooperative Bank, the Real Estate Bank, the

Savings Bank, and the Popular Credit Bank.[23] That March the government reorganized the largest public-sector manufacturing enterprises into three industrial associations: one for spinning and weaving, one for food processing, and one for chemical and mechanical production. During the course of the reorganization, Syria's 45 state-run spinning and weaving mills were consolidated into 14 companies; the 21 state-run food-processing enterprises were reduced to 11; and the 43 chemical and mechanical firms merged into 23.[24]

At the same time, the Council of Ministers issued a series of decrees that transferred wholesale trade into the public sector. A government Supply Board took over the distribution of sugar, cooking oil, and salt on domestic markets at the beginning of March 1967. A month later, the police arrested several large private wholesalers for stockpiling tea. Ba'th Party cadres were instructed to keep shopkeepers under close scrutiny in the wake of these arrests and to report any irregularities in the availability or pricing of staple goods.[25] In the wake of widespread shopkeepers' strikes in Aleppo, Damascus, and Hamah during the first week of May, government agents seized the assets of 45 of the richest merchants based in the capital. The party newspaper branded these individuals "Syria's biggest capitalists" and charged that they had been working to undercut the country's economic well-being. Other prominent members of the commercial elite had their properties confiscated and liquid assets frozen in early May as well.[26]

State control over the Syrian economy increased sharply during the months surrounding the June 1967 war with Israel. In the week just prior to the outbreak of the fighting, the government issued decrees that ordered the rationing of sugar, rice, potatoes, tea, and milk products. Subsequent directives prohibited the shipment of flour from one province to another without an official permit.[27] Immediately after the war, regulations were put in place that severely restricted the private sector's access to credit and prohibited the private importation of most consumer goods. The Supply Board made use of these regulations to tighten its hold over wholesale trade: In early September the agency started to offer subsidized credit to tradespeople as a way to draw them away from private suppliers. As a result of this initiative, the Supply Board found itself in a position by early October to open branch offices in several provinces. The board's director issued orders a month later that restructured the clothing market and fixed retail prices for textiles and finished cloth goods, whether they were made domestically or overseas.[28] Consequently, Syria's central administration emerged from the June 1967 war in a stronger position than ever before. In addition, the public sector's predominance in economic affairs was reinforced when oil production got underway in early 1968.

Nevertheless, private companies steadily chipped away at the public sector over the next two years by making more efficient use of the country's scarce financial resources. State-owned enterprises found it impossible to keep up with the rising productivity of private manufacturers, particularly in textiles, food processing, and confectionery. A surge in postwar construction, one crucial area of economic activity that had remained outside the public sector, added to the dynamism and influence of the private sector.

1969–1981: RELAXATION OF STATE CONTROL

In a succession of Ba'th Party congresses between September 1968 and November 1970, radical cadres parried repeated attempts by moderates to scale back the degree of state control over economic affairs. When the moderates drew attention to the centrality of small-scale manufacturers and tradespeople to the country's economic fortunes, radicals led by Jadid and Zu'ayyin responded by proposing that the government create two new party-affiliated popular front organizations, a Federation of Craftspeople and a Federation of Small Income Earners, under the auspices of the Ministry of Economy and the Ministry of Supply, respectively.[29] The proposal ended up being implemented in November 1968.

Radicals then set up a Higher Planning Council in early 1968 and charged it with setting the broad outlines of future economic policy; a State Planning Organization was assigned the task of formulating more detailed directives.[30] These regulatory initiatives appeared on their face to work against efforts by public-sector managers to adopt the profit-oriented strategies that characterized private companies. But in fact the priorities that got generated by these two agencies differed little from those that were entertained by private manufacturers. In an analysis of the regional and sectoral distribution of investment projects carried out by the government during the late 1960s, Alasdair Drysdale finds that "considerations of economic viability and profitability, coupled with an overriding concern with the optimum use of limited financial resources to achieve national economic growth, lead [the State Planning Organization] for the most part to make locational decisions that would do credit to a private entrepreneur."[31] When radicals inside the party tried to assert control over the Higher Planning Council in November and December 1968 by appointing former Prime Minister Zu'ayyin as its chair, moderates formed special party committees to coordinate the activities of state agencies with those of private businesses.[32] The formation of these coordinating committees accompanied a comprehensive reorganization of local administration across the country, which was intended to encourage greater popular participation in policy making.

By the fall of 1968, the Ba'th Party–led regime exhibited a growing split between a radical wing associated with Jadid and Zu'ayyin and a pragmatic wing led by al-Asad. The former favored greater state supervision over economic affairs, the subordination of the armed forces to civilian leadership, and a less antagonistic posture toward the State of Israel. The latter advocated a larger role for private enterprise as a means to stimulate economic growth, continued autonomy for the Military Committee of the Ba'th Party, and a more belligerent policy toward Israel. Pragmatists took over key ministerial posts in May 1969 and pushed through measures that were aimed at reducing the degree of state control over industry and commerce. Free industrial and commercial zones were set up in Aleppo and the port city of Tartus. The Import-Export Society was broken up into five specialized trading companies: for textiles, industrial machinery, pharmaceuticals, metals, and tobacco. The turn toward deregulation was capped with the issuance of Law 348 of 1969, which reopened the country to foreign direct investment in both manufacturing and trade.

Syria's Ba'thi regime therefore started to equivocate in carrying out its socialist program by the end of 1969. In January 1970, state officials implemented two policies that illustrated the growing ambivalence. On one hand, the minister of industry announced that the government was going to take full ownership of all industrial companies that had been only partly nationalized in previous years. This move, he told reporters, was necessitated by the decision that had been reached at the Ba'th Party's September 1966 Regional (Syrian) Congress to abolish the practice of partial nationalization.[33] On the other, the directors of public foreign trading enterprises rolled back restrictions on a wide range of manufactured imports; duties on 191 products imported from neighboring Arab countries were lifted completely. Meanwhile, the Council of Ministers announced plans to offer low-interest loans and other subsidies to small-scale private manufacturers.[34] The Commercial Bank of Syria then started to allow depositors to open accounts denominated in foreign currency on condition that the funds be used to finance transactions in line with Syria's increasingly diffuse development program.[35]

As the 1960s drew to a close, efforts to generate sustained growth by means of large-scale, state-sponsored industrial and agrarian initiatives had created escalating economic problems for the regime. Syria's foreign debt increased dramatically between 1967 and 1970; agricultural production fluctuated wildly after 1965; and heightened imports of machinery and other capital goods produced yawning trade deficits beginning in 1966. Consequently, the radicals' campaign to build up the public sector at the expense of more efficient and limber private companies became unsustainable. The government's fiscal problems opened the door to a resurgence of popular discontent in the north-central cities in 1968 and 1969; new outbreaks of public disorder in turn set the stage for the coup d'état of November 1970, which catapulted al-Asad and the pragmatic wing of the Ba'th Party to power in the name of economic "relaxation" (*infiraj*) or "opening up to the people" (*al-infitah 'ala al-sha'b*).

As its first move after seizing control of the state and party apparatuses, the leadership of the self-styled Corrective Movement called on private businesspeople to assist the government in solving Syria's persistent economic troubles. Addressing a delegation of wealthy Damascene merchants in early December, al-Asad pledged to do everything he could to promote the interests of the private sector. He further promised to initiate a comprehensive reorganization of the public sector with a view to improving its overall efficiency.[36] The shift toward a more liberal economic program gained momentum in early 1971 with the adoption of revised foreign-trade regulations that permitted private companies to import up to 100,000 Syrian pounds' worth of raw materials, machinery, and spare parts on a duty-free basis.[37] That June, the minister of economy and foreign trade announced an end to government restrictions on a variety of consumer and luxury goods.[38]

During the first weeks of 1971, the new leadership compelled the Ba'th Party to form a strategic alliance with five other broadly socialist parties, which took the name the Progressive National Front. It then appointed 173 members to a new People's Council and charged it with drafting a revised constitution and guiding the transition to a system of "popular democracy." Tabitha Petran reports that "the council's first act was to endorse [Hafiz al-Asad's] nomination for the Presidency. A referendum on 12 March [1971] made [al-Asad] President by a 99.2 per cent vote."[39] Meanwhile, the Corrective Movement took steps to subordinate the workers' unions to the Ba'th Party apparatus. Recognizing which way the wind was blowing, the General Federation of Workers' Unions abandoned what it called a posture of "demanding" and accepted the role of a "political" organization on the grounds that asserting labor demands had become unnecessary now that Syria had become a true socialist order.

In the first months of 1972, the central administration eliminated import duties on most staples, including sugar, rice, and flour. Further deregulation of foreign trade took place that spring when private companies were granted permission to import electrical equipment and spare parts. At the same time, state officials stepped up their efforts to encourage private manufacturing: Between mid-1971 and mid-1972, the Ministry of Industry issued more than 100 licenses to individuals and private companies to set up new ventures. Most of these factories engaged in clothing manufacture, food processing, and plastics molding, and virtually all were quite small, with an average capital of half a million pounds.

Private enterprise reacted quickly to the al-Asad regime's economic liberalization initiatives. The private sector accounted for 29 percent of Syria's foreign trade in 1971; figures for 1972 indicate that private companies provided 35 percent of total manufacturing production and employed 62 percent of the workforce. Elisabeth Longuenesse reports that by 1973, the private sector "produced 85 per cent of the chocolate, 51 per cent of the cotton and silk, 94 per cent of the knitted goods, 70 per cent of the socks, 56 per cent of the paint, 45 per cent of the medical supplies, and 78 per cent of the soap" that appeared in the local market.[40] These figures are all the more remarkable given the priorities of the Third Five-Year Plan (1971–1976), under whose terms almost 80 percent of total investment was earmarked for public-sector industry and transportation.

Deregulation became the dominant tendency in Syrian economic policy in the spring of 1974. The Council of Ministers issued a series of decrees in March that relaxed the procedures governing currency exchange and provided incentives for foreign investment to come into the country; subsequent changes in the investment laws made it possible for private investors based inside Syria to contract with outside investors to form joint industrial and agricultural ventures, as well as for foreign firms to bid on Syrian government projects through local brokers.[41] In early 1975, U.S. petroleum-exploration and hotel-management companies were invited to begin operating in the country, while a handful of other Western firms was authorized to undertake joint ventures with public-sector enterprises by the middle of the year.[42] These openings to the international economy were reinforced the following summer by an agreement between Damascus and Washington that guaranteed the inviolability of U.S. capital invested in Syria.

Nevertheless, state officials continued to fund a wide range of large-scale, capital-intensive industrial projects. In July 1974 alone, the government announced that it would start work on the following public-sector enterprises: a factory capable of producing 100,000 tons of sodium carbonate each year, a plant designed to manufacture 10 million electric light bulbs annually, one capable of producing 25 million pencils per year, and major additions to the existing state-run ceramics and phosphate plants. The continued concentration on mechanized industry required a substantial level of investment from the state. In textiles alone, the level of public investment rose from 12 million Syrian pounds in 1971 to 311 million in 1975. This 14-fold increase accompanied a 184 percent increase in the value of public-sector cloth production. In the chemicals sector, the government invested 28 million pounds in 1971 and 883 million by 1975.[43]

Beginning in the mid-1970s, Syrian economic planners encouraged foreign firms and local moneyed interests to participate directly in the expansion of mechanized industry. Fertilizer, cement, aluminum, and phosphate factories received the greatest stimulus during this phase of the country's industrial development, but projects in the areas of textiles, hydrocarbons, and iron and steel occupied a central place in the overall economic program. By the end of 1980, at least 12 large state-run textile factories were operating in Aleppo, Damascus, Hamah, and Idlib. These factories received substantial financial support from Middle Eastern sources—especially from Libya by way of the newly established Syrian-Libyan Company for Industrial and Agricultural Investments—and were more closely linked to external lending institutions than earlier industrialization projects had been. As a result, Syria's indebtedness to the International Monetary Fund and European financial institutions soared during the late 1970s.

These policies provided the conditions under which a new class of industrialists, wholesale distributors, and contractors took root and flourished. This "new bourgeoisie" was concentrated in Damascus but emerged to a lesser extent in Homs, Latakia, and Aleppo as well.[44] Its members made their fortunes by colluding with the state officials and plant managers who controlled public-sector monopolies, either to supply public enterprises with equipment, raw materials, and spare parts or to distribute surplus products on local and outside markets. The nouveaux riches buttressed their position through speculative investments in real estate and construction, creating a booming market in unregulated housing and commercial property in the larger cities.

Small-scale private manufacturers and shopkeepers benefited from the turn toward deregulation as well. Raymond Hinnebusch observes that "the dual public and private engines of the economy drove an impressive economic expansion in the 1970s: real GNP grew 8.2 percent in 1970–75 and 6.8 percent in 1977–80, although much business took the form of real estate speculation and import-export operations, which widened consumption rather than commodity production."[45] By allowing the petite bourgeoisie to play a greater role in industry and commerce, however, state officials gradually lost their monopoly over the financial transactions and investment decisions that shaped the Syrian economy. The trend was most pronounced in the cities of the north-central provinces, where well-to-do manufacturers and tradespeople started to exercise a good deal of autonomy from the central administration.[46] At the same time, private companies increased their share of domestic and export markets at the expense of state-run enterprises. The shift was most apparent in finished cloth goods but could be seen in food processing, furniture assembly, and soap making as well.

Despite the evident resurgence of private enterprise, state officials continued to concentrate public investment in a limited number of large-scale, capital-intensive operations, particularly in the chemical and engineering sectors. The high costs associated with these projects put a greater and greater drain on state resources as the 1970s waned, making 1977 and 1978 a "disastrous" time for public-sector manufacturing. The following year saw a partial recovery in such state-run industries as glass and pottery making, cement production, and the assembly of televisions, refrigerators, and electric motors. But low rates of output and a significant underutilization of capacity persisted in such major industries as textiles, food processing, fertilizer production, and the forging of iron bars and steel cable.[47]

By the late 1970s, state-run agricultural enterprises found themselves equally unable to compete with private farmers. The cost of the irrigation complex connected to the Tabqa dam jumped sharply in 1977 and 1978, making land reclamation in the northeastern provinces virtually unaffordable. State officials therefore turned their attention to dry-land farming and revived a long-neglected proposal that had been drawn up by the Ford Foundation to experiment with innovative techniques under the auspices of the International Center for Agricultural Research in the Dry Areas (ICARDA). The government also invited the United Nations to carry out a comprehensive study of range management and forage crops in the arid districts east of Hamah.[48] At the same time, the State Planning Organization "virtually threw open the entirety of its agricultural sector to scrutiny by the US Agency for International Development [USAID], which with a team of 37 American agronomists scoured the country in 1978 in an effort to pinpoint those bottlenecks impeding the rapid growth of the agricultural sector."[49] On USAID's recommendation, the authorities dismantled the collective farms and redistributed land to their employees as independent holdings loosely connected to the existing agrarian cooperatives. By 1980, "there were fewer than ten state farms in Syria and several of these might more accurately be thought of as research stations than as production units."[50] The few surviving collective farms were subjected to severe criticism, even in official circles, on the grounds that they were too heavily bureaucratized and permeated with corruption to operate in an efficient manner.

In an attempt to revitalize state-run heavy industrial enterprises, the government instituted a program of individual incentives for public-sector employees at the outset of 1979. The program offered bonuses to workers and managers whose performance exceeded prescribed levels; it was complemented by a general raise in pay at public-sector firms, as well as an initiative to insulate daily operations at each facility from centralized supervision and enhance the authority of local managers.[51] These measures accompanied the imposition of higher tax rates on private manufacturing companies and a campaign—particularly in the north-central provinces—to channel domestically produced raw materials away from private companies and into public-sector enterprises instead.

1981–1985: REASSERTION OF CENTRAL DIRECTION

By January 1981, Syria's central administration had begun to shift resources away from new investment in heavy industry and toward current accounts spending as a way to prop up the public sector. Three months later, the Council of Ministers issued Laws No. 181 and 182, which required private importers to obtain the credit they required from state financial institutions and take out import licenses from the Ministry of Economy and Foreign Trade. These measures were implemented in a deliberate attempt to concentrate financial affairs in the hands of government agencies, stem the flood of imports, and diminish the influence of what Deputy Prime Minister for Economic Affairs 'Abd al-Qadir Qaddurah called "parasitic groups in and around the public sector."[52] Anyone who sidestepped the new regulations was arrested on charges of smuggling and tax evasion.[53] Toward the end of the year, the minister of finance announced that the regime was going to reevaluate its decision to set up free zones at Aleppo, Damascus, Tartus, and Latakia because "they have not brought tax benefits for the economy and have failed to attract foreign investment."[54] The shift toward greater state intervention in the economy precipitated a reshuffling of the cabinet in which the ministers of economy and foreign trade, industry, transportation, and agriculture and agrarian reform were all dismissed and replaced by proponents of central planning.

It was under these circumstances that the government drew up Syria's Fifth Five-Year Plan, scheduled to run from 1981 to 1985. At the heart of the plan lay a wide variety of projects aimed at improving the efficiency and productivity of agriculture. For the most part, these projects were located in regions outside the densely cultivated central plains; Dir'a and al-Qunaitirah in the south, Tartus in the west, and al-Hasakah in the northeast were targeted for new agrarian investments in the initial stages of the plan.[55] As a complement to these projects, state-run canning plants were constructed or modernized throughout the northeast as well as around Idlib and Dir'a. Rural electrification and irrigation schemes also received high priority, as did the expansion of pesticide, phosphate, and fertilizer production.

In particular, state planners encouraged the spread of sugar-beet cultivation and refining outside its traditional centers between Homs and Hamah. The government built state-of-the-art sugar factories at Tal Salhab, al-Raqqah, Maskanah, and Dair al-Zur and provided favorable terms on loans to anyone willing to introduce mechanized sugar-beet farming into districts around al-Raqqah, al-Hasakah, and Dair al-Zur.[56] This initiative was undertaken partly as a way to keep up with rising levels of sugar consumption and reduce the importation of raw sugar. But it also represented an attempt by public-sector managers to set up a network of state-affiliated farms to cultivate cash crops for export.[57] Under the terms of the Fifth Five-Year Plan, state agencies were accorded greater command over the marketing of agricultural produce, the introduction of capital-intensive farming techniques into the countryside, and the setting of priorities in the agricultural sector.[58]

New spinning and weaving factories made up most of the manufacturing projects carried out in the early 1980s. Unlike mills built in earlier years, these were not located in the larger cities. They were constructed instead in peripheral regions, most notably Idlib, al-Hasakah, and Dair al-Zur. Among the north-central cities, only Aleppo received sizable investments in heavy industry; these went to finance a steel cable factory and cement plant, while the state-run Military Housing Establishment was awarded a contract to build a storage facility for cotton seed in the city as well. Somewhat surprisingly, no major public-sector industrial ventures were slated for the governorate of Damascus during this period.

Investment capital grew more and more scarce after 1981, and state officials made a concerted effort to regain control over the accumulation and allocation of Syria's financial resources. The government raised taxes on private companies and took steps to divert locally produced raw materials away from private manufacturers and into the hands of public-sector enterprises. The authorities then set up the Committee for the Guidance of Imports, Exports, and Consumption to regulate the commercial sector of the economy. Such initiatives alienated small-scale manufacturers and shopkeepers in the north-central cities, who took to the streets in protest against heightened state intervention in economic affairs. Violent demonstrations erupted in and around Aleppo, Hamah, Homs, and Idlib throughout the summer and fall of 1981, culminating in the large-scale insurrection that broke out in Hamah in February 1982. The authorities deployed both heavily armed security forces and elite military units to crush the protests, leaving whole districts of Hamah and Aleppo in ruins.

State officials responded to the revolt of the north-central cities by tightening the government's grip on the economy. In June 1982, the Ministry of Finance revised the exchange rate for the Syrian pound in a bid to persuade both Syrians working abroad and expatriates residing in the country to turn in their holdings of foreign currency. In early October, the authorities strengthened the regulations that governed the flow of consumer and luxury goods coming into the country;[59] four months later the new prime minister declared a moratorium on the importation of industrial equipment in order to recapture control over this pivotal component of foreign trade.

State involvement in foreign trade continued to expand during the winter of 1982–83. Government officials signed an economic cooperation agreement with the Soviet Union at the end of October. North Korean and Czech companies were awarded contracts for major agricultural and petroleum projects at about the same time, despite the fact that many of these projects had originally been promised to Western consortia. In late April 1983, the minister of commerce of the Islamic Republic of Iran announced that Syria and Algeria were planning to coordinate their commercial policies with those of his country as a way of ameliorating their persistent balance-of-payments difficulties.[60] These moves sharply reduced the amount of imports coming into Syria through private channels, a trend that was furthered by the government's campaign to limit the smuggling of consumer goods across the border from Lebanon.

Government agencies maintained firm control over Syria's foreign trade until mid-November 1984, when the Ministry of Economy and Foreign Trade revised the laws that regulated the availability of letters of credit for purchases abroad. According to the new statutes, private companies that were officially registered with the Commercial Bank of Syria could open credit lines good for no fewer than 360 days. As the *Middle East Economic Digest* noted at the time, this represented "a long time for suppliers to wait to receive their money," and the new laws consequently did little to reverse the country's adverse balance of payments.[61]

Meanwhile, the commanders of elite military formations exercised greater political influence. Many of these commanders enjoyed close personal ties to President al-Asad: the Defense Brigades were led by the president's brother Rif'at al-Asad; the Republican Guard was under the command of 'Adnan Makhluf, a cousin of the president's wife; and 'Ali Haidar, an old comrade of the president from their days at the Military Academy, was in charge of the Special Forces. These formations competed with one another for predominance over security matters. The extent of interservice rivalry became apparent in early 1984. President al-Asad suffered an unexpected heart attack in November 1983; he gave orders from his sickbed that a six-person committee would take over routine policy making in his absence.[62] The committee consisted of the prime minister, the foreign minister, the defense minister, the chief of the general staff, and two senior officials of the Ba'th Party. Rif'at al-Asad was conspicuously left out and quickly mobilized the Defense Brigades to patrol key intersections in the capital. The Republican Guard and Special Forces then took up counterpositions, leaving Damascus divided and on the brink of armed confrontation.

In early March 1984, President al-Asad showed signs of recovery, and pivotal generals in the regular armed forces rallied in opposition to the Defense Brigades. In an effort to avoid outright fighting, the president appointed three vice presidents: a senior party figure (Zuhair Musharaqah), Foreign Minister 'Abd al-Halim Khaddam, and Rif'at al-Asad. The president's brother was required to relinquish command of the Defense Brigades in order to take up the vice presidency but managed to appoint his son-in-law to take his place. Chafing at his forced promotion to a largely ceremonial post, Rif'at ordered the Defense Brigades to reoccupy strategic points in the capital at the end of March. The president then put on his full dress uniform and drove unescorted to Rif'at's house, accompanied by his eldest son Basil. On the way, he commanded the Defense Brigades to return to their barracks; President al-Asad then gave his personal assurance that Rif'at's property and assets would be protected if he would back down. His brother complied, and at the end of May quietly joined a delegation of senior military commanders on a visit to Moscow. From there Rif'at went into exile in Geneva, and the Defense Brigades were broken up and reassigned to the Republican Guard and Special Forces.

1985–1987: CONTROLLED LIBERALIZATION

Rif'at al-Asad returned from exile to attend the January 1985 congress of the Regional (Syrian) Command of the Ba'th Party. Supporters of the president orchestrated the event as a celebration of Hafiz al-Asad's accomplishments, however, and widely anticipated public deliberations about Syria's political and economic future never materialized. In an extraordinary move, delegates to the congress authorized the president to appoint all 90 members to the party's Central Committee. Squeezed out of the reconfigured political elite, Rif'at decamped to Paris.

At the January congress, the Ba'th Party directed state officials to provide greater incentives for private investment as a means to shore up the faltering Fifth Five-Year Plan. The final communiqué of the gathering spelled out a number of steps that needed to be taken in order to encourage exports, including a fundamental reorganization of the complex system of exchange rates and a scheme to cut domestic petroleum consumption in order to free up more oil for sale overseas. The party openly criticized the management and performance of several state-run enterprises and called on the government to adopt more efficient and transparent policy-making procedures in the public sector.[63]

In response to the criticisms, Prime Minister 'Abd al-Rauf al-Kasm reshuffled the Council of Ministers, replacing the ministers of industry, economy and foreign trade, agriculture and agrarian reform, finance, and supply and domestic trade. The new government immediately approached foreign investors in an attempt to attract new investment capital into agriculture and services, although it continued to insist that any outside investments conform to "the horizontal and vertical integration of the economy."[64] These appeals convinced West Germany in early May 1985 to reinstate its economic assistance program, and the European Investment Bank then allocated US$20 million for the expansion of the electrical power station at Mhardah. Meanwhile, Kuwait's Arab Fund for Economic and Social Development agreed to finance the construction of a modern pesticides factory outside Damascus.

Government officials further scaled back the degree of state control over foreign trade in late September 1985 by reducing the advance deposit required from private importers to obtain letters of credit from the Commercial Bank of Syria. New regulations also permitted private companies to pay for imports using foreign currency and to set as much as half of their profits from foreign sales aside in special foreign-currency accounts. By adopting these measures, the authorities hoped to "improve the production of private-sector industries, to supply the market with essential consumer goods, and to eliminate the negative effects of smuggling on the Syrian economy."[65] At the end of the year, official delegations traveled to the Arab Gulf states to solicit investment funds, particularly in tourist ventures. Prospective investors were offered a seven-year holiday on all taxes, additional exemptions on half of any profits that might be generated after that time, variances on customs duties on construction equipment and building materials, and a variety of other inducements.[66]

By the fall of 1986, state officials had started to loosen their grip on Syria's domestic economy as well. The Jordan-based Arab Company for Drug Industries and Medical Appliances and the Syrian-Libyan Company for Industrial and Agricultural Investments signed a contract with the government in September to build a glass-bottle factory as a joint venture with a public-sector enterprise. In early October, Syria and Jordan opened a free zone along their common border into which private industry could bring equipment and raw materials on a duty-free basis and from which finished goods could be shipped to any destination without being subject to customs duties.[67] A group of Syrian, Lebanese, and Arab Gulf investors formed a new agribusiness corporation in January 1987 in which private individuals held 75 percent ownership, with the state retaining 25 percent. The company was the first one to be set up under the terms of the reinstated 1964 law that permitted the establishment of mixed-sector ventures.[68]

The government announced in May that it would allow private manufacturers to retain 75 percent of the foreign currency that they earned through export sales, provided that the funds were deposited in the Commercial Bank of Syria.[69] Official frustration with the inefficiency and waste that permeated public-sector engineering projects erupted in mid-June with the forced resignation of the minister of construction. Similar accusations led to the resignation of the minister of agriculture and agrarian reform a month later.

Private enterprise received a significant fillip at the end of April 1987 with the adoption of Law No. 279. The terms of this statute authorized the Ministry of Economy and Foreign Trade to permit private companies to export a wide range of industrial and agricultural goods and apply 75 percent of the profits to further activities.[70] When the prime minister and president of the General Federation of Workers' Unions tried to reimpose state supervision over the activities of the private sector by forming a Commission for the Rationalization of Imports, Exports, and Consumption to administer Law No. 279, proponents of greater liberalization resisted, leading to the dismissal of the prime minister and four of his closest allies in early November.[71]

Unlicensed private traders and moneychangers continued to be harassed by government agents even under the more liberal commercial and financial regulations that were adopted in the mid-1980s. Penalties for smuggling foreign currency and precious metals in and out of the country were stiffened in early September 1986, while several public-sector managers were fired for "abusing their positions" later that same month.[72] To show that they meant business in enforcing currency restrictions, the authorities ordered the security forces to raid the moneychanging establishments that had proliferated along the Damascus-Beirut highway and confiscate any Syrian banknotes held by their owners.

Controlled liberalization buttressed the position of two social forces that became pillars of Syria's ruling coalition: the "new bourgeoisie" that profited from its intimate connections to the public sector and state apparatus, and the agrarian entrepreneurs who emerged as powerful actors in the countryside during the mid-1980s. These forces joined small-scale private manufacturers and tradespeople in prospering as a result of the government's liberalization program. Private interests accounted for more than 40 percent of total fixed capital formation throughout the second half of the decade. Mixed-sector farm companies that produced cash crops for export and commercial real-estate projects turned out to be particularly lucrative at the end of the 1980s.

Greater private-sector involvement in domestic and foreign trade accompanied a marked resurgence on the part of private and mixed-sector manufacturing. Volker Perthes reports that the late 1980s saw "a significant real increase in the number of bigger industrial establishments," particularly ones that had "comparatively large capital investments" and employed more than 50 workers each.[73] The most profitable of these ventures were large-scale clothing factories that produced shirts, underwear, and socks; companies specializing in cosmetics, confectionery, and tobacco products also earned healthy profits. All of these companies carried on a thriving trade with the Soviet Union and Eastern Europe. During the late 1980s, Syrian manufacturers contracted with Soviet state trading companies to supply moderate-quality goods at premium prices, generating returns that greatly exceeded any that Syrian goods could command on the open market.

At the end of the decade, the authorities in Moscow slashed the prices they were willing to offer for Syrian products. Soviet officials also began to insist on a greater number of countertrading arrangements, whereby specified quantities of Syrian goods would be supplied to Soviet buyers in order to retire Damascus's outstanding military debts. In response to changes in the terms of trade with the Soviet Union, Syrian officials opened up the government's hard currency reserves to companies that supplied goods to Soviet markets. Consequently, Syrian exports to the Soviet Union and Eastern Europe rebounded in 1989 and 1990.

Private-sector gains altered the distribution of power inside Syria's dominant social coalition. The change was most obvious in the role played by the chambers of commerce and industry in formulating economic policy. From 1963 to 1981, the chambers had exercised little if any influence in policy-making circles. Steven Heydemann observes that in 1974, "a Syrian economist noted in a semi-official study that the chambers of commerce no longer had a meaningful place in the country's political economy, and were badly in need of reform in keeping with the new realities of Syrian socialism."[74] By the late 1980s, however, prominent members of the Damascus Chamber of Commerce had taken positions in several government agencies, most notably the Committee for the Guidance of Import, Export, and Consumption. Such posts enabled the commercial elite of the capital to voice opinions at the highest levels. As one senior member of the Damascus chamber told Heydemann in August 1991, "Whether we agree or disagree with its decisions, we are there in the room and they consult us on every step."[75]

Military commanders and public-sector managers grew increasingly concerned about the burgeoning influence of the new bourgeoisie as the 1990s opened. In his March 1990 Revolution Day address, President al-Asad himself hinted that political fissures might arise as a result of the government's liberalization policies. He remarked that "restricting freedom tarnishes it, but regulating its practice makes it brighter. Restricting freedom means dwarfing it, but regulating its practice means developing it and making it healthy. . . . Like everything else in this universe, freedom needs order."[76] His comments launched a campaign by the Ba'th Party to reinvigorate its institutional links to the General Federation of Workers' Unions, the General Farm Laborers' Union, and the Youth Federation. The presidents of the first two of these party-affiliated popular front organizations were appointed to the reconfigured Committee for the Guidance of Import, Export, and Consumption, which was charged with coordinating the week-to-week activities of the public and private sectors.

At the same time, the number of seats in the People's Assembly was increased from 195 to 250, and non-Ba'this were encouraged to run as independent candidates. The elections of May 1990 resulted in victories for a number of well-to-do businesspeople who had campaigned on a platform of furthering economic reform and ferreting out inefficiency and corruption. Confronted with a strong showing by proponents of deregulation, the two rival wings of the Syrian Communist Party announced in July that they were going to reconcile. Nevertheless, the success of independent candidates—not to mention the four seats won by religious notables from districts in Aleppo and Idlib—heralded a resumption of the contest between state officials, public-sector managers, industrial workers, farm laborers, and the new bourgeoisie on one side and private manufacturers and tradespeople on the other for control over economic policy.

1990–1999: LIBERALIZATION UNBOUND

In early 1990, Syria's balance of trade moved into the black for the first time in more than three decades. The Ministry of Economy and Foreign Trade attributed the surplus to a 60 percent rise in nonpetroleum exports the previous year, the largest share of which consisted of private-sector manufactures and private- and mixed-sector agricultural produce. Much of the surplus resulted from a dramatic increase in the value of goods shipped to the Soviet Union. In addition, output at the oil fields around Dair al-Zur reached record levels, primarily due to improved methods of extracting petroleum from existing wellheads.

Economic prospects brightened further as world oil prices jumped during the winter of 1990 and 1991. The French oil company Elf Aquitaine inaugurated production at two new wells outside Dair al-Zur in January 1991, then discovered an additional pool of light crude in the same concession. Shortly thereafter, the European Economic Community rescinded its freeze on economic assistance to Syria and released a package of concessionary loans worth almost US$200 million; at the same time, the Japanese government announced grants totaling some US$466 million. The Council of Ministers promulgated a revised investment law that May, Law No. 10 of 1991, which provided generous incentives to projects that augmented exports, reduced imports, and increased jobs for Syrian workers. The statute set up a Higher Council for Investment to award licenses to companies that agreed to abide by the regulations. More than 250 licenses were awarded during the law's first year in force, most of which involved tourism, transportation, vehicle rental, and food processing. After Law No. 10 was revised to permit Syrian citizens to invest hard currency on the same terms as nonnationals and expatriates, another 150 more applications were approved. Minister of Finance Muhammad Khalid al-Muhaini reported in early 1992 that proceeds from the sale of locally raised vegetables and livestock had more than offset the rising cost of food imports.

Meanwhile, the state-run sectors of the Syrian economy—including industry, transportation, and mining—exhibited a marked decline in capital formation. Public-sector managers took steps to reverse the trend by modernizing and replacing aging facilities: In late 1990, the General Organization for Textile Industries solicited offers to build a new cotton spinning mill at Idlib, and the General Fertilizer Company put out a tender for a new triple superphosphate fertilizer factory. In January 1991, the minister of planning announced that the fiscal 1992 budget would allocate more funds for investment in public-sector industry and mentioned in particular plans to build a new iron and steel complex outside Hamah and renovate the problem-plagued paper mill at Dair al-Zur.

Public-sector managers hoped that such projects would attract the attention of Western investors, but firms based in the United States proved reluctant to become involved outside the petroleum sector of the Syrian economy. West European capital showed a greater willingness to invest: German, French, and Spanish consortia bid on the proposed fertilizer plant; Italian and German firms made offers to build the Idlib spinning mill; and Austrian, Italian, Japanese, and German corporations tendered bids for the iron and steel complex. But Western investment proved insufficient to replace the concessionary funding and technical support that had previously come from the Soviet Union and Eastern Europe. Instead, Arab Gulf governments stepped in to finance improvements to public-sector enterprises. The Kuwait Fund for Arab Economic and Social Development agreed in July 1991 to bankroll the Idlib cotton mill, while the iron and steel works ended up being financed by Saudi Arabia. Other Arab Gulf monies paid Bulgarian, Polish, Czech, and Hungarian companies to complete long-standing irrigation and infrastructure projects.

Thanks to connections to the former Communist Bloc, Syria's public sector acquired the resources it needed to maintain its position in the face of rapidly expanding private companies. Nevertheless, friction between the two broad sectors intensified. The contest between public and private enterprise was most clearly evident in the struggle over electricity: Output by the state-run electrical power generating establishment proved less and less able to keep up with spiraling demand. The increasing incidence and length of power outages in industrial, commercial, and residential neighborhoods during the winter of 1991–1992 made it difficult for new manufacturers to keep their production lines operating. Finally, in a desperate attempt to placate consumers, the municipality of Aleppo granted two private companies permission to set up generating stations.

Radical Ba'thi and Communist deputies voiced displeasure over the government's draft budget when it was submitted to the People's Assembly for consideration in April 1992. Planned reductions in social welfare spending and the low tax rates levied on private businesses elicited strong criticism from representatives of the workers' and farm laborers' unions. Discontent inside the General Farm Laborers' Union boiled over once again in late August, when Prime Minister

Mahmud al-Zu'bi announced that the government intended to increase support for export-oriented private agriculture. In preparation for its December 1992 congress, the General Federation of Workers' Unions compiled a lengthy list of grievances concerning the adverse impact of the state's liberalization policies. An influential faction inside the organization was prepared to recommend that the federation loosen its ties to the Ba'th Party so that workers' demands could be articulated outside existing channels. The potential for unrest among industrial workers increased further in the spring of 1993 when public-sector managers started to lay off more experienced, higher-paid employees and replace them with younger laborers in an attempt to cut costs.

Faced with growing discontent inside the Ba'th Party–affiliated popular front organizations, state officials allocated additional resources to revitalize Syria's crumbling public-sector enterprises. The board of directors of the state-run tractor factory outside Aleppo announced in August 1992 that it would reopen its assembly line using diesel engines purchased from the United Kingdom. From mid-1992 to mid-1993, the government awarded contracts to the Military Housing Establishment to build grain silos throughout the country. At the same time, however, state agencies took pains to consolidate relations with the new bourgeoisie: the Ministry of Economy and Foreign Trade hinted in September 1992 that it was going to allow private companies to keep 100 percent of their export earnings to enable them to maintain or expand their operations; the Higher Council for Investment then approved 20 more licenses to private companies under the terms of the May 1991 investment law.

Stimulated by such measures, private actors moved into areas of the local economy that had previously been reserved for the public sector. In the spring of 1994, a local subsidiary of a Greek industrial-equipment corporation broke ground for a plant outside Tartus to manufacture turbines, generators, and cranes for export. That fall the Higher Council for Investment authorized construction of the first private cement factory to be built in Syria after the 1963 revolution. Flour milling and steel rolling were opened to private companies in November 1995. Such operations competed directly with existing state-run enterprises in both domestic and export markets.

Growing pressure to resolve the coordination problems plaguing the domestic economy gave state officials an incentive to rely more heavily on the armed forces. When a group of private entrepreneurs announced plans to build a new cigarette factory outside Damascus in the spring of 1993, army units led by Basil al-Asad were ordered to suppress the smuggling of tobacco products across the border from Lebanon. More predictably, when fighting broke out in a poor neighborhood of Aleppo in July 1993 following a dispute over the distribution of interrupted water supplies, troops were sent into the district to restore order. In this way, the government's twin policies of deregulating the local economy and promoting private enterprise provided opportunities for senior military officers to exercise their muscles.

Three significant political developments accompanied the economic dynamism of the early 1990s. First, President al-Asad began to cultivate his son Basil as his successor: Posters appeared across the country bearing photographs of the father and son together, the president started to be introduced on formal occasions as "the father of Basil" (*abu Basil*), and Basil was promoted to the rank of brigade commander in the Republican Guard. Second, the People's Assembly carved out a greater role for itself in policy deliberations: Debates on the assembly floor became more animated, particularly when they concerned allegations of mismanagement and corruption in the public sector; parliamentary election campaigns became increasingly competitive; and prominent businesspeople emerged as major players in the assembly in the wake of the 1994 elections. Third, the authorities took unprecedented steps to cultivate a religious aura around the regime: Alliances were forged with prominent Sunni figures, including Muhammad Sa'id Ramadan al-Buti, Ahmad Badr al-Din Hassun, Muhammad al-Habash, and 'Abd al-Latif al-Farfur; greater tolerance was shown toward cultural and social activities undertaken by religious networks, most notably the Zaid Group (*jama'ah Zaid*) founded by 'Abd al-Karim al-Rifa'i and the Abu al-Nur Institute led by the Naqshbandi Sufi shaikh Ahmad Kaftaru;[77] conversion to Shi'ism was encouraged through the rehabilitation of Shi'i monuments and the revival of long-shuttered Shi'i theological institutes outside the shrine of al-Sayyidah Zainab in southern Damascus;[78] even the wildly heterodox Yazidi community was permitted to set up an association to further its social and cultural interests.[79]

Basil al-Asad's meteoric rise to power came to a crashing halt when he was killed in an automobile accident in January 1994. The president's second oldest son, Bashshar, was immediately recalled from the United Kingdom, where he was working as an eye doctor, and inserted into the officers' training program. He found himself promoted to the rank of colonel in the Republican Guard despite having no previous military experience. More important, he was assigned responsibility for overseeing the antismuggling campaign along the Lebanese border, squeezing out Vice President 'Abd al-Halim Khaddam. At the same time, a younger generation of commanders moved into senior positions in the armed forces and security services, presumably due to their affinity to Bashshar al-Asad. The drive to displace the old guard culminated in the forced retirement of Chief of Staff Hikmat al-Shihabi in June 1998 and his replacement by a career officer who had no history of involvement in politics.

Friction between the public and private sectors resurfaced as the 1990s drew to a close. Small-scale manufacturers and shopkeepers openly criticized the Commercial Bank of Syria for rejuggling exchange rates in 1996 as a way to prop up state enterprises. Subsequent elections for the governing council of the Damascus

Chamber of Commerce provided businesspeople with a referendum on the broad shape of economic policy; Riyad Saif, an outspoken critic of government inefficiency and corruption, unexpectedly won a seat on the council. Such chronic problems were compounded by two unpleasant surprises during the course of 1997: a sharp drop in oil revenues and the outbreak of a severe drought that lingered for two years.

State officials tried to cushion the impact of slumping oil revenues and shortfalls in agricultural production by building bridges to Iraq. The government negotiated a set of commercial agreements with the authorities in Baghdad that sent Syrian-made textiles, processed food, and consumer goods to Iraqi markets in exchange for a combination of cash payments and deliveries of Iraqi oil. These transactions generated a burst of output and higher returns for state-run enterprises while profiting a wide range of private-sector manufacturers and farmers as well. As the local economy started to revive, the Council of Ministers cut public spending, particularly for social welfare and education. In addition, the authorities reopened talks with the European Union over the conditions under which Syria might join the Euro-Mediterranean Partnership.

Syria's domestic economy gained additional momentum as world oil prices began to recover in 1999. By the fall of 2000, between 150,000 and 200,000 barrels of Iraqi petroleum were moving across Syria every day to the refinery at Homs and the export terminus at Banyas. A substantial proportion of this oil was channeled through the state-run petroleum distribution system for internal use, allowing Syria's own oil to be sold overseas. The influx of Iraqi oil accompanied a steady increase in bilateral trade, which peaked at approximately US$3 billion by late 2002. Proceeds from the petroleum scheme and exports to Iraq kept public-sector enterprises afloat and enabled the government to raise wages for state employees. Remarkably, capital formation in state-run enterprises outpaced private companies by a wide margin at the end of the decade.

State officials took steps to placate private business and entice foreign investors as a way to offset measures to resuscitate public-sector enterprises. In June 1999, a special ministerial committee forwarded to the People's Assembly a set of amendments to Law No. 10 of 1991 that made it possible for foreign firms to own the land on which their plants were sited; a package of additional tax incentives for companies that engaged in exports quickly followed. When Minister of Economy and Foreign Trade Muhammad al-'Imadi rejected calls from the Damascus Chamber of Commerce to abolish the awkward system of dual exchange rates, President al-Asad riposted by granting an amnesty for persons convicted of holding and using foreign currency. More important, state officials in October 1999 took an important step toward enforcing trade regulations in a uniform manner by shutting down an illegal port facility that had been operated at Latakia by the family of Rif'at al-Asad.

At the same time, increased food exports to Iraq combined with Syria's growing population to give agrarian entrepreneurs and small farmers alike a strong incentive to expand grain production. Much of the augmented cereals cultivation took place on marginal land that required intensive irrigation, but heightened demand for wheat and barley prompted landholders in the central plains to boost output by irrigating their fields as well. By the same token, rising demand for textiles both at home and in Iraq resulted in a substantial expansion of cotton production. These trends dramatically escalated rates of water use in the countryside, compounding recurrent shortages of water in the cities. In a desperate bid to augment rapidly shrinking water supplies, the Ministry of Irrigation in early 1999 resumed work on a massive dam across the Khabur River south of al-Hasakah.

Meanwhile, President al-Asad appeared in public less and less often. In February 1999, he came away with 99.98 percent of the vote in a plebiscite for his fifth term as president. The president ventured out of the presidential palace to come to the People's Assembly to be sworn in but uncharacteristically did not deliver an inaugural address. Anxieties about the health of the president, combined with heightened intersectoral rivalry and uncertainties about the future of agriculture, precipitated conflict in the political arena. At the end of November 1999, the president's third son, Mahir al-Asad, shot and wounded the chief of Military Intelligence, the president's son-in-law 'Asif Shawkat. The shooting was reported to have arisen out of a heated argument about the closure of Rif'at al-Asad's private port, with Shawkat—a close ally of Bashshar al-Asad—defending the dismantling of the facility. A month later, members of the People's Assembly publicly derided the minister of finance after he introduced the annual budget for 1999 a mere three days before the end of the year. Riyad Saif complained in an open letter to the state-sponsored daily *Tishrin* in late January 2000 that Syria's banks had become nothing more than "a channel for providing loans to those who do not deserve them" and that private businesspeople were increasingly "afraid, confused, shackled and unable to perform [their] hoped-for role in the development process." More ominously, the powerful chief of Internal Security, 'Ali Duba, unexpectedly resigned his command.

Under these circumstances, a new Council of Ministers that was widely reported to reflect the reformist inclinations of Bashshar al-Asad was formed in mid-March 2000. Twenty-two new faces could be found among the 36 ministers, including Prime Minister Muhammad Mahmud Miru, who had previously served as governor of Aleppo province and did not hold a senior position in the Ba'th Party. The head of the free-zone establishment, who was said to be intimately "acquainted with the concerns of private business," was promoted to the influential post of deputy prime minister for economic affairs. Bashshar al-Asad remarked that the Miru government's top priority would be to "modernize the administration and decrease the level of corruption."[80] Nevertheless, long-serving ministers retained the crucial portfolios for foreign affairs, defense, interior, economy and foreign trade, and finance.

Rumors then started to circulate that the Ba'th Party was going to convene a congress of the Regional (Syrian) Command for the first time since the landmark 1985 gathering. *Middle East Economic Digest* observed that such a meeting "will provide an opportunity to hold a searching internal policy debate, as well as to bring figures from the younger generation into positions of political influence."[81] Major reforms looked imperative in light of the country's growing population, which was pumping an estimated 250,000 job seekers into the local market each year. There were reports of sporadic street protests against cuts in food subsidies and medical care in some impoverished communities, and in early May former prime minister al-Zu'bi was expelled from the Ba'th Party and arrested on charges of siphoning public funds into his family's businesses. The news that al-Zu'bi had managed to commit suicide in the presence of Damascus's chief of police fueled speculation that he had been silenced before he could testify in open court to widespread corruption on the part of other senior officials.

NOTES

1. Itamar Rabinovich, *Syria under the Ba'th 1963–66: The Army-Party Symbiosis* (New York: Halsted Press, 1972), 64.

2. Ibid., 93–94.

3. Tabitha Petran, *Syria* (New York: Praeger, 1972), 176.

4. V. V. Vavilov, "The Nature of the Socioeconomic Changes in Syria," in *Problems of the Economy and History of the Countries of the Near and Middle East*, ed. E. S. Tefimov et al. (Washington, DC: Joint Publications Research Service, 1967), 52.

5. Rabinovich, *Syria under the Ba'th*, 139.

6. Ibid., 140–42; Petran, *Syria*, 179.

7. Rabinovich, *Syria under the Ba'th*, 140.

8. Petran, *Syria*, 179.

9. Vavilov, "Nature of the Socioeconomic Changes," 53.

10. *Arab Report and Record* (ARR), February 15–28, 1966.

11. Rabinovich, *Syria under the Ba'th*, 207.

12. Syrian Arab Republic, Ministry of Planning, *Statistical Abstract 1966* (Damascus: Government Printing Office, 1967), 330–31; Ziad Keilany, "Land Reform in Syria," *Middle Eastern Studies* 16 (October 1980), 212.

13. Bichara Khader, "Propriete agricole et reform agraire en Syrie," *Civilisations* 25 (1975), 72–73; Francoise Metral, "Le monde rural syrien a l'ere des reformes," in *La Syrie d'Aujourd'hui*, ed. Andre Raymond (Paris: CNRS, 1980), 30; *Middle East Record* 3 (1967), 504.

14. Robert Springborg, "Baathism in Practice: Agriculture, Politics and Political Culture in Syria and Iraq," *Middle Eastern Studies* 17 (April 1981), 192–93.

15. United Nations Economic and Social Office in Beirut, *Studies on Selected Development Problems in Various Countries of the Middle East* (1969), 85–86.

16. ARR, June 16–30, 1966, October 1–15, 1966, and November 16–30, 1966.

17. E. Kanovsky, *Economic Development of Syria* (Tel Aviv: University Publishing Projects, 1977), 47.

18. ARR, September 1–15, 1966.

19. Ibid.

20. ARR, October 16–31, 1966, and November 16–30, 1966.

21. Syrian Arab Republic, Ministry of Planning, *Second Five-Year Plan 1966–1970* (Damascus: Office Arabe de Presse et de Documentation, n.d.), 65.

22. Ziad Keilany, "Socialism and Economic Change in Syria," *Middle Eastern Studies* 9 (January 1973), 67; ARR, May 16–31, 1966.

23. Economist Intelligence Unit, *Quarterly Economic Review of Syria* (QERS), first quarter 1967.

24. *Middle East Record* 3 (1967), 505.

25. Ibid., 501.

26. Ibid., 500.

27. Ibid., 502.

28. Ibid., 501; *Economic Review of the Arab World* (Beirut) 1 (December 1967).

29. *Middle East Record* 4 (1968), 722.

30. Fred Gottheil, "Iraqi and Syrian Socialism: An Economic Appraisal," *World Development* 9 (September–October 1981), 831.

31. Alasdair Drysdale, *Center and Periphery in Syria: A Political Geographic Study*, unpublished doctoral dissertation, University of Michigan, 1977, 180.

32. *Middle East Record* 4 (1968), 718–19.

33. *Middle East Record* 5 (1969–1970), 1182.

34. QERS, first quarter 1970.

35. QERS, second quarter 1970.

36. *Middle East Record* 5 (1969–1970), 1164.

37. QERS, second quarter 1971.

38. *Economic Review of the Arab World* 5 (June 1971).

39. Petran, *Syria*, 250.

40. Elisabeth Longuenesse, "The Class Nature of the State in Syria," *MERIP Reports*, no. 77 (May 1979), 7.

41. QERS, June 7, 1974.

42. Syed Aziz al-Ahsan, "Economic Policy and Class Structure in Syria: 1958–1980," *International Journal of Middle East Studies* 16 (August 1984), 311.

43. "L'Industrie: Secteur pilote de l'economie," *Syrie et Monde Arabe*, no. 348 (February 25, 1983).

44. Eric Rouleau, "Syria: Clubbing Together to Beat the System," *Guardian Weekly*, July 24, 1983; Hanna Batatu, "Syria's Muslim Brethren," *MERIP Reports*, no. 110 (November–December 1982), 19–20.

45. Raymond A. Hinnebusch, "The Political Economy of Economic Liberalization in Syria," *International Journal of Middle East Studies* 27 (August 1995), 311.

46. Eric Rouleau, "La Syrie ou le miroir aux alouettes II: Le club d'Alep," *Le Monde*, June 30, 1983.

47. David W. Carr, "Capital Flows and Development in Syria," *Middle East Journal* 34 (Autumn 1980), 459–64.

48. Springborg, "Baathism in Practice," 193.

49. Ibid., 194.

50. Ibid., 197.

51. Carr, "Capital Flows and Development," 465.

52. *Middle East Economic Digest* (MEED), May 22, 1981.

53. QERS, second quarter and fourth quarter 1981; *Wall Street Journal*, July 23, 1981.

54. MEED, November 20, 1981.

55. "Etude analytique de l'economie Syrienne: 1981," *Syrie et Monde Arabe*, no. 345 (November 25, 1982), 2–5.

56. "La culture de la betterave et la fabrication du sucre," *Syrie et Monde Arabe*, no. 347 (January 25, 1983).

57. "Les fermes d'etat," *Syrie et Monde Arabe*, no. 349 (March 25, 1983).

58. "Les transformations economiques et les perspectives de developpement agricole," *Syrie et Monde Arabe*, no. 349 (March 25, 1983).

59. MEED, October 22, 1982.

60. MEED, May 6, 1983.

61. MEED, November 16, 1984.

62. Alasdair Drysdale, "The Succession Question in Syria," *Middle East Journal* 39 (Spring 1985).

63. MEED, February 1, 1985.

64. MEED, April 12 and 26, 1985.

65. MEED, November 2, 1985.

66. *Economic Review of the Arab World* 19 (December 1985).

67. *Economic Review of the Arab World* 20 (October 1986).

68. MEED, January 24, 1987.

69. MEED, May 9, 1987.

70. *Syrie et Monde Arabe*, no. 399 (May 1987).

71. *New York Times*, November 2, 1987.

72. MEED, September 6 and 13, 1986.

73. Volker Perthes, "The Syrian Private Industrial and Commercial Sectors and the State," *International Journal of Middle East Studies* 24 (May 1992), 212–13.

74. Steven Heydemann, "Taxation without Representation," in *Rules and Rights in the Middle East*, eds. Ellis Goldberg, Resat Kasaba, and Joel S. Migdal (Seattle: University of Washington Press, 1993), 89–90.

75. Ibid., 92.

76. Fred H. Lawson, *Why Syria Goes to War* (Ithaca, NY: Cornell University Press, 1996), 139.

77. Leif Stenberg, "Naqshbandiyya in Damascus: Strategies to Establish and Strengthen the Order in a Changing Society," in *Naqshbandis in Western and Central Asia*, ed. Elisabeth Ozdalga (Istanbul: Swedish Research Institute, 1999); Thomas Pierret, "Sunni Clergy Politics in the Cities of Ba'thi Syria," in *Demystifying Syria*, ed. Fred H. Lawson (London: Saqi Books, 2009).

78. Myriam Ababsa, "The Shi'i Mausoleums of Raqqa," in *Demystifying Syria*, ed. Lawson; Abdulrahman Alhaj, *State and Community: The Political Aspirations of Religious Groups in Syria 2000–2010* (London: Strategic Research and Communication Centre, n.d.), 42 note 62.

79. Alhaj, *State and Community*, 48.

80. Eyal Zisser, *Asad's Legacy* (New York: New York University Press, 2000), 47.

81. MEED, March 24, 2000.

FURTHER READING

Hanna Batatu. *Syria's Peasantry, the Descendants of Its Lesser Rural notables and Their Politics.* Princeton, NJ: Princeton University Press, 1999.

Raymond A. Hinnebusch. *Peasant and Bureaucracy in Ba'thist Syria.* Boulder, CO: Westview Press, 1989.

Raymond A. Hinnebusch. *Authoritarian Power and State Formation in Ba'thist Syria.* Boulder, CO: Westview Press, 1990.

Volker Perthes. *The Political Economy of Syria under Asad.* London: I. B. Tauris, 1995.

Tabitha Petran. *Syria.* London: Benn, 1972.

Itamar Rabinovich. *Syria under the Ba'th, 1963–66.* Jerusalem: Israel University Press, 1972.

Nikolaos van Dam. *The Struggle for Power in Syria*, 4th ed. London: I. B. Tauris, 2011.

CHAPTER 2

Syria's Contemporary Political Economy

On June 10, 2000, President Hafiz al-Asad died in his bed after three decades as Syria's unrivaled leader. Later that same day, the People's Assembly ratified an amendment to the constitution that lowered the age requirement for the presidency from 40 to 34, exactly the age of the former president's eldest surviving son, Bashshar. The Regional (Syrian) Command of the Ba'th Party announced that evening that Bashshar al-Asad had been named head of state. The next day, Vice President 'Abd al-Halim Khaddam proclaimed that Bashshar al-Asad had been designated commander in chief of the Syrian armed forces and promoted to the rank of lieutenant general. At the long-planned but hastily convened Ba'th Party congress a week later, the new lieutenant general was voted onto the Regional Command and elected to the post of secretary general. He was then nominated to be the Ba'th Party's sole candidate for the presidency, a nomination that was ratified by the People's Assembly on June 26.

Presidential elections in the form of a popular referendum took place on July 10, 2000. Bashshar al-Asad came away from the balloting with the approval of 97.3 percent of the electorate and on July 17 took the presidential oath of office in front of a special session of the People's Assembly. The remarkably smooth transition of power reflected not only the absence of viable alternative candidates but also the high degree of complementarity that had taken shape among various components of the regime in the decades after the coup d'état of November 1970. Unlike November 1983, when Hafiz al-Asad had suffered a heart attack and abruptly disappeared from the scene, no tanks rolled through the streets of Damascus.

Nevertheless, considerable jockeying among top military commanders and security officers took place in the weeks immediately following Hafiz al-Asad's death. Colonel Manaf Tlas, son of long-time Minister of Defense Mustafa Tlas, joined Bashshar al-Asad on the Regional (Syrian) Command of the Ba'th Party despite having no previous command experience. The head of the National Security Council, Muhammad Sa'id Bukhaitan, also took a seat on the Regional Command, while the head of Military Intelligence retired in early July. Such changes have generally been interpreted as part of a coordinated effort to usher supporters of the new president into key posts and squeeze out potential rivals and adversaries.

THE "DAMASCUS SPRING"

In his inaugural address, President Bashshar al-Asad promised to continue to prosecute the anticorruption campaign that he had supervised during his father's last years in office. He underscored the importance of "present[ing] new ideas in all areas, while also improving ideas that no longer suit the existing reality, or even relinquishing old ideas that are no longer useful."[1] More provocatively, the new president expressed a commitment to furthering democratic governance, albeit "a democracy distinctive to us, founded on our history, culture and personality and stemming from the needs of the society and reality in which we live." He then solicited proposals from the political parties in the Progressive National Front for opening up the domestic arena to a broader range of public expression and greater popular participation in policy making.[2]

Taking the president at his word, intellectuals, academics, and artists started to organize public forums to discuss political, economic, and social issues. A collection of these groups, led by Riyad Saif and Michel Kilu of the Communist Action League, announced plans to organize a Committee of the Friends of Civil Society to push for civil rights and fundamental institutional reform. Other groups simultaneously petitioned to be recognized by the Ministry of Social Affairs as the Committee for Environmental Protection. In late September, 99 prominent civil rights activists published an open letter in a Beirut newspaper, which called for freedom of assembly and expression as well as the immediate release of all political prisoners. By the end of the year, the Tuesday Economic Forum run by the Association for Economic Science in Damascus had started to circulate scholarly treatises that questioned specific aspects of government economic policy, and even the official newspapers began to print articles that criticized long-standing administrative practices.

Meanwhile, independent representatives in the People's Assembly took steps to set up a liberal political party that would operate outside the purview of the Progressive National Front. The initiative was blocked by the leadership of the assembly, but the 21 prospective members of the new party continued to voice objections to ministerial reports and introduce motions for reforms in existing bureaucratic procedures throughout the winter of 2000–2001. A collection of Nasirist and socialist parties concurrently coalesced into the National Democratic Bloc, whose members subjected cabinet ministers to formal questioning and complaints from the left.

In response to these developments, local branches of the Ba'th Party convened public rallies to rebut the points that had been raised by the civil rights activists and liberal reformers. Party officials also made overtures to the Syrian Social National Party, one of the primary rivals of the Ba'th that had gradually rehabilitated itself and quietly resumed activities inside Syria. President al-Asad ordered the release of 600 imprisoned members of the Communist Workers' Party, the Iraq-leaning Democratic Ba'th, the Muslim Brothers, and the Lebanon-based Islamic Liberation Party. Such conciliatory moves were soon overtaken by harsher measures. Minister of Information 'Adnan 'Amran charged in early January 2001 that the public forums were being funded by the embassies of foreign governments.[3] As the winter of 2000–2001 drew to a close, organizers of forums were told by the security forces that they must obtain permits for meetings in advance and then found it impossible to navigate the byzantine vetting process that such permits required. By May 2001, almost all of the public forums had shut down; at the end of the summer, several outspoken members of the nascent opposition in the People's Assembly found themselves under arrest.

CONSOLIDATING THE POST-HAFIZ ORDER

Two overlapping dynamics sealed the fate of the short-lived "Damascus spring." First, and not surprisingly, senior commanders in the military and the security forces chafed at the drift away from orderliness that the discussion groups and parliamentary critics both epitomized and furthered. At the same time that President al-Asad was hinting at the need for more openness in political affairs, the former heads of several key security agencies came out of retirement and began to act as his political advisers. Among these were 'Ali Duba, the former commander of Military Intelligence; Muhammad al-Khuli, the past chair of the Presidential Intelligence Committee; and Muhammad Nasif, the former chief of the internal branch of General Security.

Potential dangers inherent in loosening up the political arena were illustrated in early November 2000 when fighting abruptly flared in the countryside around Dir'a. A band of Sunni tribespeople attacked Druze inhabitants of the village of Rahi in a dispute over property rights, prompting the Druze to retaliate by setting fire to houses and mosques belonging to the local Sunni population. Druze residents then seized control of the municipality and provincial administration office, while others staged a rowdy protest in front of the People's Assembly in Damascus. Druze students at the University of Damascus joined the demonstrators in demanding that President al-Asad disarm the tribespeople and enforce existing landholding arrangements. In the end, a task force of some 5,000 troops and security personnel had to be dispatched to the southern highlands to restore order. The incident convinced senior military and security officers that unregulated public activism was likely to lead directly to outbreaks of violent unrest.

Second, a jump in world oil prices and a burst of financial assistance from the European Union provided the central administration with sufficient resources to offer economic incentives to those citizens who restrained themselves. The influx of higher oil revenues enabled state officials to raise public-sector wages by 25 percent in September 2000. The Ninth Five-Year Plan (2001–2005) earmarked more than two-thirds of new investment funds to public-sector projects. The plan boosted total spending on public transportation infrastructure by some 400 percent over the amount that had been allocated in the Eighth Five-Year Plan.

More important, crude oil started flowing across Syria from the oilfields of northern Iraq in the fall of 2000. The authorities distributed the Iraqi oil, estimated at 150,000 to 200,000 barrels per day, inside the country to satisfy local demand at subsidized rates, and exported Syrian petroleum overseas for sale at market prices. The influx of Iraqi oil accompanied a marked increase in Syrian exports of processed food, clothing, plastic wares, and other manufactured goods to Iraq. Due to the severe constraints associated with UN economic sanctions, Iraqi consumers enjoyed little if any access to goods from other countries and were therefore forced to settle for Syrian products.

Exports to Iraq bolstered Syria's obsolescent public-sector manufacturing plants but did little to halt the general slide in per-capita gross domestic product. As improvements in foreign trade failed to diminish the country's rising unemployment, state officials turned to private entrepreneurs to engage in new industrial and commercial ventures. The Higher Council for Investment approved licenses for 31 companies in August and September 2000, which were expected to create some 2,000 jobs. At the same time, the government welcomed the formation of the Saudi-sponsored Islamic Institution to Promote the Private Sector to encourage further investment in the free zones. October saw the opening of an investors' conference under the auspices of the Ministry of the Economy and Foreign Trade and the chambers of commerce of Damascus and Aleppo. More important, a draft banking-reform bill was presented to the People's Assembly in January 2001, the first step toward deregulating the state-dominated financial system. The resulting Law No. 28, which was ratified by the assembly in April, authorized the formation of both private banks and partnerships between public and private financial institutions.

In the countryside, state officials started to allow private farmers to take control of agricultural land that had previously been worked by the state-run collective farms. Law No. 83, issued by the Ba'th Party in December 2000, ordered all government landholdings to be transferred to heirs of their former owners, laborers who worked on the collective farms, and technical employees of the General Administration of the Euphrates Basin, in that order. Myriam Ababsa reports that in the northeastern provinces, along the Euphrates river and its tributaries, the law "triggered considerable tension and competition among these three categories [of beneficiaries], as each feared being excluded from the land redistribution process. As implementation proceeded, more than 250 complaint letters were addressed to the Syrian President's office and a peasant revolt took place in the village of Disbi Afnan in December 2002."[4]

Many of the opportunities that arose out of initiatives to bolster private enterprise were seized by close relatives and long-time comrades of President al-Asad. The introduction of mobile telephones, expansion of duty-free shops, and spread of Western-style franchise restaurants rapidly enriched one of the president's wife's cousins. Highly profitable food processing and real estate ventures ended up in the hands of sons of Vice President Khaddam and Minister of Defense Tlas. Cousins of the president snapped up lucrative contracts to provide services for the oil sector and construct public housing, while a son of the head of Internal Security became the owner of the country's largest advertising agency. This trend enhanced the economic weight and political influence of an assortment of well-connected individuals whom Salwa Ismail aptly calls "the children of authority" (awlad al-sultah).[5]

December 2001 saw a significant reshuffling of the Council of Ministers. The portfolios for economy and foreign trade and finance were put in the hands of two Western-trained economists, Ghassan al-Rifa'i and Muhammad al-Atrash. A firm champion of the public sector was removed as minister of industry and replaced by the more market-oriented minister of planning, 'Isam al-Za'im. At the same time, comrades of the president from university days and from the Syrian Computer Society took over as minister of higher education and ambassador to the United States, respectively.

State officials attempted to mask, and perhaps also to dilute, the expanding prerogatives of the president's relatives and political allies by ramping up the anti-corruption campaign. In March 2002, the Council of Ministers announced that all government employees over the age of 60 would be required to step aside so that their positions could be turned over to younger individuals. At the same time, several senior figures in the public sector were dismissed on charges of embezzlement and other forms of malfeasance. They included the director general of the Commercial Bank of Syria, who was placed under arrest, and the head of Syrian Arab Airlines, who was merely removed from his post. Moreover, Minister of the Interior 'Ali Hamud launched a campaign to root out corruption inside the security forces: Some 220 mid-level officers and 40 senior commanders were forced to retire, mostly for exhibiting "undisciplined and immoral behavior."[6] The campaign coincided with the promotion of several powerful military and security chiefs to ceremonial positions in the Ministry of Defense.

Official actions aimed at weeding out corruption got derailed in early June 2002, when a recently constructed dam across the al-'Asi (Orontes) River north of Hamah suddenly collapsed. The resultant flooding killed more than 20 people and devastated hundreds of hectares of productive farmland. Preliminary reports that the dam's failure had been caused by shoddy building materials, compounded by negligence in performing routine maintenance on the part of the state-run Orontes Basin Company, prompted the People's Assembly to demand a thorough investigation. Reporters who visited the scene came away impressed by "the utter poverty and deprivation of the surrounding countryside. It [was] as if virtually everyone there [was] in need, yet after some 30 years of authoritarian rule, the state had not yet reached the area."[7]

RESURGENT CHALLENGES

Spontaneous demonstrations broke out in Syria's larger cities in July 2002 to protest Israeli military activities in the West Bank. Ostensibly pro-Palestinian protests quickly displayed the slogans and symbols of organizations that stood opposed to the Ba'thi regime. Dissidents took advantage of the demonstrations to distribute handbills that called on the authorities to release political prisoners, end martial law, and relax restrictions on public assembly and expression. Faced with signs of simmering popular restiveness, senior officials in the Ba'th Party orchestrated a succession of mass rallies and marches that highlighted the party's unwavering struggle against Zionism. And for good measure, public-sector wages were raised another 20 percent in late October.

Members of the Kurdish Democratic Unity Party in Syria (Yakiti) staged a protest outside the People's Assembly in December 2002 after their formal request to meet with the minister of the interior had been denied.[8] Julie Gauthier notes that this demonstration, "though modest, represented a marked contrast to the usual gatherings and memorial ceremonies undertaken by the Kurdish parties. Because of the messages on the placards, the ideology of the regime was displaced from the street, a space that had long been confiscated and manipulated by the state for its own glorification."[9] In the wake of this incident, a group of civil rights activists announced the creation of the Committee to Free Political Prisoners. Faced with these challenges, the authorities clamped down on campaigning in the run-up to elections for the People's Assembly in the spring of 2003. New regulations stipulated that in order to be eligible to run for a seat in the assembly, candidates had to have been a member of one of the parties in the Progressive National Front for at least 10 years.[10] Still, electoral competition turned out to be remarkably fierce, and the balloting ended up bringing 177 new faces to the 250-member body, 125 of whom were under 50 years of age.

Shortly after U.S. troops occupied Iraq in March 2003, the oil pipeline from Kirkuk in northeastern Iraq to Banyas on the Syrian coast was shut down.

Largely due to the collapse of the oil distribution scheme, "the year 2003 was gloomy with all external factors—declining oil exports, a bad harvest and regional conflict—being negative and contributing to an economic slowdown."[11] Moreover, the Iraq war severely disrupted the flow of capital investment and economic assistance from the Arab Gulf states. Spreading popular discontent was reflected in a silent protest against corruption and government ineffectiveness by 100 young people in the capital, which was quickly broken up by the security forces.[12]

Faced with the prospect of having to adjust to dramatically reduced resources, the Council of Ministers created a Credit and Monetary Council to accelerate the formation of private- and mixed-sector banks.[13] The government then released a revised economic development plan that set an objective of 6 percent annual growth rates over the following five years. Steps were taken to boost tax collection by setting new assessments that were low enough to encourage compliance while at the same time toughening the penalties for evasion.[14] More important, the prohibition against carrying out transactions in foreign currency, which had been promulgated in 1986, was lifted in early July. Two months later, the Council of Ministers was reshuffled, with ministers who had expressed doubts about joining the European Union–sponsored Mediterranean Trade and Investment Initiative replaced by pro-EuroMed politicians. The speaker of the People's Assembly, Muhammad Naji' al-'Utri, was given a mandate to rationalize and accelerate the liberalization of the economy. A Western-trained, proreform economist on the staff of the United Nations Development Program in Damascus, 'Abdullah al-Dardari, became director of the State Planning Organization.

Trade with Iraq revived briefly during the fall of 2003 by order of the U.S. military commander in Musil, Colonel David Petraeus. The influx of resources prompted the Ministry of Industry to invite foreign investors to set up joint operating agreements with public enterprises in several areas of manufacturing,[15] and plans were drawn up to reduce average tariff rates as a means to promote trade. But by early 2004, escalating violence in northwestern Iraq made routine transactions between the two countries almost impossible. The permanent cut-off of Iraqi oil, combined with the absence of alternative outlets for Syrian industrial products, threatened to send the local economy into a tailspin. The one bright spot in the local economy was the arrival of well-to-do refugees from Iraq, who pushed up real estate prices in the cities and boosted demand for staples and household items.

State officials undertook a variety of initiatives to cope with the prospects of a prolonged economic downturn. In February 2004, the government announced that it would no longer guarantee permanent employment for all university graduates. The announcement propelled students in the College of Engineering at the University of Aleppo into the streets in a rare public protest. The Council of Ministers then introduced a plan whereby state employees who held only a secondary school diploma would be retired from their posts with a lump sum payoff so that positions could be freed up for university graduates. At the same time, the government disbanded the Economic Security Courts, whose primary task had been to enforce the laws against the holding and use of foreign currency. In mid-February, Syrian officials contracted with Iran's largest automobile company to build an assembly plant outside Damascus.[16] The first quarter of 2004 also saw the initial set of three private banks receive clearance to start operations, while consumption taxes were eliminated on a wide range of goods and services later in the year.

That April, responsibility for setting the prices of key commodities was transferred from a mixed commission made up of officials from the Higher Economic Committee, the Ministry of Supply, and the provincial administrations to the Ministry of Economy and Foreign Trade, which immediately signaled that it was going to rely more heavily on market dynamics to set prices. Meanwhile, public-sector enterprises were authorized to collaborate directly with foreign companies. The Syrian Arab Electronics Industries Company and the General Organization of Tobacco both signed contracts to carry out combined operations with external partners.[17] In October, the Syrian government at last accepted the terms of the Euro-Mediterranean economic partnership and initialed a formal agreement to deregulate trade and investment with the European Union. And a month later, the General Authority for Free Zones announced plans to construct a dozen new duty-free markets at various border crossings.[18]

None of these measures succeeded in generating a sustained economic recovery, so in February 2005 President al-Asad traveled to Moscow for talks with senior Russian officials about the future of bilateral relations. He persuaded his hosts to write off almost three-quarters of Syria's outstanding debt and returned home with an agreement whereby Russian companies would take the lead in exploring for new hydrocarbon deposits inside Syria.

Efforts to stimulate the economy were overshadowed by outbreaks of unrest among Syria's previously quiescent minority communities. During a March 2004 soccer match in the northeastern city of al-Qamishli, Kurdish fans of the home team taunted Arab supporters of the visiting team by waving the flag of the Kurdish autonomous region in northern Iraq and chanting slogans in praise of U.S. President George W. Bush. The Arabs then assaulted the Kurds, and fighting spilled outside the stadium into the surrounding streets.[19] The incident precipitated rioting in several northern towns, which threatened to spread to the predominantly Kurdish suburbs of Aleppo; there were even reports of agitation in Dumar, a largely Kurdish enclave on the outskirts of Damascus. Security forces stepped in and arrested hundreds of Kurds, prompting civil rights activists to organize sporadic demonstrations to restore constitutional liberties. Restiveness then percolated into other minorities: Assyrian Christians around al-Hasakah in the northeast took to the streets in an unprecedented public demonstration in October 2004, followed by an outbreak of rioting at Masyaf in Hamah province that pitted Isma'ilis against 'Alawis.

Simmering tensions across the northern provinces set the stage for the appointment of a new minister of interior, Ghazi Kan'an, who had commanded Syrian security forces in Lebanon since 1982 and had been acting as head of Political Security in Damascus since October 2002. The change followed the resignation of Minister of Defense Mustafa Tlas, who was replaced by the chief of staff, Hasan al-Turkmani. In March 2005, President al-Asad's brother-in-law 'Asif Shawkat took over as chief of Military Intelligence. The new security team adopted a hard line in dealing with civil rights activists at Tishrin University in Latakia as well as with Kurdish activists who staged a sit-in outside the High Court in Damascus; in both cases cadres of the Ba'th Party's student union armed with clubs were dispatched to break up the protests.

Kurds in the northeastern provinces took to the streets once again in April 2005 to celebrate the election of the historic leader of the Patriotic Union of Kurdistan, Jalal Talabani, to the presidency of Iraq. Kurdish activists at the same time entered into discussions with prominent civil rights activists, which led to the formation of the National Coordination Committee for the Defense of Basic Freedoms and Human Rights, Syria's "most inclusive opposition alliance to date."[20] In early June, a prominent religious figure in the Kurdish community, Muhammad Ma'shuq al-Khaznawi, went so far as to tell a reporter, "Either the regime must change or the regime must go. . . . The reason I and others can speak out is because the Americans are trying to get rid of dictators and help the oppressed" of the region, including the Kurds.[21] Al-Khaznawi dropped out of sight on May 10, sparking renewed protests in al-Qamishli.

REFORGING THE SOCIAL CONTRACT

Delegates from all parts of Syria gathered in Damascus in June 2005 for the first general congress of the Ba'th Party to take place in five years. On the first day of the congress, Vice President 'Abd al-Halim Khaddam unexpectedly resigned his post. Other major changes followed in quick succession: Vice President Zuhair Musharaqah was relieved of his office; the party disbanded its pan-Arab leadership, the so-called National Command, and reduced the size of the Regional (Syrian) Command from 21 to 14 members. The head of the State Planning Organization, 'Abdullah al-Dardari, was promoted to the post of deputy prime minister for economic affairs despite not being a member of the party. Moreover, there were intimations that the state of emergency that had been in force since March 1963 might soon be rescinded and that political parties outside the Progressive National Front might be permitted to contest the People's Assembly elections scheduled for 2007.

Perhaps the most salient outcome of the 2005 party congress was the transformation of the Ba'th Party's long-standing socialist program into a pledge to construct a "social market economy." The adoption of social market principles signaled a renewed commitment to encourage private enterprise throughout the domestic economy so long as profit-oriented companies acted in a socially responsible way. No explicit guidelines were drafted to say what exactly was entailed by the notion of the social market economy. Consequently, Deputy Prime Minister al-Dardari and other proponents of deregulation sat down to hammer out a Tenth Five-Year Plan (2006–2010) that would meld economic reform, export promotion, investment in agriculture, and support for existing social welfare programs into a more or less coherent package.[22]

More important, the 2005 party congress marked a change in the distribution of power between the armed forces and the security services. Bassam Haddad points out that prior to the congress, the Regional (Syrian) Command had always included among its members the minister of defense and chief of the general staff. These two figures found themselves dismissed from the Regional Command during the course of the gathering and replaced by the heads of General Intelligence and Military Intelligence.[23] At the same time, the Republican Guard, under the command of the president's younger brother Mahir, established itself as the central actor inside the military establishment, further undercutting the position of more senior officers in regular combat formations.

Hints that the Ba'th Party might relinquish its monopoly over party politics prompted a group of liberal notables in Aleppo to announce plans to form a new political organization, the Movement of Free Patriots.[24] Civil rights activists in October 2005 issued a more ambitious manifesto, known as the Damascus Declaration. This document demanded an immediate end to the 40-year state of emergency, along with the appointment of a constitutional commission to draw up a basic law that would guarantee the liberties of citizens. The declaration was signed by representatives of a broad range of organizations, including Kurdish political parties and the outlawed Muslim Brothers. According to Joe Pace and Joshua Landis,

> Socialists, communists, liberals and Islamists were willing to unite over a single platform of democratic change and respect for one another. Civil society activists who had previously turned their noses up at political parties joined forces with them and a deliberate effort was made to ensure that signatories of the declaration hailed from a majority of Syria's provinces.[25]

State officials responded to the call for political liberalization by demonizing the individuals and groups that had affixed their signatures to the Damascus Declaration. The signers were denounced as traitors to the nation and stooges of the United States and Israel. "Unfortunately," Pace and Landis remark, "indictments of the opposition's loyalty still resonated with an anxiety-ridden public."[26] The presence of the Muslim Brothers among the sponsors of the declaration greatly diminished the appeal of the civil rights movement for many citizens, particularly in the wake of armed clashes at Hamah and al-Hasakah between the security forces and a radical Islamist organization, the Army of Syria (*jund al-Sham*). Other military operations that targeted cells of Islamist radicals took place in early December in poor districts of Aleppo and the countryside around Idlib.

Renewed disorder in the north-central provinces was eclipsed by former Vice President 'Abd al-Halim Khaddam's scathing condemnation of the Ba'th Party–led regime, which was broadcast on regional television at the end of December 2005. Khaddam, who had decamped to Paris following his resignation, three months later presided over the inaugural conference of an umbrella opposition alliance, the National Salvation Front. The front appealed to dissident Ba'this, Muslim Brothers, civil rights activists, and Kurdish nationalists to work together to overthrow the family-based clique that was ruling Syria and replace it with a pluralist political system.[27] Prominent critics of the Ba'thi order inside Syria tended to keep their distance from the National Salvation Front, partly due to lingering suspicions about Khaddam—who had played a key role in terminating the "Damascus Spring" of 2000–2001—and partly out of mistrust of the Muslim Brothers. Nevertheless, the emergence of the front prompted the authorities to crack down hard on local civil rights activists, particularly individuals who had established relations with outside governments and international human rights organizations.[28] The systematic arrest and imprisonment of leading dissidents continued into the spring and summer of 2006.

Forcible suppression of civil rights activists and Islamist militants accompanied redoubled measures to liberalize the domestic economy. In early 2006, price supports for gasoline and cement were drastically reduced, leaving prices for these two crucial commodities to fluctuate in accordance with local demand.[29] A Council of Ministers consisting primarily of technocrats was formed in February; the new government finalized the Tenth Five-Year Plan, which mandated a substantial reduction in the number of products that would be subject to import duties. The curtailment of tariffs precipitated a sharp rise in Turkish manufactured goods entering the local market, almost all of which competed directly, and successfully, against items produced by Syria's public-sector enterprises.

State officials also emphasized religious themes and symbols more forcefully as the spring of 2006 went by. President al-Asad told a congress of Arab socialist parties in early March that their strength derived from "Islam, which is strongly connected to Arabism."[30] Andrew Tabler reports that "on March 13, Syria held its first competition for reading the Koran in the auditorium of Damascus University—a venue traditionally reserved for Ba'th Party occasions and presidential speeches."[31] On April 1, the Ministry of Defense announced that Islamic scholars would be permitted to discuss religious matters with military personnel in their barracks; four days after that, a presidential decree authorized the creation of an Islamic college in Aleppo. Ceremonies to commemorate the founding of the Ba'th Party were auspiciously held on the Prophet's birthday rather than the usual date of April 7, and President al-Asad joined other senior members of the party along with Grand Mufti Ahmad Badr al-Din Hassun in praying at the Hassibi Mosque to mark the anniversary. More important, several Islamic societies, some of which had exercised considerable political influence during the 1970s, were allowed to resume operations; these included Islamic Civilization (*al-Tamaddun al-Islami*), the League of Religious Scholars of the Levant (*Rabitah 'Ulama Bilad al-Sham*), and the League of Advocates for the Good in the Blessed Levant.[32]

Officials in the Ministry of Finance announced in the summer of 2006 that the Commercial Bank of Syria would be accorded greater flexibility to pursue promising investments. The bank's total capital was increased, and its managers were authorized to use these monies to purchase shares in private financial institutions. The troubled state-run Industrial Bank received a massive injection of capital as well.[33] The turn toward market dynamics in the financial sector was supervised by the Syrian Central Bank, whose authority to regulate public and private banks steadily expanded as sanctions imposed by foreign governments crippled the Commercial Bank. At the end of 2006, the governor of the Central Bank issued a revised set of regulations that raised the minimum capitalization required of all private banks to US$100 million.[34]

New laws designed to encourage private manufacturing and trade were issued on a regular basis during the course of 2007 and 2008. These included Law No. 8 of 2007, which guaranteed that foreign investors could repatriate all of their profits overseas and own the land on which their operations took place, and a revised commercial code that updated the one that had been drawn up in 1949. April 2008 saw the promulgation of Law No. 3, which set rules for mergers and acquisitions in the private sector, and the even more significant Law No. 7, which was designed to promote competition and eliminate monopolies. The latter prohibited the formation of cartels or other forms of collaboration that interfered with the operation of the market, and it directed that market dynamics—not state agencies—should set prices. The law created a Competition and Anti-Monopoly Committee to enforce its provisions, made up of eight government officials, three representatives of the chambers of commerce and industry, and one member each from the General Federation of Workers' Unions and General Farm Laborer's Union.[35]

Meanwhile, the Council of Ministers encouraged public-sector enterprises to engage in public-private partnerships.[36] Such arrangements initially took shape in areas related to infrastructure: housing, electricity, water, and sanitation projects steadily slipped into the hands of foreign companies working hand in hand with state-run enterprises. Next, the General Organization of Free Zones announced that it was going to collaborate with private companies to build and manage five additional industrial and commercial enclaves. In the summer of 2008, the Construction Projects Holding Company formed a joint venture with a Saudi manufacturer to produce prefabricated steel buildings,[37] while the Syrian-Iranian

Company for Automobiles opened a second assembly facility outside Homs. Several public-sector industrial enterprises subsequently unveiled plans to shut down underused facilities and contract with private tourism companies to transform them into tourist resorts.[38]

Developments in the countryside held a good deal less promise for the future. Agriculture's share of total gross domestic product slipped from approximately 25 percent in the years before 2007 to less than 20 percent after that date. By 2008, it was estimated that three-fifths of the population in the agricultural areas of the northeast were living in poverty.[39] The UN Food and Agricultural Organization reported that three-quarters of farms in the provinces of al-Raqqah, al-Hasakah, and Dair al-Zur experienced "total crop failure" during the 2007–2008 growing season.[40] In an effort to prop up flagging output, the Ministry of Agriculture and Agrarian Reform in 2008 created the Agricultural Support Fund to rationalize the distribution of crop subsidies and low-interest loans to small farmers. The fund's governing board was given the authority to decide which crops would be granted state support each year, a major change from earlier policy, which specified that only profitable crops were eligible for subsidies.[41] Fiddling with the allocation of loan monies did little to offset the damage done to farmers by the government's decision to reduce price supports on diesel fuel. The resultant jump in prices made it impossible for many cultivators to keep their irrigation pumps running, much less to transport produce to the cities.

Elections to the People's Assembly in April 2007 sparked violent protests in Homs, al-Raqqah, and al-Hasakah after local officials took steps to rig the balloting in favor of proregime independents. Nine Kurdish parties boycotted the electoral process, charging that the authorities had tried to undermine them by putting pressure on government employees to vote for candidates from parties in the Progressive National Front. On the other hand, moderate Islamists won several seats with support from the newly revived religious societies.[42] Shortly after it convened, the assembly nominated President al-Asad for a second seven-year term; the referendum that took place in late May accorded the president almost 98 percent approval. The successive electoral campaigns accompanied a wholesale crackdown on civil rights activists: Anwar al-Bunni, Kamal Labwani, and Michel Kilu were all sentenced to prison on charges of defaming the nation and, in Kilu's case, for "inciting sectarian sentiments."[43]

At the end of September 2007, an influential figure in the country's Islamist movement, Mahmud Qul Aghasi, popularly known as Abu al-Qaʻqa, was assassinated in Aleppo. Aghasi had urged his followers, who called themselves the Strange Ones of Syria, to engage in militant struggle (*jihad*) against U.S. military forces throughout the Muslim world. Rumors spread that he had been killed on orders from the U.S. Central Intelligence Agency, although knowledgeable observers speculated that the culprits were instead radical Islamists who had been incensed by his calls for reconciliation between Sunnis and Shiʻis. In a bid to quiet the waters, President al-Asad issued a decree in October that awarded a 50 percent salary increase to all government employees and military personnel. Complementing this carrot, the security forces in early December rounded up 40 civil rights activists, who had constituted themselves as the National Council of the Damascus Declaration group.[44]

GLOBAL RECESSION AND INTERNAL CRISIS

Hydrocarbons constituted the pivotal sector of the Syrian economy as the first decade of the twenty-first century came to a close. As world oil prices plummeted in 2008, so did the country's economic growth rate. In addition, the inexorable exhaustion of local petroleum deposits diminished the likelihood that the rebound in world prices that occurred in mid-2009 was going to generate enough revenue to continue to subsidize industry and agriculture. In an effort to increase efficiency in the hydrocarbons sector, a pair of new agencies, the General Organization of Oil and the General Organization for Oil Refining and Distribution of Petroleum Products, was established by presidential decree in February 2009 and given responsibility for managing all upstream operations. The Petroleum Ministry observed that the two agencies would devote particular attention to "the construction of new oil refineries, in joint venture with private investors, as well as the establishment of petrol stations operated by international firms."[45]

Global financial difficulties depressed manufacturing in Syria during the winter of 2008–2009. Turkish manufactures continued to flood into the country, while even cheaper goods from the People's Republic of China had started to penetrate local markets as well. As a result of such trends, "domestic demand for most [Syrian-made] industrial products crashed (falling 80 percent between October 2008 and March 2009)."[46] Forty-one textile factories in Aleppo shut their doors during the last quarter of 2008, followed by as many more during the winter of 2009–2010.[47] State officials responded by raising tariffs on imported textiles and setting up a special commission to come up with ways to augment industrial exports. Prime Minister al-'Utri pledged at the end of March 2009 that no public-sector workers would lose their jobs as a result of the economic slump. Nevertheless, the General Federation of Workers' Unions reported that inflation had gobbled up the recent raises that its members had received, and a pronounced rise in unemployment led to an unprecedented surge in armed robberies and other violent crimes across the north-central cities.[48] Minibus drivers in Damascus carried out a two-day strike in September 2009 after the municipality prevented them from raising fares to keep up with soaring gasoline prices.[49]

By the fall of 2009, broad areas of the northeast and the central plains were suffering from persistent drought, which brought agricultural production to a halt.[50] Villages along the Euphrates River and its now-barren tributaries the

Balikh and Khabur Rivers turned into ghost towns as local residents fled to Aleppo and Damascus in search of sustenance. The effects of the drought forced the government to open the domestic market to imported wheat for the first time since the early 1990s, while UN agencies distributed emergency supplies of food, fodder, and seed. To make matters worse, yellow rust struck the wheat fields of al-Hasakah province during the summer of 2010, wiping out between one-third and one-half of the summer harvest.[51] In an attempt to come up with alternative jobs for rural laborers, President al-Asad issued a decree in September 2009 that granted manufacturers a 10-year tax exemption on all new projects set up in al-Raqqah, al-Hasakah, and Dair al-Zur.[52]

Growing desperation in the northeastern provinces exacerbated tensions between Kurdish activists and local officials. Members of the Yakiti and Azadi parties organized a demonstration in Damascus in November 2008 to protest new restrictions on Kurdish landowners in districts along the border with Turkey. In March 2010, riot police shot into a crowd celebrating the new year (Nawruz) in al-Raqqah after demonstrators refused to exchange the Kurdish flags they were waving for Syrian ones.[53] In mid-June the security forces rounded up a large number of Kurds who were suspected of sympathizing with the radical Kurdistan Workers' Party. Seven months later, two members of the Organization of Western Kurdistan were killed in al-Raqqah, sparking protests in cities and towns across the northeast that threatened to spread as far as the predominantly Kurdish suburbs of Aleppo and Hamah.

January 2011 brought reports that President al-Asad had instructed the Ba'th Party to give greater weight to district and provincial elections in selecting representatives to the upcoming party congress. At the same time, a series of presidential decrees raised the penalties on a variety of crimes against women, including familial retaliation against women alleged to have engaged in extramarital sexual activity. Local access to the Internet websites Facebook and YouTube was unexpectedly opened in early February. As popular uprisings gathered momentum in Egypt and Bahrain, state officials reduced import duties on a wide range of staples and lowered taxes on rice, sugar, tea, coffee, and cooking oil. These measures sparked an epidemic of hoarding by local distributors and shopkeepers, which pushed prices for these commodities to unprecedented heights.

Widespread popular disorder shook Syria throughout the spring of 2011 (see Chapter 4). As clashes between protesters and the security forces escalated, Minister of Agriculture and Agrarian Reform 'Adil Safar was appointed to the post of prime minister, despite having been severely criticized for his handling of problems associated with the ongoing drought. Several outspoken proponents of economic liberalization were dismissed from their administrative posts; salaries for government employees and public-sector workers were hiked another 30 percent; the subsidy on heating oil was increased substantially; and state funds were earmarked to provide electricity and water to the shantytowns that had sprung up around Aleppo and Damascus as newly impoverished farmers and rural laborers flocked to the two metropolises looking for work.[54] At the same time, deposits in Syria's private banks plummeted[55] and foreign investment dried up.

As economic difficulties mounted, popular resentment focused on the activities of the "children of authority." Rami Makhluf, who had made his fortune running the country's largest private telecommunications company, elicited particular opprobrium and was blamed for a sharp drop in the value of the Syrian pound at the end of April 2011.[56] The fact that two of his brothers occupied command positions in Air Force Intelligence and State Security helped to keep public anger within limits, although Makhluf announced in June that he was going to give up his career in business and devote his energies to charity work in future.[57]

June 2011 also saw the publication of a revised political parties statute, which envisaged the creation of a multiparty order in place of the Ba'th Party's longstanding monopoly of the electoral system. The statute complemented a draft media law that proposed the dismantling of the Ministry of Information and guaranteed "independence and freedom" to all forms of mass media.[58] Both laws were reported to reflect the proclivities of President al-Asad but aroused the antipathy of hardliners in the state administration and Ba'th Party.[59] A collection of former government and party officials then met to form a nascent rival to the Ba'th; former Minister of Information Muhammad Salman emerged as head of the prospective party and in a public statement called on President al-Asad to convene a national congress to deal with the crisis that was gripping Syria, asserting that "the Ba'thi leaders who reached power and leading positions after 2000 are unworthy of leading the country and being in charge of top positions in the [Ba'th] party."[60]

Confronted with a highly uncertain future, government officials once again tried to revitalize the public sector. Subsidies on staples were reinstated and plans drawn up to increase employment in state-run enterprises.[61] Preliminary reports indicated that the Eleventh Five-Year Plan would target investments at the public sector, particularly in manufacturing and infrastructure.[62] The General Organization for Desert (al-Badiya) Management and Development was set up to find ways to improve economic conditions in the wastelands around Palmyra, while a Fund for Mitigating the Impact of Drought and Natural Disasters on Agricultural Production was created to deal with the problems plaguing the northeastern provinces. President al-Asad ordered the state-run Industrial Bank to permit faltering manufacturers to reschedule their outstanding obligations. The draft 2012 budget raised total government expenditures by almost 60 percent over the previous year's level.[63]

In addition, the Ministry of Economy and Foreign Trade ordered a "temporary" ban on the importation of a wide range of consumer and luxury goods as a way to preserve scarce holdings of foreign currency. As a result of this initiative, imports dropped off dramatically and remained suppressed as sanctions imposed by the United Nations, the European Union, and the United States started to take effect. Prices for locally produced foodstuffs, coffee, and sugar quickly sky-rocketed, prompting officials in the economy ministry to warn that they would "step in and regulate the markets whenever there is an artificial price increase" in staples.[64] An immediate outburst of anger on the part of private wholesalers and shopkeepers persuaded the government to lift the import ban within days.[65] Shortages of diesel fuel and heating oil nevertheless pushed the cost of operating machinery and heavy vehicles, not to mention keeping houses and workplaces warm, out of the reach of most citizens.[66]

Even as fighting raged across broad swaths of the country, local council elections took place in mid-December 2011. The authorities pointed to the voting as the first outcome of the revised political parties statute; in deference to the new order, candidates who represented minor parties in the Progressive National Front changed their affiliation to the National Unity List.[67] As 2012 opened, a presidential decree transferred several thousand Ba'th Party functionaries to permanent positions in the state bureaucracy; the directive also moved the staff of the party newspaper *al-Ba'th* into the Ministry of Information, while officials in the party-affiliated popular front organizations were assigned new jobs in the government ministries that were most closely connected to their respective unions.[68]

Meanwhile, persistent fighting in Homs and Hamah forced recent migrants to return to the parched countryside of the northeastern provinces. Despite adequate rainfall during the winter 2011–2012 growing season, insecurity along the high-ways and surging fuel prices prevented farmers in al-Raqqah and al-Hasakah from obtaining vital seeds and fertilizer and kept most irrigation pumps silent.[69] Short-falls of grain production ended up being aggravated by international sanctions, which blocked the importation of wheat and barley from Russia.[70] Economic deprivation in the countryside contrasted sharply with the windfall profits that were reaped by private building contractors as a wave of unlicensed construction washed through the cities and towns. The virtual closure of the private banks generated even greater profits for a well-organized network of informal lenders and moneychangers.[71]

As campaigning for seats in the People's Assembly got underway in April 2012, a large number of candidates from minor parties in the Progressive National Front abandoned the race in deference to representatives of the National Unity List.[72] The Syrian Social National Party formed an electoral alliance with the National Committee for Unity of Syrian Communists, which presented itself as the primary opposition bloc.[73] In total, nine new political parties took part in the contest under the terms of the revised parties statute. Nevertheless, the number of assembly seats allocated to independents remained unchanged, boosting the degree of rivalry between candidates who were sponsored by the new parties and nonpartisan candidates.

Thanks to the termination of reserved seats for parties in the Progressive National Front, the Ba'th Party ended up winning greater representation than ever before. Of the opposition parties, only the Syrian Democratic Party emerged victorious, winning one of the electoral districts for Aleppo. The People's Assembly elections set the stage for the June 2012 appointment of a senior Ba'th Party figure, Riyad Hijab, to the post of prime minister. Hijab had served as governor of Latakia from February to April 2011 and after that as minister of agriculture and agrarian reform. The Council of Ministers that surrounded Hijab included only one new face: Qadri Jamil of the Popular Will Party became deputy prime minister in a nod to Russia, where his family had extensive investments.[74]

Hijab took on the premiership in the context of spiraling prices for fuel, which hobbled transportation and led many households to revert to kerosene for heating and cooking. Reports that the ubiquitous butane gas canisters were being modified for use as bombs led the authorities to restrict the distribution of gas even more tightly.[75] A combination of fuel shortages, transportation difficulties, and general chaos across many regions of the country resulted in a plunge in agricultural output, particularly in Homs province (poultry), the north-central plains (fruits and vegetables), and the far northeast (wheat and cotton). Imports of foodstuffs and industrial raw materials from Lebanon correspondingly soared.[76] Syria's growing dependence on trade with Lebanon reflected not only short-term disruptions associated with the 2011–2012 uprising but also and more profoundly the country's economic connections to the outside world, which had steadily proliferated and deepened during the first decade of the twenty-first century.

Shortly after Hijab took office, General Manaf Tlas, the commander of the 105th Division of the Republican Guard, fled across the border to Turkey. It was rumored that he had fallen out with other key military commanders for attempting to negotiate with opposition forces operating in the Damascus suburbs of Harasta and Duma at the outset of the uprising instead of resorting immediately to force to crush the revolt. On July 18, 2012, another four senior officers were fatally wounded in a bombing at the headquarters of the National Security Council in Damascus. Minister of Defense Daud Rajiha, Chief of the Bureau of Crisis Management Hasan al-Turkmani, and Deputy Minister of Defense 'Asif Shawkat were all killed instantly by the blast, while the head of the National Security Council, General Hisham Ikhtiyar, died in hospital two days later. General Fahd al-Fraij was then appointed defense minister; General 'Ali Ayyub, who had preceded Manaf Tlas as commander of the 105th Division, became chief of staff; and General 'Ali Mamluk assumed the post of head of national security.

Prime Minister Hijab defected to Jordan on August 6. He was succeeded by Minister of Health Wail Nadir al-Halqi, a 48-year-old Sunni from Dir'a province.

NOTES

1. Eyal Zisser, *Commanding Syria: Bashar al-Asad and the First Years in Power* (London: I. B. Tauris, 2007), 41.

2. *al-Sharq al-Awsat*, August 5, 2000.

3. Abdulrahman Alhaj, *State and Community: The Political Aspirations of Religious Groups in Syria 2000–2010* (London: Strategic Research and Communication Centre, n.d.), 11, note 3.

4. Myriam Ababsa, "Agrarian Counter-Reform in Syria (2000–2010)," in *Agriculture and Reform in Syria*, eds. Raymond Hinnebusch, Atieh El Hindi, Mounzer Khaddam, and Myriam Ababsa (Boulder, CO: Lynne Rienner Press, 2011), 84.

5. Salwa Ismail, "Changing Social Structure, Shifting Alliances and Authoritarianism in Syria," in *Demystifying Syria*, ed. Fred H. Lawson (London: Saqi Books, 2009), 18.

6. *Middle East International*, July 26, 2002.

7. *Middle East International*, June 28, 2002.

8. Associated Press (AP), December 19, 2002.

9. Julie Gauthier, "The 2004 Events in al-Qamishli: Has the Kurdish Question Erupted in Syria?" in *Demystifying Syria*, ed. Lawson, 107.

10. ArabicNews.com, January 18, 2003.

11. Ferdinand Arslanian, "Growth in Transition and Syria's Economic Performance," in Samer Abboud and Ferdinand Arslanian, *Syria's Economy and the Transition Paradigm* (Boulder, CO: Lynne Rienner, 2009), 67.

12. Alhaj, *State and Community*, 64.

13. *Syria Report*, May and July 2003.

14. Arslanian, "Growth in Transition," 65.

15. *Syria Report*, January 2004.

16. *Syria Report*, March 2004.

17. Samer Abboud, "The Transition Paradigm and the Case of Syria," in Abboud and Arslanian, *Syria's Economy*, 19.

18. *Syria Report*, November 1, 2004.

19. Carsten Wieland, *A Decade of Lost Chances* (Seattle: Cune Press, 2012), 112–13.

20. Joe Pace and Joshua Landis, "The Syrian Opposition," in *Demystifying Syria*, ed. Lawson, 129.

21. Agence France Presse (AFP), June 2, 2005.

22. Oxford Business Group, July 13, 2005.

23. Bassam Haddad, "Syria's Curious Dilemma," *Middle East Report*, no. 236 (Fall 2005); Bassam Haddad, *Left to Its Domestic Devices: How the Syrian Regime Boxed Itself In*, Working Paper 43/2005, Real Instituto Elcano, March 10, 2005, 7.

24. *Asia Times*, July 21, 2005.

25. Pace and Landis, "Syrian Opposition," 130.

26. Ibid., 131.

27. Ibid., 136–38.

28. Ibid., 136–38.

29. *Syria Report*, first quarter 2006.

30. Andrew Tabler, *In the Lion's Den* (Chicago: Lawrence Hill, 2011), 134.

31. Ibid.

32. Alhaj, *State and Community*, 67–68; Thomas Pierret, *Baas et Islam en Syrie* (Paris: Presses Universitaires de France, 2011), 258.

33. *Syria Report*, third quarter 2006.

34. *Syria Report*, fourth quarter 2006.

35. Joshua Landis, "Will the Anti-Trust Law Make a Difference in Syria?" *Sada*, May 12, 2008.

36. Samer N. Abboud and Fred H. Lawson, "Antinomies of Economic Governance in Contemporary Syria," in *Governance in the Middle East and North Africa*, ed. Abbas Kadhim (London: Routledge, 2012).

37. *Syria Report*, third quarter 2008.

38. *Syria Report*, fourth quarter 2008.

39. Husain Ammash, *Hazimah al-Aman al-Ijtima'iyyah fi Suriya* (Damascus: Syrian Economic Society, March 2008). I owe this reference to Samer Abboud.

40. *Syria Today*, May 2009.

41. I owe this information to Samer Abboud.

42. Thomas Pierret and Kjetil Selvik, "Limits of Authoritarian Upgrading in Syria," *International Journal of Middle East Studies* 41 (November 2009): 600–1.

43. Tabler, *In the Lion's Den*, 178.

44. Ibid., 209.

45. *Syria Report*, first quarter 2009.

46. Bassam Haddad, "The Political Economy of Syria: Realities and Challenges," *Middle East Policy* 18 (Summer 2011): 52.

47. *Institute for War and Peace Reporting* (IWPR), March 10, 2009; *Syria Now*, March 4, 2010.

48. Haddad, "Political Economy," 54; IWPR, April 23, 2009.

49. IWPR, October 29, 2009.

50. *Daily Star*, February 20, 2010.

51. "Syria: Yellow Wheat Rust Hits Supplies," Integrated Regional Information Networks (Nairobi) (IRIN), August 19, 2010.

52. IWPR, September 14, 2009

53. *Daily Star*, March 30, 2010.

54. Jihad Yazigi, "No End in Sight to Syria's Economic Woes," in *Syria's Revolution: Society, Power, Ideology: Perspectives No. 3* (Beirut: Heinrich Böll Stiftung February 2012), 24.

55. *al-Akhbar*, August 24, 2011.

56. Cham Press, April 29, 2011.

57. *al-Akhbar*, June 17, 2011.

58. *RIA Novosti*, June 7, 2011.

59. *al-Quds al-'Arabi*, July 15, 2011.

60. *al-Rai al-'Amm* (Kuwait), August 9, 2011.

61. *Guardian*, May 23, 2011.

62. IRIN, October 27, 2011; Haddad, "Political Economy," 48.

63. *Syria Report*, September 26, 2011.

64. *al-Akhbar*, October 3, 2011.

65. *New York Times* (NYT), October 4, 2011; *Syria Report*, October 10, 2011.

66. *al-Akhbar*, December 15, 2011.

67. *al-Watan* (Damascus), December 12, 2011.

68. *al-Quds al-'Arabi*, January 5, 2012.

69. IRIN, February 17, 2012.

70. Reuters, May 8, 2012.

71. Reuters, March 21, 2012.
72. *al-Watan*, April 30, 2012.
73. *al-Akhbar*, May 15, 2012.
74. *al-Sharq al-Awsat*, June 24, 2012.
75. *al-Akhbar*, June 23, 2012.
76. *al-Akhbar*, June 13, 2012.

FURTHER READING

Alan George. *Syria: Neither Bread nor Freedom*. London: Zed Press, 2003.

Bassam Haddad. *Business Networks in Syria*. Stanford, CA: Stanford University Press, 2012.

Fred H. Lawson, ed. *Demystifying Syria*. London: Saqi Books, 2009.

David W. Lesch. *The New Lion of Damascus: Bashar al-Asad and Modern Syria*. New Haven, CT: Yale University Press, 2005.

Flynt Leverett. *Inheriting Syria: Bashar's Trial by Fire*. Washington, DC: Brookings Institution, 2005.

Volker Perthes. *Syria under Bashar al-Asad: Modernization and the Limits of Change*. London: Oxford University Press for the International Institute of Strategic Studies, 2004.

Eyal Zisser. *Commanding Syria: Bashar al-Asad and the First Years in Power*. London: I. B. Tauris, 2007.

CHAPTER 3

Vicissitudes of Syria's Islamist Movement

Syria's variegated Islamist movement has gone through five distinct phases over the last seven decades. The first accompanied the emergence of the Muslim Brothers as a major political actor in the mid-1940s. A second, more militant phase took shape during the late 1960s, inspired by the writings of the influential Islamist intellectual Sa'id Hawwa. The third got underway at the beginning of the 1980s with the formation of the Islamic Front in Syria and the publication of the charter of the National Alliance for the Liberation of Syria. A fourth phase can be discerned in a series of pronouncements issued by the leadership of the Muslim Brothers in the mid-1990s, which signaled a willingness to engage in a rapprochement with the Ba'thi regime. The fifth phase started to unfold as large-scale popular unrest erupted across Syria in the spring of 2011.

MUSLIM BROTHERS AS LIBERAL REFORMERS

During the mid-1940s, a cluster of disparate Islamist welfare societies and civic associations coalesced to form a Syrian incarnation of the Muslim Brothers (*Ikhwan al-Muslimin*), which quickly affirmed fraternal ties to the Society of Muslim Brothers that had been established in Egypt 15 years earlier under the leadership of Hasan al-Banna.[1] The emergence of the Syrian Ikhwan was orchestrated by the prominent Damascene religious scholar and activist Mustafa al-Siba'i, who was elected general supervisor of the organization in the summer of 1946.[2]

At the outset, the Syrian Muslim Brothers envisaged itself as a popular movement rather than a political organization. General Supervisor al-Siba'i observed in early 1947 that "our movement is neither a jam'iyah [benevolent society] nor a political party, but [is instead] a ruh [spirit] that permeates the very being of the ummah [community of believers]: It is a new revolution."[3] The movement's primary objective was to establish an Islamic order that could succeed at last in liberating Syria from foreign domination. Freedom from French control was expected to be complemented by a variety of administrative reforms that would promote the full independence of the country and facilitate the political, economic, and social progress of the Syrian people. In addition, the Muslim Brothers advocated the redistribution of agricultural land, the expansion of public education, and the development of a prosperous and progressive economy. To accomplish this ambitious program, the movement set up a network of local committees to carry out community-based projects that would mobilize the public to action. The Muslim Brothers encouraged the work of these committees by publishing several newspapers, along with a substantial collection of books and pamphlets offering practical advice on a wide range of economic and social matters.

Supplementing this package of domestic objectives was the movement's call for a fully independent armed forces that could defend the security and strategic interests of the Syrian nation.[4] The construction of a military free from outside interference was expected to enable Syrians to assist their Palestinian neighbors in prosecuting the ongoing struggle against Zionism. Muslim Brothers repeatedly appealed to the members of Syria's disparate Christian communities to join them in combating Zionist initiatives.[5] As for the broader international arena, the Brothers championed a foreign policy of strict neutralism with regard to the burgeoning conflict that pitted the United States and United Kingdom on one side against the Soviet Union and its East European allies on the other.

Candidates sponsored by the Muslim Brothers contested the parliamentary elections that took place in July 1947. The leadership of the Ikhwan al-Muslimin publicly endorsed such well-known Islamist activists as Ma'ruf al-Dawalibi and 'Umar Baha al-Amiri from Aleppo, Muhammad al-Mubarak from Damascus, and Mahmud al-Saqafa from Hamah.[6] The platform on which these figures campaigned was comparatively moderate, both in content and in tone. As Joshua Teitelbaum observes, "The fact that the Ikhwan operated within a parliamentary system forced upon it certain limitations. It had to more or less eschew political violence, and avoid alienating even those who were not part of its natural constituency, namely Syria's sizeable Christian minority."[7] In particular, during its earliest years "there was a surprising lack of emphasis on Islam per se in the activities of the Ikhwan; indeed," Teitelbaum remarks, "at times their activities could not be differentiated from common nationalist politics."

Soon after the parliament convened, the government of Prime Minister Jamil Mardam introduced an ambitious program that called for an integrated, autonomous national economy, the implementation of agrarian reform, and greater orderliness and transparency in the operations of the central bureaucracy. The

Ikhwan al-Muslimin's Muhammad al-Mubarak immediately criticized this reformist program on the grounds that it looked impractical and did not rest on firm "socialist foundations."[8] The Muslim Brothers proposed instead to carry out policies that furthered the interests of the common people while undermining the prerogatives enjoyed by what it called the "feudal clique" that had dominated the nationalist movement since the 1920s.[9] Representatives of the Ikhwan then joined the leaders of the liberal People's Party in organizing a cluster of popular demonstrations in August 1948 to protest President Shukri al-Quwwatli's bid to secure a second term in office.

Meanwhile, the Muslim Brothers turned its attention more and more to the realm of foreign affairs. In mid-September 1948, the Ikhwan al-Muslimin organized a large public rally at the historic 'Umayyad Mosque in central Damascus to denounce U.S. policy in Palestine and castigate Saudi Arabia for collaborating with American military and economic interests in the Middle East.[10] At the same time,

> the Muslim Brotherhood had issued a National Charter declaring that an Arab state must be established in Palestine, free of Jews who entered on the basis of the Balfour Declaration. The Charter also opposed the "imperialistic" Greater Syria plan of Transjordan's King Abdallah and his proposal for an "Arab Liberation Army for the Salvation of Palestine."[11]

Ikhwani representatives joined both the liberal opposition and the newly emerging Ba'th Party in criticizing steps taken by the government of Prime Minister Khalid al-'Azm to conclude a monetary agreement with France and grant a long-term concession to American oil companies that would enable them to extend the Trans-Arabian Pipeline across Syrian territory.[12]

When news reached the Syrian capital that the UN Security Council had voted to partition Palestine into separate Jewish and Arab states, the leaders of the Ikhwan al-Muslimin helped to organize a mass protest in which "about three hundred turbaned and white banded Moslem Brothers marching in formation behind Syrian, Lebanese, and Iraqi flags arrived" in front of the US legation.[13] A small group of protesters forced its way into the building and tore down the American flag that was flying from the roof. The U.S. chargé d'affaires reported on December 4, 1947, that "the flag seems to have been the main objective of the break into the building, and no serious attempt was made to get into the locked offices to destroy property. However, an attempt was made to [set] fire [to] the building. Rags soaked in gasoline were ignited and thrown against first and second floor shutters. These failed to catch fire." In the end, the charge remarked that "the demonstration was magnificently organized. All observers are unanimous on this point. Students marching in ranks of four, with instructors alongside urging them on, bicycle squadrons in the streets, as well as the drilled formation of Moslem Brothers, all confirm this impression." Other, equally well-disciplined protests occurred outside the French and Belgian legations. The next day, General Supervisor al-Siba'i addressed a crowd gathered in front of the 'Umayyad Mosque and warned the people to refrain from attacking foreign embassies "because they are our guests and the Arab is generous to his guest." Further Ikhwan-sponsored protests took place throughout the spring and summer of 1948,[14] most of which were comparatively orderly and all of which focused on such external matters as events in Palestine and Saudi Arabia's ties to the United States.

Immediately after the March 1949 coup d'état that brought Colonel Husni al-Za'im to power, the Muslim Brothers "called upon Za'im to enact 'true democratic government' [along with] reforms and [other measures that might] improve the lot of the people."[15] When the new leader ignored these entreaties and instead cracked down on Ikhwani and Ba'thi activists alike, the Brothers turned against the military regime and started to agitate against it. "Even [al-Za'im's] Kurdish ancestry became an issue, with the Muslim Brotherhood joining those who accused him of attempting to set up some sort of Kurdish republic and of favouring Circassian and Kurdish units of the army over Arab ones."[16]

Husni al-Za'im's ouster in August 1949 at the hands of military officers led by Colonel Sami Hinnawi led to a reemergence of parliamentary politics in which the Ikhwan al-Muslimin moved away from its tactical alliances with the liberal People's Party and the radical Ba'th Party. Teitelbaum points out that

> on 11 November [1949], the Muslim Brotherhood announced the formation of the Islamic Socialist Front and published its platform—which was conspicuous in its lack of reference to Islam. The platform instead emphasized the problem of corruption and the need for social equality, supporting progressive taxation, land reform, limitation of ownership and workers' rights.[17]

When elections took place later that same month for a Constituent Assembly charged with drafting a revised constitution, "the Islamic Socialist Front presented a full list [of candidates] only in Damascus, and it included Siba'i, Mubarak, and Arif al-Taraqji of the Muslim Brotherhood and Abd al-Hamid al-Tabba' of the Jam'iyat al-Gharra. In Aleppo, Dawalibi and Baha al-Din al-Amiri were supported by the Ikhwan," despite their lingering ties to the People's Party.[18]

Rivalry between the Muslim Brothers and the People's Party heated up as soon as the assembly opened. The People's Party endorsed closer relations, and eventual political amalgamation, with neighboring Iraq, whereas the Ikhwan al-Muslimin allied itself with the Arab Socialist Party of Akram al-Hawrani in wholehearted defense of Syrian independence and sovereignty.[19] The Islamic Socialist Front and Arab Socialist Party likewise joined forces to criticize the People's Party–led government on the grounds that it intended to abandon Syria's republican political system in favor of the sort of monarchies that existed in Iraq and Transjordan.

Despite the growing rift between the Islamist movement and the People's Party, General Supervisor al-Siba'i accepted a seat on the constitutional committee that was chaired by the People's Party's Nazim al-Qudsi. With regard to the work of this committee, "the main points of the Ikhwan's position were set out by Siba'i in February 1950, and his tone was above all else pragmatic. Islam, wrote Siba'i, should be the state religion, since this was a prerequisite to restoring the confidence of the country. Israel, which was also based on religion, . . . had successfully defeated the Arabs, who should therefore be aware of the power of having a state religion. . . . Siba'i argued further that declaring Islam to be the state religion would increase Syria's commercial markets in the Islamic countries and further [the flow of] economic assistance" coming into the country.[20]

Persistent skirmishing with the People's Party, the Arab Socialist Party, and the officers' corps sapped the strength and prestige of the Muslim Brothers during the course of 1951 and 1952. As a result, the leaders of the Islamist movement eventually "decided to refrain from all overt political activity and to concentrate solely on social and religious activities."[21] The Ikhwan al-Muslimin thus took no part in the parliamentary elections that were held in October 1953 and once again refrained from fielding candidates in the subsequent September 1954 elections. This markedly passive orientation was reaffirmed at the general congress that convened in June 1955,[22] and it continued to characterize the Muslim Brothers on into the early 1960s under the leadership of General Supervisor 'Isam al-'Attar.[23]

RISE OF THE MILITANTS

Syria's Islamist movement changed course sharply during the late 1960s. The economic crisis that gripped the country in 1968 and 1969 generated widespread discontent among tradespeople and small manufacturers, who made up the primary constituency of the Muslim Brothers.[24] Growing restiveness on the part of its supporters engendered disagreements over strategy among the leadership of the Ikhwan al-Muslimin, which became evident at a clandestine congress in 1969. As reported by Umar Abd-Allah,

> a split developed between the Muslim Brothers of Damascus and those of the north, that is, the cities of [Homs], Hamah, [Aleppo], [Latakia], and so forth to the north of Damascus. The Damascus group opposed armed confrontation with the Ba'thist regime and followed the line of [General Supervisor] al-'Attar. . . . The northern circle, however, which . . . included prominent figures like Sa'id Hawwa, 'Abd al-Fattah Abu Ghuddah, 'Adnan Sa'd al-Din, and others, firmly supported jihad [armed struggle] and called for al-'Attar's replacement.[25]

Rivalry between the two factions persisted until 1972 when Abu Ghuddah emerged as the new general supervisor after a succession of disputed internal elections.

At the same time, a network of younger activists sprung up in the north-central provinces, led by Marwan Hadid, who had been profoundly influenced by the radical Egyptian Islamist Sayyid Qutb during the years that he had studied agricultural engineering in Cairo.[26] Hadid and his lieutenants moved to Jordan in 1968 and went through basic training at a camp operated by Palestinian commandos. Upon returning to Syria, they set up a string of underground cells whose cadres carried out sporadic attacks against state and party facilities. After the Muslim Brothers of Damascus and Homs publicly welcomed the November 1970 coup carried out by Hafiz al-Asad and his allies, the militants around Hadid coalesced into a Fighting Vanguard of the Party of God and launched a campaign of armed struggle against the Ba'thi leadership.

Militants of the Fighting Vanguard found inspiration in the writings of Sayyid Qutb's Syrian counterpart, Sa'id Hawwa. Hawwa was born into a family of modest means in the north-central city of Hamah and studied at the College of Islamic Law in Damascus University.[27] After graduation, he returned to Hamah to work as a religious scholar and issued rulings on questions brought to him by residents of the city and its surrounding districts. He also gained a reputation as an accomplished Sufi of the Naqshbandiyyah order. Being a Naqshbandi master (*shaikh*) accorded him extensive contacts inside the local religious establishment, whose members harbored pronounced respect for Sufi principles and practices.

Beginning in 1968, Hawwa published a series of books that focused on the oneness of God (*tawhid*) and the contemporary relevance of the message of the Prophet Muhammad.[28] These publications, which appeared under the general rubric "Purposeful Methodological Studies,"[29] emphasized the importance of sustained struggle (*jihad*) to combat injustice and strongly implied that all good Syrian Muslims should engage in active opposition to the Ba'th Party–led regime. As a preliminary step toward forging a broad-based Islamist movement, Hawwa proposed that the most committed and courageous members of the community should form a Party of God (*hizbullah*), which could act as the vanguard of com-batant believers (the Army of God, or *jund Allah*) in the battle against Islam's adversaries.

Despite such radical—virtually Leninist—political notions, the economic pro-gram that one finds in Hawwa's writings retains a distinctly liberal character. Its underlying vision reflects both the earlier platform of Mustafa al-Siba'i and the reformist ideas of Muhammad al-Hamid, who had acted as Hawwa's intellectual mentor during the initial stages of his academic career.[30] Hawwa argues that cer-tain economic functions are essential to the survival of the community and should be centrally regulated in order to ensure that they get carried out efficiently. Nevertheless, individuals enjoy a variety of natural rights, including the right to own property or, more accurately, the right of each person to control his or her own means of livelihood. Although Hawwa carefully avoids using the term "means of production," whose connotations are clearly Marxian and there-fore antithetical to Islam, his conception of personal autonomy and initiative corresponds quite closely to the conception of possessive individualism that

Karl Marx associates with a capitalist political-economic order. Hawwa asserts that laws must to be codified to buttress and guarantee the rights of individuals. One of the major functions of government is therefore to protect and facilitate the operation of private enterprise.

Itzchak Weismann offers a succinct statement of the main thrust of Hawwa's thinking:

> During the entire course of his activity under the Ba'th[,] Hawwa tried to curb the influence of Marwan Hadid, the man who had brought Qutb's message to Syria, and who declared an unconditional war against its regime. Hawwa regarded this as a rash and irresponsible policy, suggesting instead a long and fundamental preparation before taking any action.[31]

It is not clear that Weismann is correct when he goes on to say that "the core of the dispute [between the more moderate Hawwa and the more radical Hadid] was not the struggle [against the Ba'thi regime] itself, as both believed in its necessity, but its timing." But he is on firmer ground to assert that Hawwa got "drawn into" political action during the late 1970s "by the enthusiastic younger members of the [Islamist] movement, who were no longer willing to wait" for the confrontation with the regime to get underway.

In February 1973, elite army units surrounded Hamah, where violent popular disorder had flared in response to the deletion of all references to Islam in Syria's newly revised constitution. Security forces moved into Homs two months later to put down protests in that city. Fighting between the military and Islamist militants surfaced again in July 1975 when security forces arrested "a number of members of the right-wing [sic] Muslim Brotherhood" for plotting to overthrow the regime and other "anti-government activities."[32] During the course of the summer 1975 crackdown, 'Adnan Sa'd al-Din assumed the post of general supervisor. The election of yet another radical northerner further alienated comparatively moderate Brothers in Damascus, who from that time on, in the words of Hanna Batatu, "went their own way."[33]

Units of the Fighting Vanguard stepped up attacks against party and state installations in the last weeks of 1975. Rioting erupted in several north-central districts in February 1976, but the most severe disturbances occurred in Hamah, where security forces clashed repeatedly with tradespeople and students. Widespread disorder persisted through the spring, culminating in a wave of arrests of suspected Islamist activists at the end of April. Looking back on these months, the official journal of the Syrian Muslim Brothers marked February 1976 as the date when the leadership of the movement declared war (*jihad*) against the Ba'thi regime.[34]

Sporadic fighting between the Fighting Vanguard and the Syrian armed forces and security services continued through 1977 and 1978, then escalated sharply in the spring of 1979. Mainstream Muslim Brothers orchestrated a succession of large-scale demonstrations and strikes in Aleppo, Hamah, and Homs during the second half of 1979 and early 1980. March 1980 saw several districts of Aleppo "break loose from the regime's control" and become Islamist enclaves;[35] at the same time, violent protests erupted in Jisr al-Shughur, which were only suppressed when the military's elite Special Units took up positions throughout the town. Four months later, the Special Units deployed to Aleppo to break up a cell of suspected militants. The ruthlessness with which the regime retaliated against the radicals persuaded moderate Muslim Brothers to express guarded support for the armed struggle, and in December 1980 a 12-member Joint Command was set up to coordinate the activities of the various wings of the Islamist movement. Hasan Huwaidi, a long-time ally of al-'Attar, took over the post of general supervisor from Sa'd al-Din, who retained a seat on the Joint Command. Among the other major figures on the council were Hawwa, 'Ali Sadr al-Din al-Bayanuni from Aleppo, and 'Adnan 'Uqlah from the Golan, the most energetic commander of the Fighting Vanguard.

Militants loyal to 'Uqlah carried out a wave of attacks against government installations in Aleppo and Hamah during March and April 1981. Armed clashes resumed in October and November, setting the stage for an all-out confrontation at the beginning of February 1982. When troops from the Special Units and the Defense Brigades raided suspected Islamist hideouts in the center of Hamah, Ikhwani militants pushed the soldiers back with small arms and grenade launchers. The Islamists then attacked the main police station, the local headquarters of the Ba'th Party, and the military airfield on the outskirts of the city. By the second day of fighting, mosques in some neighborhoods had begun to broadcast calls for a general uprising against the authorities. Whole districts joined the revolt, and fighters barricaded themselves in the labyrinthine alleyways of the old city. House-to-house battles lasted for five days, followed by what *Middle East Watch* calls an additional three days of "fierce collective punishment," in which "troops pillaged stores and homes and fired weapons indiscriminately, treating all citizens as responsible for the insurrection."[36] In the end, some 5,000 to 10,000 of Hamah's residents died in the rebellion, and the homes of more than 60,000 people were destroyed.

REASSERTING LIBERAL PRINCIPLES

At the height of the armed struggle undertaken by the Fighting Vanguard, a group of respected religious scholars initiated discussions among divergent factions of the Islamist opposition to find a less provocative and destructive way to effect fundamental change. The talks led to the emergence of the Islamic Front in Syria, with Muhammad Abu al-Nasr al-Bayanuni of Aleppo as its secretary general. The Islamic Front's initial proclamation in October 1980 charged that the Ba'th Party–led regime was not only unnecessarily brutal in its response to challengers but also wholly incompetent to govern the country.[37] The Islamic

Front called on the Syrian people to join it in setting up a network of patriotic committees to resist what it referred to as the "tyrannical oppressor" and to work toward the reinstatement the rule of law as the foundation for domestic politics.[38]

This proclamation was followed by the publication a month later of a manifesto that called for the reestablishment of the full rights, freedoms, and dignity of all Syrian citizens, including those of minority communities. The document affirmed that the kind of political system that was appropriate for Muslims—that is, a system rooted in the principle of consultation between rulers and ruled (*shura*)—was one that "guaranteed the separation of the legislative, executive and judicial authorities. It would further ensure freedom to form political parties, provided 'these parties are not opposed to the nation's faith and are not bound up in loyalty to a foreign state.' "[39] The Islamic Front called on the authorities to adhere to the provisions of Syria's 1973 constitution and demanded an end to sectarianism and partisanship in public policy making. The strongest condemnation of sectarianism was articulated by the leadership of the Ikhwan al-Muslimin toward the end of this third stage of the Islamist opposition:

> Sectarian rule is the rule of a religious or sectarian minority on which the ruler relies and from which he receives strength, help and support in order to rule autocratically over the majority. The sect makes common cause with those in power, defends them and shuns no material or immaterial burden in order to help them and to support them. . . . We can say . . . that in a democracy, for example, the ruler derives his power from the people, who voted for him . . . while in a sectarian regime he derives his power from the sect which supports the regime and which the regime supports. . . . If we suppose that a ruler is based on a religious or sectarian minority on assuming power . . . then he will no longer rule the people with justice; he will take their equality from them and the members of the sect will have more rights than others.[40]

Most important, the November 1980 manifesto called for the elimination of sectarianism from the ranks of the Syrian armed forces, which had to be purged of all sectarian divisions and animosities, and transformed into a unified, popular army.[41] To this end, every citizen should be required to complete a period of military training and service so that the entire populace would be prepared to bear arms in defense of the nation.[42]

Hans Günter Lobmeyer notes that

> the most conspicuous thing about [the October 1980 proclamation and the November 1980 manifesto of the Islamic Front] is that nowhere do they demand the introduction of Islamic law, the shari'a. It is merely mentioned a few times—one could almost say: in passing. They do not even demand that Islam be declared [the] state religion[,] although seven years previously Islamists had protested violently over the lack of such a passage in the 1973 draft constitution. At best some points are presented as being "based in word and spirit on Islam". . . . The programme largely contains elements that are rather more bourgeois-liberal in character than Islamic, including for instance legal guarantees for human rights and in particular the demand for the classical liberal [principle] of the division of power.[43]

With regard to economic affairs, the platform of the Islamic Front exhibited four significant features. In the first place, it asserted that there exists a fundamental right to private property ownership.[44] The activities of the private sector were to be encouraged by means of government policy. In particular, smaller private companies were to be granted the same kinds of state support that were enjoyed by public-sector enterprises, especially unhindered access to credit and subsidies for raw materials and other vital inputs. Furthermore, the manifesto called for the state-run collective farms to be broken up and their lands to be distributed among small-scale private farmers.[45] Second, the Front proposed that workers in public-sector industrial enterprises be given a fair share in the ownership of these companies and be provided with incentives to encourage them to increase overall productivity.[46] Third, improvements in working conditions were to be made in both the public and the private sectors. At the same time, comprehensive health benefits were to be extended to all citizens indiscriminately. Fourth, the manifesto called for government spending to be distributed according to the needs of particular regions, not on the basis of sectarian or partisan considerations, and state expenditures were to be made in such a way as to avoid generating further corruption among administrative personnel.

Several attempts at reconciliation between the Islamic Front in Syria and the Joint Command of the Muslim Brothers were made during the winter of 1980–1981, to little avail. Meanwhile, the Joint Command dispatched delegations to Iraq and Jordan to solicit military and financial assistance.[47] These missions obtained few if any additional resources for the movement, and in the wake of the Hamah revolt sentiment inside the Islamist movement shifted decidedly against the strategy of armed struggle. 'Adnan 'Uqlah himself was dismissed from the Joint Command at the end of April 1982 on the grounds that his actions had inflicted unnecessary suffering on the residents of Aleppo and Hamah.[48]

With the Joint Command in disarray and the Fighting Vanguard in full retreat, the Islamic Front in Syria turned its attention toward a motley collection of groups that stood opposed to the Ba'thi regime. The new coalition adopted the designation of the National Alliance for the Liberation of Syria and included dissident cells of the Ba'th Party and an assortment of independent Arab socialist (Nasirist) parties, along with the vestiges of al-Hawrani's Arab Socialist Party.[49] The platform advanced by the National Alliance was on the whole sketchy, although its components tended to mirror the principles that were contained in the manifesto of the Islamic Front.

In general, the National Alliance demanded that the Ba'th Party–led regime be overthrown but that other aspects of Syria's domestic political-economic order be marginally reformed rather than subjected to any kind of fundamental restructuring. It called for the revival of an elected parliament, as well as for the drafting of a revised constitution that would guarantee all citizens the freedoms of public association, expression, and religion.[50] It also advocated an end to official corruption and promised that the new order would provide various kinds of assistance to industrial workers and agricultural laborers. On the whole, the National Alliance retreated from the detailed economic program that had been advanced by the Islamic Front and offered instead incremental changes to the country's domestic affairs. More important, as Thomas Mayer observes, "only one paragraph [of the National Alliance's 1983 charter] directly referred to Syria's Islamic nature. No mention was made of the Islamic Front's intention to establish a shura system in Syria. The Front's detailed economic program also was ignored. Instead, the Alliance made a vague promise to reform the Syrian economy."[51]

Militants found themselves steadily marginalized by the Islamist movement in the aftermath of the Hamah revolt. The remnants of the Fighting Vanguard asserted that its goal continued to be "the establishment of an Islamic state, through jihad."[52] 'Uqlah's supporters expressed particular contempt for the liberal principles that permeated the platforms promulgated by the Islamic Front and the National Alliance. In their view, "To set up a democratic state is not our problem. We have already had experience with these parties and they are mere dictators." Furthermore, the radical Islamists claimed that "men have no right to choose to govern themselves; they must [instead] be ruled by the order of God."[53] With regard to economic issues, the Fighting Vanguard expressed an equally radical viewpoint. When asked about the group's economic policy, one spokesperson answered simply, "What I make by my own efforts, legally, I keep; otherwise the state has the right to take it back. This is very precise in Islamic books."[54] In 1986, the few remaining militants, led from Germany by Sa'd al-Din, formally broke with the Muslim Brothers, headed by General Supervisor Abu Ghuddah, who was living in exile in Saudi Arabia.

LIBERALISM'S APOGEE

By the early 1990s, the authorities in Damascus had started to make overtures to prominent Islamist opponents of the Ba'th Party–led regime. Such moves prompted the leadership of the Muslim Brothers to draw up a list of relatively moderate demands, which included the release of all political prisoners, an end to martial law, and guarantees of freedom of political expression and religious practice.[55] As time went by, spokespeople for the Islamist opposition increasingly emphasized such liberal principles as heightened "respect for human rights," "equality among all citizens," and "political pluralism to enable the people to choose . . . the governmental system."[56] Islamist activists also underscored the need to restore national unity in order to carry on the struggle against Zionism.

Halting rapprochement between the Ikhwan al-Muslimin and the regime set the stage for General Supervisor Abu Ghuddah's return to Syria in December 1995. In exchange for permission to reenter the country, Abu Ghuddah promised not to engage in any kind of political activity and settled down to teach theology and Islamic law in Aleppo.[57] The leadership of the Muslim Brothers then met in London and elected 'Ali Sadr al-Din al-Bayanuni, a former radical member of the Joint Command, to the post of general supervisor.[58]

Persistent reports of contacts between the authorities and the Muslim Brothers prompted the Ikhwan al-Muslimin to issue a statement that urged the government "to open the doors for more freedom and political pluralism, so that the people will be able to foil the schemes of the enemies" of the nation.[59] A subsequent statement underscored the Ikhwan's interest in "achiev[ing] a national reconciliation which will bolster the steadfastness of the Syrian domestic front in the face of outside pressures aimed at undermining Syria's security and stability."[60] The major external threat was said to come from the State of Israel, although the consolidation of a strategic partnership between Israel and Turkey eventually focused the Ikhwan's opprobrium on Ankara as well.[61]

As the 1990s drew to a close, leading figures of Syria's Muslim Brothers reiterated an appreciation for the virtues of political pluralism and liberal democracy. Senior figures issued a communiqué in August 1999 that demanded that the authorities in Damascus take steps to "renounce autocracy and opt for democracy, freedom and political pluralism as part of reform."[62]

Shortly after the death of Hafiz al-Asad in June 2000, the Ikhwan al-Muslimin issued a statement that called on Syria's new leader, Bashshar al-Asad, to adopt measures that would promote "general national unity within a framework of political pluralism and public freedoms."[63] The incoming president was exhorted to show a "willingness to reverse the despotic approach [to government] and carry out genuine reforms," as well as to move quickly to "close national ranks [in order] to confront outside threats and challenges." At the same time, General Supervisor al-Bayanuni told reporters that the Muslim Brothers did not even have to be permitted to operate legally inside Syria; it would be enough to have some sort of "formula" that would allow the organization to "express its views" concerning public issues. "We would welcome any move to rectify the situation," al-Bayanuni remarked, "even if this has to be done gradually."

A Covenant of National Honor for Political Action, issued by the leadership of the Muslim Brothers in May 2001, asserted that "the time has passed when a single party claimed [ownership of the homeland]. From now on, each political group should be able to have its place on the national map in keeping with its relative strength as expressed in clean and democratic elections."[64] The document went on to advocate the creation in Syria of a "modern state," that is, "a state of rotation" in which "free and honest ballot boxes are the basis for the rotation of power between all the homeland's sons."[65] It also called for the establishment of "the supremacy of law" and "the separation of powers." As Alan George notes, the Covenant of National Honor "made no mention of the Ikhwan's long-standing demand [sic] for the application of Shari'a law."[66] In July 2002, the London office of the Muslim Brothers invited a wide range of groups that had actively opposed the Ba'thi regime to meet to endorse the Covenant. In the end, so many of the invitees declined to attend the gathering that the document quickly dropped out of sight.[67]

April 2005 saw the release of a statement by the leadership of the Ikhwan al-Muslimin that called for "free and fair elections" and the immediate termination of the state of emergency that had been imposed in the wake of the March 1963 revolution.[68] Nine months later, General Supervisor al-Bayanuni announced that the Islamist opposition had decided to join forces with Syria's exiled former vice president, 'Abd al-Halim Khaddam, in a campaign to replace the existing Ba'thi regime with a democratically elected leadership. The Ikhwan al-Muslimin thus became one component of Khaddam's umbrella National Salvation Front. In taking this step, the Muslim Brothers effectively allied itself with the liberal reform movement that in October 2005 issued the Damascus Declaration. Such a posture reaffirmed the organization's demand that Ba'thi authoritarianism be replaced by a "modern state," "that is, a 'contractual' state, based on citizenship, the rule of law, representation, pluralism, institutions, and the peaceful transfer of power."[69]

Radical Islamists upset with the London-based leadership for adopting such an accommodating posture toward the regime reverted to armed struggle in an attempt to discredit al-Bayanuni and his allies. Militants attacked a United Nations building in Damascus in April 2004; a year later, the security forces raided a house full of weapons in a suburb of the capital. Clashes broke out between radical cadres and security personnel around Hamah in the summer of 2005, and a firefight erupted on the outskirts of Aleppo that December. Under pressure from the radicals and finding the Ikhwan al-Muslimin unable to exert much influence inside the National Salvation Front, the general supervisor announced in April 2009 that the Muslim Brothers was no longer part of the Front.

RESURGENCE OF ARMED STRUGGLE

In May 2010, an influential Islamist preacher castigated the Muslim Brothers for negotiating with the government and warned that a resumption of armed struggle might prove to be the only way "to force the Ba'thist regime into introducing serious political reforms." The leadership council of the Ikhwan al-Muslimin in July 2010 replaced General Supervisor al-Bayanuni with Muhammad Riyad al-Shaqfah, a 66-year-old engineer from Hamah. The new general supervisor appointed Muhammad Faruq Taifur, also from Hamah, to be his deputy. Both men had taken part in armed struggle against the regime during the early 1980s as cadres of the Fighting Vanguard, and Taifur had more recently been an outspoken critic of al-Bayanuni's dealings with the authorities.

Initial manifestations of popular discontent in Aleppo and Damascus in February and March 2011 elicited no response from the Muslim Brothers. In fact, when large-scale unrest flared around Dir'a in mid-March, government officials quickly charged that General Supervisor al-Shaqfah had played a part in instigating the uprising; al-Shaqfah responded by issuing a carefully worded statement that expressed sympathy for the objectives of the protesters but kept the Ikhwan al-Muslimin at arm's length from the disorders.[70] The general supervisor reiterated the organization's backing for the protesters after the security forces opened fire on students at the University of Damascus in early April.[71]

Representatives of the Muslim Brothers traveled to the Turkish city of Antalya at the end of May 2011 to take part in negotiations with other opposition groups based outside Syria to form a united front opposed to the Ba'thi regime. Four months later, senior Ikhwani figures returned to Antalya to engage in the deliberations that resulted in the formation of the Syrian National Council. Of the 29 seats in the Council's original secretariat, 4 were assigned to the Muslim Brothers, a number matched only by liberal activists associated with the 2005 Damascus Declaration.

Meanwhile, inside Syria, local militias composed largely of former soldiers started to carry out armed attacks against Ba'th Party offices, military facilities, and other targets beginning in June 2011. Virtually all of these guerrilla formations took names drawn from the early days of Islam: the 'Umar bin al-Khattab Brigade outside Dair al-Zur, the 'Ali bin Abi Talib and Abu Bakr al-Sadiq Brigades in Jabal al-Zawiyyah, the Khalid bin al-Walid Brigade at al-Rastan, and the Allahu Akbar Brigade of Al Bu Kamal. Such militias had few if any ties to the Muslim Brothers and received inspiration instead from independent preachers of a more radical, populist disposition. One such figure, 'Adnan al-'Ar 'ur, called on the shopkeepers of Hamah to stage a general strike in mid-June in sympathy with the embattled residents of Duma and Jisr al-Shughur.[72] Al-'Ar 'ur galvanized the crowd at a public rally in Idlib in early November, prompting General Supervisor al-Shaqfah to invite the Turkish army to intervene in northern Syria to protect the civilian population, an invitation that he quickly rescinded.[73]

Religious notables who might have mobilized internal opposition to the Ba'thi regime during the spring and summer of 2011 for the most part refrained from doing so. Thomas Pierret reports that the al-Hasan mosque in the Midan district of Damascus provided the staging point for a series of popular protests that July, but those preachers who dared to speak out in support of the demonstrations found themselves forced out of their official positions and sometimes subjected to physical violence. "After August 2011," Pierret continues,

> mosques gradually lost their importance in the uprising for at least two reasons: first, in Damascus and Aleppo, repression succeeded in making demonstrations increasingly rare in rebellious places of worship; second, in the regions where the opposition was most

powerful (the governorates of Homs, Hama, Idlib, and [the countryside around] Damascus), it became increasingly militarised and took control of several towns and neighbourhoods, thus reducing the importance of mosques as "safe" zones for demonstrations.[74]

Disagreements inside the Muslim Brothers over the strategy of aligning with liberal and radical parties under the auspices of the Syrian National Council led to a short-lived campaign in early July to oust General Supervisor al-Shaqfah in favor of the more radical Faruq Taifur.[75] A month later, a collection of prominent religious scholars (*'ulama*) in Aleppo issued a public statement that sharply condemned the ongoing "blood-spilling and violation of public rights" and urged "the different Syrian groups to be keen on the unity of the children of this precious nation and to work on consolidating it and to preserve the public and private properties of the nation."[76]

By the end of 2011, the Muslim Brothers started to be challenged by other Islamist movements that had firmer networks inside Syria. One of these was the Islamic Liberation Party (*Hizb al-Tahrir al-Islami*), which had been active in Homs since the early 1980s. This party's platform diverged sharply from that of the Ikhwan al-Muslimin, most notably in its insistence that government policy reflect the tenets of Islam and its demand that autonomous states subordinate themselves to an overarching Islamic authority, the Caliphate.[77] A second rival to the Muslim Brothers was the Believers Join In movement (*al-Muminin Yusharikun*), led by Lu'ai al-Zu'bi. Yet another was the Strange Ones of Syria (*Ghuraba al-Sham*), which took shape largely to resist U.S. military intervention in Iraq. Arguably more important was the cluster of "neofundamentalist" religious scholars who occupied key posts in the official religious hierarchy and used their positions to advocate social justice and community orderliness. Prominent members of this body of scholars, including the grand mufti of Aleppo, Ibrahim al-Salqini, distanced themselves from the regime as the violence escalated, and a number of them affixed their names to petitions in support of political reform.[78]

February 2012 saw the detonation of massive car bombs outside two security forces headquarters in Aleppo. Responsibility for the bombings was subsequently claimed by a self-declared affiliate of al-Qa'idah, which took the name the Assistance Front for the People of Syria.[79] Shortly after the attacks, al-Qa'idah's head of operations 'Ayman al-Zawahiri released a video recording that bore the striking, and perhaps ironic, title "Onward, Lions of Syria." The video extolled the bravery of the fighters who were engaged in armed struggle against the Ba'th Party. A previously unknown personage calling himself al-Fatih (The Conqueror) Abu Muhammad al-Gawlani ("from the Golan") presented himself as the secretary general of the Assistance Front.

In the wake of such developments, Syria's Muslim Brothers turned its sights on the Islamic Republic of Iran. In an April 2012 interview with the Turkish newspaper *Zaman*, General Supervisor al-Shaqfah claimed to possess hard evidence

that Tehran had provided extensive "political, financial and military support" to
the Ba'thi regime. Taifur added that Iranian arms had come into Syria by way
of Iraq and that the brightest hope for his country's future lay in Turkey, whose
governing AK Partisi he praised as "the ideal Islamic model" of governance.

Meanwhile, Syria's major opposition groups gathered in Istanbul at the end of
March 2012 to work out a coordinated strategy to guide the future of the uprising. In the days leading up to the congress, the Muslim Brothers released a
revised Covenant of National Honor, which laid out a "new social contract" that
promised to "protect the fundamental rights of individuals and groups from any
abuse or excesses, and ensure equitable representation of all components of society." The document envisaged the establishment of "a republican parliamentary
system of government," in which representatives would be selected through
popular elections. It advocated a "separation of powers" among the executive,
legislature, and judiciary, and stipulated that the rights of citizens would be
"endorsed by heavenly religions and international conventions."[80]

Elements of the Ikhwan al-Muslimin's new covenant were clearly evident in
the platform that the Syrian National Council drew up at the Istanbul congress.
Furthermore, the rhetoric of Council Chairman Burhan Ghalioun's closing
address, which called on delegates to take a formal oath to support the proposed
Transitional Authority in Syria, evoked the medieval Islamic ceremony of swear-
ing public allegiance to the ruler. Such symbols reinforced the conviction of
liberal activists inside the National Council that the Muslim Brothers occupied
a dominant position in the coalition and intended to exert control over its agenda
and activities for the foreseeable future.

Growing apprehension on the part of its political allies about the organization's
influence and objectives prompted leaders of the Muslim Brothers to reiterate the
liberal principles that it had championed during the 1940s. One member of the
organization told reporters in early April that in the post-Ba'thi era, Syria's
president might even be a Christian. "She can be a Christian woman," Mulham
al-Durubi insisted. "She can, but she has to win the elections. Any Syrian citizen
can be a president."[81] When the Christian George Sabra was suggested as a
replacement for Barhun Ghalioun as head of the Syrian National Council in
May 2012, former General Supervisor al-Bayanuni opined that "the Muslim
Brothers movement had no veto against George Sabra in case he is selected to head
the council. The important thing is for everyone to co-operate for the interest of
Syria and the resistance of its people."[82] In the end, representatives of the Ikhwan
al-Muslimin threw their weight behind Ghalioun, ensuring his reelection.[83]
Nevertheless, General Supervisor al-Shaqfah took pains to reassure Syria's 'Alawi,
Isma'ili, Druze, and Christian communities that their civic interests would be
fully protected in the future: "After we are rid of this murderous regime, they will
benefit even further. The rights of all Syrian sects will be guaranteed and we will
not differentiate between the citizens, neither on sectarian nor on ethnic bases."[84]

NOTES

Portions of Chapter 3 first appeared in Fred H. Lawson, "Syria's Islamist Movement and the 2011–12 Uprising," *Origins* 5, no. 10 (July 2012), http://ehistory.osu.edu/osu/origins/article.cfm?articleid=70. Used by permission.

1. Ishak Musa Husaini, *The Moslem Brethren* (Beirut: Khayat's, 1956), 76; Umar Abd-Allah, *The Islamic Struggle in Syria* (Berkeley, CA: Mizan Press, 1983), 91.

2. Johannes Reissner, *Ideologie und Politik der Muslimbrüder Syriens* (Freiburg, Germany: Klaus Schwarz Verlag, 1980), 124–26; Suechika Kota, "The Syrian Muslim Brotherhood and Mustafa al-Siba'i," *Asian and African Area Studies* 2 (2002).

3. Abd-Allah, *Islamic Struggle*, 93.

4. Ibid., 149.

5. Ibid., 142.

6. Reissner, *Ideologie und Politik*, 183.

7. Joshua Teitelbaum, "The Muslim Brotherhood and the 'Struggle for Syria', 1947–1958," *Middle Eastern Studies* 40 (May 2004), 136.

8. Reissner, *Ideologie und Politik*, 196.

9. Ibid., 197.

10. United States National Archives, Record Group 59 (USNA), 890.00/9-1547.

11. Teitelbaum, "Muslim Brotherhood," 138.

12. Ibid.; Reissner, *Ideologie und Politik*, 282.

13. USNA, 890.00/12-447.

14. USNA, 890.00/7-2448.

15. Teitelbaum, "Muslim Brotherhood," 139.

16. Ibid., 140.

17. Ibid., 140–41.

18. Ibid., 141; Reissner, *Ideologie und Politik*, 316.

19. Teitelbaum, "Muslim Brotherhood," 142.

20. Ibid., 143; R. Bayly Winder, "Islam as the State Religion: A Muslim Brotherhood View in Syria," *Muslim World* 44 (July 1954).

21. Teitelbaum, "Muslim Brotherhood," 150.

22. Husaini, *Moslem Brethren*, 152; Teitelbaum, "Muslim Brotherhood," 153.

23. Thomas Mayer, "The Islamic Opposition in Syria, 1961–1982," *Orient* 32 (December 1983), 590–91.

24. Hanna Batatu, "Syria's Muslim Brethren," *MERIP Reports*, no. 110 (November–December 1982).

25. Abd-Allah, *Islamic Struggle*, 107–8.

26. Mayer, "Islamic Opposition," 592.

27. Itzchak Weismann, "Sa'id Hawwa: The Making of a Radical Muslim Thinker in Modern Syria," *Middle Eastern Studies* 29 (October 1993), 603–7, 614; Annabelle Böttcher, *Syrische Religionspolitik unter Asad* (Freiburg, Germany: Arnold Bergsträsser Institut, 1998), 131–44.

28. Mayer, "Islamic Opposition," 594; Weismann, "Sa'id Hawwa," 617.

29. Mayer, "Islamic Opposition," 594 note 25.

30. Weismann, "Sa'id Hawwa," 607–11.

31. Ibid., 620.

32. *Arab Report and Record* (ARR), July 16–31, 1975.

33. Hanna Batatu, *Syria's Peasantry, the Descendants of Its Lesser Rural Notables and Their Politics* (Princeton, NJ: Princeton University Press, 1999), 264.

34. Abd-Allah, *Islamic Struggle*, 109; *Le Monde*, March 26, 1976.

35. Batatu, *Syria's Peasantry*, 269.

36. Middle East Watch, *Syria Unmasked* (New Haven, CT: Yale University Press, 1991), 20.

37. Abd-Allah, *Islamic Struggle*, 115.

38. Mayer, "Islamic Opposition," 597.

39. Ibid., 600.

40. Hans Günter Lobmeyer, "Islamic Ideology and Secular Discourse: The Islamists of Syria," *Orient* 32 (September 1991), 405.

41. Abd-Allah, *Islamic Struggle*, 151.

42. Ibid., 152.

43. Lobmeyer, "Islamic Ideology," 412–13.

44. Mayer, "Islamic Opposition," 601.

45. Lobmeyer, "Islamic Ideology," 413.

46. Abd-Allah, *Islamic Struggle*, 160.

47. Batatu, *Syria's Peasantry*, 268–69.

48. Ibid., 269.

49. Hans Günter Lobmeyer, "Al-dimuqratiyya hiyya al-Hall? The Syrian Opposition at the End of the Asad Era," in *Contemporary Syria*, ed. Eberhard Kienle (London: British Academic Press, 1994), 87.

50. Mayer, "Islamic Opposition," 607.

51. Ibid.

52. Chris Kutschera, "Syria: Muslim Brothers, The Question of Alliances," *The Middle East*, no. 103 (May 1983).

53. Ibid.

54. Ibid.

55. Chris Kutschera, "When the Brothers Fall Out," *The Middle East*, no. 162 (April 1988).

56. Lobmeyer, "Al-dimuqratiyya," 90.

57. Eyal Zisser, "Syria, the Ba'th Regime and the Islamic Movement," *Muslim World* 95 (January 2005), 52.

58. Gary C. Gambill, "The Syrian Muslim Brotherhood," lebanonwire.com, 2006.

59. *al-Rai* ('Amman), February 18, 1997.

60. *al-Quds al-'Arabi*, April 3, 1997.

61. *al-Sabil* ('Amman), October 7, 1998.

62. *Jordan Times*, August 26, 1999.

63. British Broadcasting Corporation (BBC), July 14, 2000.

64. Zisser, "Syria," 56.

65. Alan George, *Syria: Neither Bread nor Freedom* (London: Zed Books, 2003), 92.

66. Ibid.

67. Eyal Zisser, *Commanding Syria* (London: I. B. Tauris, 2007), 86.

68. *Christian Science Monitor*, June 10, 2005.

69. Scott Lasensky and Mona Yacoubian, *Syria and Political Change* (Washington, DC: United States Institute of Peace, 2005).

70. *al-Sharq al-Awsat*, March 23, 2011.

71. *Los Angeles Times*, April 11, 2011.

72. *al-Watan* (Damascus), June 16, 2011.

73. *al-Sharq al-Awsat*, November 19, 2011.

74. Thomas Pierret, "The Role of the Mosque in the Syrian Revolution," *Near East Quarterly*, no. 7 (February 2012).

75. *al-Quds al-'Arabi*, July 5, 2011.

76. *al-Rai al-'Amm*, August 9, 2011.

77. *al-Akhbar*, May 3, 2012.

78. Line Khatib, "Syria's Islamic Movement and the Current Uprising: Political Acquiescence, Quietism and Dissent," *Jadaliyya*, February 21, 2012, http://www.jadaliyya.com.

79. Associated Press, March 21, 2012.

80. *Syria Comment*, March 26, 2012; *al-Rai al-'Amm*, March 27, 2012.

81. *The National* (Abu Dhabi), April 2, 2012.

82. *al-Rai al-'Amm*, May 15, 2012.

83. *al-Rai al-'Amm*, May 17, 2012; *al-Sharq al-Awsat*, May 25, 2012.

84. *al-Sharq al-Awsat*, June 14, 2012.

FURTHER READING

Umar F. Abd-Allah. *The Islamic Struggle in Syria*. Berkeley, CA: Mizan Press, 1983.

Hanna Batatu. "Syria's Muslim Brethren." *MERIP Reports*, no. 110 (December 1982).

Line Khatib. *Islamic Revivalism in Syria*. London: Routledge, 2011.

Hans Guenter Lobmeyer. "Islamic Ideology and Secular Discourse: The Islamists of Syria." *Orient* 32 (September 1991).

Thomas Mayer. "The Islamic Opposition in Syria, 1961–1982." *Orient* 24 (December 1983).

Itzchak Weismann. "Democratic Fundamentalism?: The Practice and Discourse of the Muslim Brothers Movement in Syria." *Muslim World* 100 (January 2010).

Eyal Zisser. "Syria, the Ba'th Regime and the Islamic Movement: Stepping on a New Path?" *Muslim World* 95 (January 2005).

CHAPTER 4

Popular Uprising and Regime Response

Simmering discontent exploded into popular disorder across the Arab world during the winter of 2010–2011. First Tunisia and Bahrain and then Egypt and Yemen experienced large-scale opposition movements that demanded an end to autocratic rule and the immediate implementation of liberal-democratic reforms. As protesters flooded into Liberation (Tahrir) Square in Cairo in late January 2011, President Bashshar al-Asad sat down with two reporters from the *Wall Street Journal* to discuss current developments in the region. "Syria is stable," the president asserted. "Why? Because you have to be strongly linked to the beliefs of the people. . . . If you didn't see the need for reform before what happened in Egypt and Tunisia, it's too late to do any reforms. . . . [W]e are outside of this; at the end we are not Tunisians and we are not Egyptians. We are not a copy of each other."[1] And indeed, when Syria exploded into violence several weeks later, the trajectory of the uprising diverged sharply from the pattern found in Tunisia, Egypt, Bahrain, or Yemen.

INITIAL PROTESTS

At the end of January 2011, a group calling itself the Movement of Democratic Youth organized a torchlight march in the northeastern city of al-Raqqah to protest the killing of two members of the Organization of Western Kurdistan by the security forces. In the neighboring city of al-Hasakah, a man named Hasan 'Ali 'Aqlah doused himself with gasoline and set himself on fire, following the example of Tunisia's Muhammad Bu 'Azizi. The demonstrations in the northeast provinces prompted civil rights activists in the north-central

metropolis of Aleppo to call for public protests against police practices and official corruption; activists in Damascus announced plans to organize a march in
front of the People's Assembly on February 5.[2] Units of the regular armed forces
quickly moved into Kurdish neighborhoods of Aleppo to dissuade residents from
making any open display of antiregime sentiment, and the day designated for
protests in the capital came and went without incident.

On February 17, shopkeepers around Hariqah Square in Damascus ran to the
defense of a young man who was being assaulted by the police, and on March 1
Hussam al-Din Mansur walked into the square and held up a banner that read,
"We have had enough. Bashshar, save us from the gang." Mansur was arrested,
charged with "writing expressions that undermine public security," and then
released after three days in jail. While Mansur was still in custody, the Council
of Ministers reinstated the policy of guaranteeing employment to all university
graduates and pledged to create 10,000 additional job opportunities for young
people in the private sector.[3] Two days after Mansur's release, President al-Asad
issued a general pardon for prisoners who had not been convicted of political
crimes.[4] Detainees who remained incarcerated in 'Adra prison then launched a
hunger strike to demand that political prisoners be pardoned as well.[5] On
March 8, an independent representative in the People's Assembly suggested that
the state of emergency that had been in force since March 1963 be brought up
for reconsideration.

When the Ministry of the Interior adjacent to Martyrs' Square in downtown
Damascus opened its doors for business on the morning of March 16, eight
women related to political prisoners went into the building to ask about the
health and condition of their relatives. They were joined by 33 other women
who attempted to gain entry to the building as well. Before the second group
could get inside, some 50 people gathered around it, holding photographs of
other prisoners and chanting slogans that in the words of the official *al-Watan*
newspaper "had nothing to do with the detainees or their parents." Security personnel, shopkeepers, and passersby rushed to the scene, and almost immediately
"fistfights erupted, and one could no longer differentiate between the supporters,
the opponents and the families of the detainees."[6] The security forces arrested
several people involved in the melee, including a handful of prominent civil
rights activists. A smaller crowd gathered outside the interior ministry the next
day, surrounded by a greatly reinforced security presence.

This initial cycle of protest and response in the capital was eclipsed when more
serious disorder erupted around the southern city of Dir'a in the third week of
March. The unrest in the south flared into violence after the security forces
harassed 15 schoolchildren who had scrawled the battle cry of Egypt's revolution-
aries—"The people want the fall of the regime"—on a wall.[7] The detention and
physical mistreatment of the children sparked a succession of demonstrations
around the 'Umari Mosque in the center of Dir'a, during the course of which

the local headquarters of the Ba'th Party was taken over and set on fire, along with the storefront of the mobile telephone company owned by Rami Makhluf. Regular army units then advanced into the city and seized control of the mosque. The direct intervention of the armed forces prompted the inhabitants of towns and villages surrounding Dir'a to take to the streets, where they were met by riot police who shot into the crowds with small arms.

Officials in Damascus tried to calm the situation by claiming that local commanders had acted against explicit orders when they used live ammunition against the protesters. Representatives of the interior ministry traveled to Dir'a to express the government's condolences and to confer with regional notables. The latter were reported to have demanded the immediate dismissal of both the head of provincial security, who was a cousin of President al-Asad, and the provincial governor. Prime Minister Muhammad Naji' al-'Utri acknowledged that the southern highlands had been treated unfairly by government agencies, and promised that "very soon a new program will be put in place to ensure that the working forces and university graduates in the province find appropriate jobs."[8] State-sponsored news media at first blamed the troubles on "Palestinian radicals" from a refugee camp outside Dir'a, then alleged that "an armed gang" with links across the border in northern Jordan had provoked the violence. The government news agency further asserted that the new head of Syria's Muslim Brothers bore responsibility for inciting the unrest by proclaiming the organization's intention to resume militant activity against the regime.[9]

Public disorder almost immediately spread to Latakia on the Mediterranean coast, where protesters clashed with groups of government supporters. Early reports claimed that the police were being fired upon by shadowy "Sunni elements." Such reports accompanied the deployment of units of the Republican Guard and regular armed forces to various parts of the city. After protesters set fire to the Ba'th Party headquarters, snipers started to target young people milling in the streets. As in the case of Dir'a, the authorities initially blamed the outbreak of violence on "armed gangs" and Palestinian militants, then pointed to the prominent Qatar-based preacher Yusif al-Qaradawi, who had praised Syrian demonstrators in his Friday sermon on March 25.[10] The persistence of sporadic, small-scale protests in Damascus, along with growing signs of popular restiveness in Homs, Hamah, and Dair al-Zur, set the stage for reports that the authorities had taken steps to mobilize cadres of the party-affiliated workers' and students' unions into militias to maintain order.[11]

As fighting escalated in Latakia, protests broke out in Duma, the administrative center of the Damascus countryside province. The protesters were met by proregime demonstrators, who quickly fled in the face of the crowd. Opposition activists then seized control of the town's main square and renamed it Freedom Square. Here the crowd chanted for an end to the state of emergency that had been in effect since 1963, the release of all political prisoners, constitutional guarantees of civil rights, and measures to eliminate official corruption. Local commanders dispatched security personnel, religious notables, and a member of the People's Assembly to convince the crowd to disperse, but all such efforts failed. Shortly after midnight,

> the street lights went out so that no one could take pictures or shoot any videos. Then [the security forces] attacked in the dark, with heavy sticks. They even chased [the protesters] down the side streets and alleys. . . . The police pursuit and arrests carried on until the early hours. Traces of blood and shattered glass were all over the streets, although the municipality cleaned everything up the next morning in an attempt to wipe away all evidence of the brutality.[12]

On March 30, 2011, President al-Asad delivered a televised address to the country. He admitted that the reform process that he had outlined at his inauguration in July 2000 had stalled but blamed the evident lack of progress on the Palestinian uprising of 2000, U.S. military offensives in Afghanistan and Iraq, and the 2006 Israel-Hizbullah war in Lebanon. He went on to charge that the disorders gripping Syria were the result of "conspiracies" and pledged that he would redouble the government's efforts to carry out political and economic reforms. On the other hand, the president cautioned, "announcing a timeframe for any issue is a technical matter. We could announce a timeframe that might be tighter than necessary, and the end result would be rushing things at the expense of quality. . . . We need to be quick, but not rush things." The day after the president's speech, the Council of Ministers set up a special committee to determine whether or not the state of emergency should be lifted, and raised wages for public-sector workers and state employees; at the same time, a commission was formed to review the 1962 census that had denied citizenship to some 150,000 Kurds in the northeastern provinces. On the recommendation of the latter, the government on April 7 issued a law that conferred full citizenship on those members of Syria's Kurdish community who had previously existed in limbo.

THE UPRISING GATHERS MOMENTUM

Two days after the president's speech, several hundred Kurds in the northeastern cities of al-Hasakah, al-Qamishli, Ras al-'Ain, and 'Amudah marched through the streets chanting "We do not want only citizenship, but freedom as well."[13] Protesters in Duma and Kafr Susah outside Damascus, Dir'a, and Latakia were attacked by club-wielding thugs and elicited gunfire from the police, while marches in Homs and the coastal city of Banyas took place more peacefully. These incidents were followed by two days of calm, during which President al-Asad appointed Minister of Agriculture and Agrarian Reform 'Adil Safar as prime minister of a new government. Rumors circulated that a cluster of new ministers would be selected, including individuals drawn from the provinces of Dir‘a and al-Suwaida.[14] Shortly thereafter, the head of Military Intelligence for the two southern provinces was quietly reassigned.[15]

A week of minor events came to an end on April 10, when a skirmish occurred between heavily armed men and the security forces in Banyas. The authorities imposed a blockade around the city and the nearby town of Baidah after a group of women marched from Baidah to the coastal highway demanding the release of spouses and sons who had been swept up in a mass arrest. Meanwhile, back in the capital, President al-Asad met with a delegation of 50 notables from Dir‘a, including the prayer leader of the ‘Umari Mosque. He "assured [the delegation] that [an] investigation committee was working in a transparent way and will hold accountable all those who are proven to be involved in these incidents," and then issued a presidential pardon for all those who had been arrested in the province up to that point but had "not been involved in criminal acts."[16]

One week later, thousands of residents of Homs occupied the central Clock-tower Square. The crowd took to the streets after police opened fire on partici-pants of earlier protests, which had in turn been sparked by the death of the chief of the Fawara Bedouin clan, Shaikh Badr Abu Musa, while he was in official custody. After renaming the place Liberation (Tahrir) Square, civil rights activists pledged that they would continue to occupy the area until the state of emergency was rescinded and all political prisoners set free. Security forces peppered the area with tear gas and occasional shots fired into the air but for the most part kept their distance. Just before dawn on the second day of the protest, however, police, security forces, and armed thugs moved into the square in force and shot at the demonstrators.[17] Officials in the capital told reporters that Islamist militants had launched "an armed insurrection" in Homs and Banyas, backed by "armed criminal gangs." Military units then deployed throughout the northeastern suburbs of the capital, and when coordinated demonstrations in Duma, Zamalka, and al-Ma‘adamiyyah took place after Friday prayers on April 22, troops fired into the crowds in those towns as well. The assaults were followed by systematic house-to-house sweeps through residential neighborhoods and a wave of arrests of suspected activists.

Around this time, clusters of dissidents started to set up clandestine councils to orchestrate protests and coordinate popular action across different districts. The disparate groupings, which called themselves the Local Coordinating Commit-tees, communicated with one another by means of Internet chatrooms and mobile telephones smuggled into Syria from Lebanon and Jordan.[18] The mem-bership of the committees consisted overwhelmingly of young proponents of civil rights and constitutional government, including both men and women. Older, established critics of the regime played little if any part in creating and maintaining the network, nor did the Local Coordinating Committees have connections to the Muslim Brothers. Several competing networks of activists coa-lesced as well: the Union of Coordinating Committees of the Syrian Revolution, the Free Committees, the Tomorrow (Ghad) Democratic Coalition, and the Committees of National Action.[19]

Regular army units returned to Dir'a in force on April 25, supported by tanks and other heavy weapons. The troops seized control of the 'Umari Mosque and cut off the supply of electricity to the city and its environs.[20] They then undertook house-to-house searches for dissidents and began to troll local hospitals for anyone who might have been injured while taking part in protests. The city was cordoned off, and shipments of food and medicine interdicted. The military offensive against Dir'a was followed by the envelopment of Banyas by armored units, and after that by reports that a column of tanks was headed for Homs. At this point, two members of the People's Assembly representing electoral districts in Dir'a resigned their posts, as did the city's senior religious official (*mufti*), Shaikh Rizq 'Abd al-Rahim Abazaid. One of the parliamentary representatives, Nasir Hariri, told reporters that "if I cannot protect the chests of my people from these treacherous strikes, then there is no meaning for me to stay in the People's Assembly."[21] In addition, students at the University of Aleppo and University of Damascus organized campus demonstrations, which were dispersed by police firing tear gas and rubber bullets.[22]

Fighting broke out in Homs between armed protesters and security forces during the first week of May 2011. The clashes centered on the district of Baba 'Amru, a working-class neighborhood in the southeastern corner of the city. Residents of the northeastern city of al-Qamishli held a torchlight march to demand an end to military operations at Dir'a, Banyas, and Homs.[23] But despite this protest, the armed forces stepped up the assault on Baba 'Amru, subjecting the neighborhood to sustained tank, mortar, and heavy machine-gun fire. The shelling sparked a sizable demonstration in the dormitory area of the University of Aleppo, which was broken up by cadres of the Ba'th Party's students' union and security forces.[24] Armed skirmishes then spread to the area around Idlib, including the town of Tal Kalakh at the junction of the main north-south and east-west highways. Troops advancing into Tal Kalakh were accompanied by substantial numbers of proregime thugs, popularly referred to as phantoms (*shabbihah*), who exercised indiscriminate violence against local residents. The brutality of the assault on Tal Kalakh, and widespread rumors of outright butchery inflicted on local Sunnis, sent most residents of the town fleeing across the border into northern Lebanon.[25] At the end of May, tanks surrounded the strategically situated town of al-Rastan, but residents prevented the armored forces from moving into the town by firing back with automatic rifles and rocket-propelled grenades.

Representatives of several organizations opposed to the Ba'th Party–led regime, all of them based outside Syria, gathered in the Turkish city of Antalya on May 31. The conference was reported to have been sponsored by a number of wealthy Syrian businesspeople whose commercial interests had been harmed by the actions of relatives of the president.[26] Among the attendees were members of the Muslim Brothers, the United States–based Syrian National Coalition for Change, and the London-based Movement for Justice and Development. Notably absent from the meeting were the primary Kurdish political parties, whose leaders warned activists in the northeastern provinces to scale back street protests lest they provoke the kind of retaliation that was present in Banyas and Homs.[27] As the delegates arrived in Antalya, President al-Asad proclaimed a general amnesty for political prisoners, including members of the Muslim Brothers. The amnesty accompanied a government proposal to allocate US$65 million to improve infrastructure and public services in Dir'a province.[28]

At the same time, the president met with a succession of delegations from southern and northeastern Syria and proposed that a set of "national dialogues" be convened across the country to discuss pressing economic and social problems. Civil rights activists inside the country who were critical of the effort to set up an external opposition organization, and worried that the activities of the groups that met in Antalya would set the stage for foreign military intervention, formed the National Coordinating Committee of the Forces for Democratic Change (NCCFDC) under the leadership of Hasan 'Abd al-'Azim; this organization attracted the support of the Kurdish parties that had stayed away from Antalya and voiced guarded support for the state-sponsored dialogues, which it asserted could provide the impetus for a gradual transition to democratic rule. Independent civil rights campaigners like Michel Kilu, 'Arif Dalilah, and Haitham al-Mana' eventually gravitated toward the NCCFDC as well.[29]

These developments were overshadowed by the rise of a movement honoring Hamza 'Ali al-Khatib, a 13-year-old boy from Dir'a province who had been tortured and killed while in the custody of the security forces. By the end of May, some 49,000 individuals had joined a Facebook page called "We are all the martyr child Hamza 'Ali al-Khatib."[30] Following Friday prayers on June 3, tens of thousands of residents of Hamah marched to al-'Asi Square in the center of the city to commemorate "Children of Freedom Day." Security forces shot into the crowd at several points in and around the square, killing some 200 civilians. That same day, protests occurred in the Damascus suburbs of Rukn al-Din, Barzah, Dar'ayya, and Zamalka, as well as the southern end of the Midan district. Demonstrations were also reported in al-Zabadani, Idlib, al-Qamishli, and Dair al-Zur; around Dir'a "hundreds defied a military curfew and took to the streets chanting 'No dialogue with killers.' "[31]

On June 4, 2011, snipers on the roof of the post office in the town of Jisr al-Shughur northwest of Hamah fired on a passing funeral procession. The enraged mourners torched the building, killing eight security officers, then took control of the main police station and confiscated the weapons stored inside. The actions of the crowd led Syrian state television to report that "hundreds of gunmen had taken over the town."[32] Over the next few days, some 120 troops were killed in skirmishes and gun battles with armed townspeople. In response, the armed forces launched a major assault against Jisr al-Shughur, followed by a wave of mass arrests. The offensive generated a flood of refugees across the border into the Hatay region of Turkey. During the course of the battle, Lieutenant Colonel Husain Harmush defected from the Syrian armed forces with the troops under his command; he then proclaimed from Hatay the formation of an antiregime military formation, which adopted the name the Free Officers' Movement. In pursuit of the defectors, regular army units pushed past Jisr al-Shughur and swept through the surrounding towns of Bdama, Ma'arah al-Nu'man, and Khan Shaikhun, all of which boasted long histories of resistance to the forced imposition of external authority.[33]

As fighting raged at Homs and in Jabal al-Zawiyyah—the mountainous region around Idlib and Jisr al-Shughur—popular protests escalated in the largely Kurdish cities and towns of the northeast. Most of these demonstrations called for an end to tyranny and government corruption, but on a few occasions the participants raised banners that proclaimed allegiance to Kurdistan rather than to Syria.[34] The authorities in Damascus took note of the growing restiveness of the country's Kurdish community and, in early June, set up a special commission to draw up regulations whereby unlicensed Kurdish political organizations could gain recognition as official parties.[35] At the same time, a proregime group in al-Qamishli that called itself the Free Arab Youth warned Kurdish activists to put an end to public protests and "return to their senses and resort to the language of reason and dialogue."[36] Sporadic eruptions of popular protest nonetheless took place in Salah al-Din and Saif al-Dawlah, two predominantly Kurdish districts of Aleppo, as well as in the surrounding towns of Hraitan and A'zaz.[37] Farther east, residents of Dair al-Zur who had defaced posters of the president were chased off by soldiers in armored vehicles.

On June 20, 2011, President al-Asad once again addressed the country by television. He repeated the allegation that "conspiracies" and "vandals" lurked behind the unrest, and added that "conspiracies are like germs. They proliferate every moment and everywhere. They cannot be eradicated, but we can strengthen the immunity of our bodies against them." He went on to reiterate his proposal that a national dialogue be undertaken to hash out Syria's persistent problems. Residents of Hamah, Homs, and Dair al-Zur poured into the streets on the Friday after the president's speech to voice their rejection of the proposed dialogue; marchers in Hamah chanted "This speech was sponsored by Dettol [a local brand of household disinfectant]," while those in Dir'a preferred "The germs want the fall of the regime."[38] Outside the north-central town of al-Kaswah, units of the regular army were reported to have skirmished with the security forces and armed proregime thugs.[39]

At the end of June, government forces in Hamah abruptly withdrew from the city, and crowds of protesters surged back into al-'Asi Square. The square took on a carnival atmosphere and was renamed Freedom Square; residents of surrounding villages streamed into the city center to join the movement. By the third day, demonstrators started to chant, "O youth of Damascus, we in Hamah have toppled the regime."[40] But a day later the provincial governor was replaced by the city's chief of General Security,[41] and on July 4 armored and security forces advanced to the edge of the city and set up roadblocks on the main arteries. Government agents in plain clothes then swept through town, "searching homes and detaining suspects." In some neighborhoods, residents tried to interfere with the sweeps by setting tires alight, but "the military deployed trucks full of more security personnel and dispatched bulldozers to force open the streets [that] the residents had tried to close off."[42] A tense stalemate ensued, with troops and neighborhood watch committees peering warily at one another across the barricades.

In Damascus, government officials convened the initial session of the national dialogue on July 11, which was broadcast live on national television. Vice President Faruq al-Shar' told the participants that several new political parties would be authorized in the near future to compete against the Ba'th for seats in the People's Assembly.[43] More strikingly, critics of the regime's policies openly complained of instances in which excessive force had been exercised by the security forces and the shabbihah, and demanded that the authorities take steps to limit the use of violence against unarmed protesters.

TURN TO ARMED STRUGGLE

On July 17, 2011, reports came from Al Bu Kamal in the far eastern corner of the country that a group of opposition activists had stormed the district administration and captured a cache of heavy weapons. The detachment of security personnel that had been assigned to guard the building was said to have joined the dissidents and taken up positions to protect the city from the military units that were poised to counterattack.[44] Two weeks later, several regular army units in neighboring Dair al-Zur also defected and engaged in firefights with units that remained loyal to the regime.[45]

At the same time, Colonel Riyad As'ad and six other officers joined the opposition and set up headquarters outside Antakya in the Hatay for a military formation that took the name the Free Syrian Army (FSA). Soldiers at al-Rastan who had defected under the leadership of Major 'Abd al-Rahman Shaikh 'Ali, and had assumed the name the Khalid bin al-Walid Brigade, allied themselves with the new opposition army. Captain Qais Qatanah in Dir'a shortly thereafter announced the formation of the Southern Sector of the Free Officers' Movement; this unit subsequently transformed itself into the 'Umari Battalion of the FSA.[46]

Military and security forces backed by tanks rolled back into central Hamah on August 3, overwhelming the barricades that had been raised in their path.

Protesters retreated to the alleyways of the residential neighborhoods surrounding al-'Asi Square, closely pursued by troops. Armored units carried out a parallel assault on the heart of Dair al-Zur in the east, advancing in the company of pro-regime thugs. As the government regained control over Hamah and Dair al-Zur, scattered protests broke out in the countryside around Aleppo and in poorer districts of the metropolis itself. Meanwhile, in Damascus the People's Assembly convened an extraordinary session on August 7 to ratify the presidential decrees that opened the door to licensing new political parties.[47] Both the capital and Aleppo experienced a dramatic increase in residential and commercial construction as building inspectors stopped enforcing codes and property owners rushed to put up structures without permits; street vendors who had previously been harassed by the police found themselves free to practice their trade as well.[48]

Mid-August 2011 saw a coordinated land and sea attack on the coastal city of Latakia, whose initial target was a pair of restive Sunni neighborhoods. Several days of intense shelling by tanks and gunboats inflicted severe damage on a Palestinian refugee camp located in one of these districts.[49] Nighttime protest marches in Homs gathered strength, and residents replaced street signs with notices honoring the individuals who had been killed by the security forces.[50] Tense localities around the capital like Kafr Susah and Midan, by contrast, remained quiet, patrolled by large numbers of security forces and shabbihah.[51] Protests in Kurdish areas of the northeast also trailed off.[52]

At the beginning of September, the mufti of Aleppo, Ibrahim al-Salqini, died while under police watch. Several days earlier, he was reported to have delivered a "defiant" Friday sermon, which prompted a visit to his house by a team of security agents.[53] Confronted by the agents, Shaikh al-Salqini suffered a heart attack and was rushed to the hospital, where he passed away with police officers standing guard outside his room. Several hundred young people accompanied al-Salqini's coffin to the cemetery, chanting one of the slogans of the Hamah protesters: "Death, but not indignity." The youths were set upon by shabbihah and beaten up. At almost the same time, Syrian commandos carried out a raid inside Turkish territory, abducting former Lieutenant Colonel Harmush and spiriting him away to a secret location.

Under these circumstances, representatives of a variety of opposition groups took steps to form an umbrella organization to coordinate their activities. Leading figures in the movement included the France-based academic Burhan Ghalioun, the influential 'Alawi civil rights activist Wajdi Mustafa, the Kurdish leftist 'Abd al-Basit Sidah, and the prominent Muslim Brothers Muhammad Riyad al-Shaqfah and Muhammad Faruq Taifur. These individuals joined some 100 others in announcing that the organizational meeting of a Syrian National Council (SNC) would take place in Antalya in mid-September 2011. The organizers' initial manifesto appealed to the Local Coordinating Committees to align themselves with the SNC, which elicited only a lukewarm response.[54]

Influential civil rights activists inside Syria, including Michel Kilu, 'Arif Dalilah, and 'Ubaidah Nahhas, continued to express doubt that any organization operating outside the country could improve the prospects for fundamental reform.[55]

Meanwhile, armed confrontations between security forces and opposition fighters associated with the Khalid bin al-Walid Brigade took place outside al-Rastan. Members of the brigade carried out a pair of ambushes of military vehicles north of Homs in early September. Reports that a senior official in the Hamah attorney general's bureau had resigned in protest against the indiscriminate use of violence by the security forces prompted renewed demonstrations in villages around the city; protesters also took the streets in the northeastern town of 'Amudah to condemn Russia's ongoing support for the regime.[56] Anti-Russian marches subsequently took place in Homs and Dir'a.[57]

As September drew to a close, the Khalid bin al-Walid Brigade again attacked military convoys outside al-Rastan and seized the house of the head of Military Intelligence inside the town. Units of the regular armed forces then surrounded al-Rastan and initiated a sustained bombardment by tanks and artillery. Faced with superior firepower, the brigade abandoned the town; most of its fighters melted into the countryside, although one component that called itself the Faruq Battalion took up positions in the Baba 'Amru district of Homs.[58] The dispersed components of the Khalid bin al-Walid Brigade joined a diverse collection of guerrilla forces operating in different parts of the country: the Hamza al-Khatib Brigade outside Idlib, the 'Ali bin Abi Talib and Abu Bakr al-Sadiq Brigades in Jabal al-Zawiyyah, the 'Udai al-Tayyib Brigade at al-Hasakah, the 'Umar bin al-Khattab Brigade around Dair al-Zur, the God is Greatest (*Allahu Akbar*) Brigade outside Al Bu Kamal, and the Mu'awiyya bin Abi Sufyan and Aba 'Ubaidah bin al-Jarah Brigades in the countryside around Damascus.[59]

As government troops took control of al-Rastan, some 300 opposition figures met in Antalya to hammer out the organizational structure of the SNC. The SNC's provisional head, Burhan Ghalioun, announced that the council would consist of a 140-member general assembly and a 29-member secretariat. The latter would include representatives of seven major groups, most notably the supporters of the 2005 Damascus Declaration, the Muslim Brothers, the Kurdish Future Movement Party, and a handful of independent liberal and Kurdish activists.[60] The NCCFDC kept its distance from the new organization, as did the Union of Coordinating Committees of the Syrian Revolution headed by Muhammad Rahhal. Links to the Local Coordinating Committees inside Syria remained tenuous, as did the relationship between the SNC and the FSA, which in late September had merged with the Free Officers' Movement. The Union of Coordinating Committees of the Syrian Revolution complicated matters further by setting up the Salah al-Din Army and insisting that it exercised authority over guerrilla formations in the field.[61]

On October 7, the leader of the Future Movement Party, Mish'al Tam'u, was assassinated at his home in al-Qamishli. Tam'u was not only a vocal critic of the regime but had also publicly criticized rival Kurdish parties for adopting a neutral posture in the escalating internal conflict.[62] His death was reported to have come shortly after he announced his intention to join the SNC.[63] Tens of thousands of Kurds marched in Tam'u's funeral procession, and outbreaks of popular protest in Kurdish districts started to occur more frequently over the next few weeks.

Elements of the 'Ali bin Abi Talib Brigade carried out a series of raids on government convoys in the al-Hulah district of Jabal al-Zawiyyah in mid-October, while another militia attacked military outposts around al-Qusair on the border with Lebanon. These operations—and the wave of protests that washed through Ma'arah al-Nu'man, Khan Shaikhun, Kfar Takharim, and Jisr al-Shughur in their wake—led army and security forces to launch a large-scale sweep across the region around Idlib, which entailed mass arrests of residents in the towns and villages of the area.[64] The offensive encouraged the authorities in Idlib to mobilize a mass demonstration in support of the regime similar to ones that had taken place in Aleppo and Damascus.[65] Perhaps in response to this rally, the FSA for the first time claimed credit for an attack on an army vehicle on the highway between Hamah and Salamiyyah that killed nine soldiers; an ambush of a bus transporting security personnel took place northwest of Idlib two days later.[66]

On October 28 and 29, tanks and artillery stepped up the bombardment of the Baba 'Amru district of Homs. By the first week of November, there were reports of growing sectarian violence in the city, particularly arson attacks and kidnappings involving rival gangs of Sunnis and 'Alawis.[67] The first day of the religious holiday of 'Id al-Adha saw the start of a large-scale military offensive around Baba 'Amru; fighters of the Faruq Battalion retreated to the countryside in the face of the onslaught, resulting in the occupation of most parts of Baba 'Amru and the envelopment of the adjacent district of al-Khalidiyyah.[68] Groups of shabbihah fanned out in the aftermath of the assault, looting businesses and rounding up suspected dissidents.[69] At the same time, security forces and shabbihah cracked down on neighborhoods in Latakia, villages around Dir'a, and the Damascus suburb of Kafr Susah. In response, opposition militias struck police stations and government offices at Khan Shaikhun and Ma'arah al-Nu'man, and two new formations—the Abu al-Fida' Battalion and 'Usama bin Zaid Battalion—started operating west of Hamah. Some 40 troops were killed in mid-November in ambushes around Dir'a carried out by the Ahmad Khalaf and Martyrs of Freedom Battalions.[70]

Almost 1,200 individuals whom the authorities alleged to have been "involved in recent events" were released from prison on November 15, 2011, adding to the 500 who received a presidential pardon on the eve of 'Id al-Adha. But such conciliatory gestures failed to diminish the fighting. The day after the prisoners' release, the FSA attacked the headquarters of Air Force Intelligence at Harasta outside the capital with machine guns and shoulder-fired rockets. The raid took place shortly after the FSA's leader arrived in Ankara to propose that the formation be formally recognized as the military wing of the SNC.[71] Government commanders deployed large numbers of troops and security forces throughout Damascus in the wake of the raid and carried out a further set of operations in the suburbs of Kafr Susah, Jisrin, and Duma.[72] Despite the reinforced military presence, the FSA managed to fire two rocket-propelled grenades at the Ba'th Party headquarters in the Mazra'ah district of the capital on November 20.[73]

In Idlib, a mass rally voiced support for the radical Islamist 'Adnan al-'Ar'ur, prompting the head of the Muslim Brothers, Muhammad Riyad al-Shaqfah, to invite the Turkish armed forces to intervene in northern Syria to protect the civilian population.[74]

CIVIL WAR

By late November 2011, instances of peaceful protest had virtually disappeared from Syria's cities and towns. In its place one saw attacks and counterattacks between regular armed forces, the security services, and companies of shabbihah on one side and elements of the FSA, independent local militias, and bands of neighborhood fighters on the other. Poorer 'Alawis in the disadvantaged towns and villages of the mountainous west found themselves increasingly driven toward unquestioning support for the regime, largely to protect themselves against attacks from Sunni militants and threats of retaliation for actions undertaken by the government. The International Crisis Group observes that the confluence of growing 'Alawi solidarity and pervasive state brutality

> conformed to the worst anti-Alawite stereotypes [held by the Syrian public]. It revived age-old prejudices about the community's 'savagery'. It exacerbated historic grievances regarding ownership of land, which in some parts of the country had been transferred from Sunni feudal elites to Alawite serfs during the agrarian reform that began in the 1950s.[75]

Large parts of the provinces of Dir'a, Homs, Hamah, and Idlib, along with most of Jabal al-Zawiyyah, fell out of government control, while tribespeople around Dair al-Zur began to act as intermediaries between the provincial authorities and armed dissidents.

Battle lines hardened as the FSA set up a joint committee with the SNC to coordinate their respective military and political activities, and General Hasan al-Turkmani took charge of a Ba'th Party crisis management team consisting of senior military and security officers, diplomats, and academics.[76] Mid-level FSA commanders almost immediately started to complain that the SNC was trying to put too many restrictions on field operations, and fighting flared around

Homs, Hamah, Idlib, and Dir'a in early December.[77] The violence appeared to belie President al-Asad's remarks in an interview with the U.S. television network ABC, in which he asserted that "Most of the people who have been killed are supporters of the government" and "Every brute reaction was by an individual, not by an institution. . . . There is a difference between having a policy to crack down and having some mistakes committed by some officials."[78]

Rather bizarrely, local council elections took place on December 12, 2011. Some 43,000 candidates were listed on ballots for 17,588 council seats. The Local Coordinating Committees boycotted the proceedings and called for a general strike to demand "dignity" for the country's citizens. Workers at a factory outside Aleppo complied with the strike call, prompting the security forces to set fire to the factory.[79] Skirmishing between the armed forces and the FSA intensified following the elections, particularly in the provinces of Idlib, Homs, and Hamah. After troops shot a dozen residents of Ma'arah Masrin and Kafar Yahmul north of Idlib, FSA fighters ambushed a convoy in the northern town of Bab al-Hawa, killing a half-dozen security personnel, and then attacked a military convoy outside Hamah.[80] Regular army units in reply launched a sustained offensive in Jabal al-Zawiyyah, which resulted in the deaths of more than 70 FSA guerrillas and some 200 civilians.[81]

In the capital, a pair of car bombs exploded at two installations of General Security in Kafr Susah on December 23.[82] The blasts occurred just as an advance contingent of Arab League monitors arrived to assess the extent to which troops and security forces had started to pull out of populated areas, as mandated by the terms of a ceasefire agreement that had been concluded in November. Teams of monitors visited Homs, Hamah, Idlib, Dir'a, and the Damascus suburbs of Duma and Kiswah during the final week of the year.[83] At each stop, residents organized public marches to demand an end to violence and the ouster of the Ba'th Party–led regime. Despite the overall lull in the fighting that surrounded the Arab League mission, a suicide bomber set off a powerful explosion alongside a police bus in the Midan district of Damascus on January 6, 2012.[84]

At the end of the first week of January, the SNC and FSA appealed to the international community to establish a safety zone along the Syrian-Turkish border, which would be patrolled by foreign troops. The *Christian Science Monitor* reported from Beirut that prices for AK-47s and rocket-propelled grenade launchers had soared to unprecedented heights.[85] Meanwhile, in the countryside outside Homs, opposition fighters set up a new Special Tasks Battalion to strike at oil pipelines running through the area. The calm was broken on January 12, when the regular army advanced on the town of al-Zabadani on the Lebanese border northwest of Damascus following reports that a company of soldiers in the area had defected to the FSA.[86] The assault was beaten back by FSA fighters, who then found themselves surrounded and subjected to massive artillery bombardment before a ceasefire could be negotiated. The battle for al-Zabadani sparked an outbreak of public demonstrations in the other Damascus suburbs of Dar'ayya and Mazzah, and an FSA unit gained a foothold in Duma as well.[87] Government forces regained control of Duma a day later, only to be pushed out of neighboring Saqbah.[88] While troops were struggling to wrest the environs of Damascus from the hands of the FSA, tanks and artillery resumed shelling of suspected FSA positions in the Baba 'Amru neighborhood of Homs.

On January 27, the 'Abd al-Rahman al-Ashtar Battalion moved back into al-Rastan and two days later inflicted significant damage on the armored forces that were besieging the town.[89] The Faruq Battalion shortly thereafter announced that it had captured seven Iranians who had been operating with army units in Homs.[90] Fighting then flared in the countryside around Dir'a, where the 'Umari Battalion, the Martyrs of Freedom Battalion, and the Ahmad Khalaf Battalion carried out a succession of ambushes and strikes against military patrols and outposts. On February 3, the Faruq Battalion attacked three checkpoints ringing Homs, capturing a tank in the operation; government forces responded by unleashing an all-night artillery barrage on the city that killed some 50 civilians. The following day, troops resumed the offensive against al-Zabadani, inflicting severe damage on the town, and continued the bombardment of Baba 'Amru. Taken together, these battles marked the peak of organized violence by both sides in the 10 months after March 2011.

At the height of the fighting, former Brigadier General Mustafa Ahmad al-Shaikh, who had defected to the opposition in early January, announced that he was forming a unified military command, the Syrian Revolutionary Military Council, which "will include all the soldiers who have fled the regular army."[91] He went on to say that Major Mahir al-Nu'aimi, who had been appointed as official spokesperson for the FSA, would act in the same capacity for the new council. Colonel al-As'ad of the FSA immediately issued a press release in which he stated that al-Shaikh " 'does not belong to the Free Syrian Army' and only represents himself." The SNC, meeting in Qatar, did its best to paper over the disagreement.[92] General al-Shaikh replied in a somewhat confusing fashion: "Along with the Free Syrian Army, we represent one formation and one entity, but we might have diverging views over a number of issues, especially in relation to the way the Free Army was organized because we think this was done in a very chaotic way."[93]

Residents of Aleppo reacted to the upsurge of violent activity by staging sporadic demonstrations, which were somewhat larger and more frequent on the campus of the University of Aleppo.[94] These episodes of unrest were quickly suppressed by the security forces and shabbihah, and the pounding of Baba 'Amru and al-Zabadani went on. Massive car bombs detonated outside two security forces headquarters in Aleppo on February 10.[95] The FSA claimed that the bombings had accompanied a raid against shabbihah in the city but that FSA fighters had left the area around the two buildings before the explosions occurred. Two new FSA units appeared at mid-month: the Yazid bin Mu'awiya Battalion at Saraqib and the Ansar Allah Brigade outside Hamah. In honor of the diplomatic and material support that the opposition was receiving from Qatar, another unit in Ma'arah al-Nu'man was christened the Shaikh Hamad bin Qasim Brigade after that Arab Gulf emirate's prime minister. In early March, arguably as a counterweight to the Mu'awiya Battalion, the FSA set up the Husain bin 'Ali Battalion.[96]

Mid-February 2012 saw the formation of an alliance of opposition groups critical of the SNC, which took the name the Syrian Democratic Platform. Prominent members of the alliance included the civil rights activists Michel Kilu and 'Arif Dalilah.[97] At almost the same time, yet another opposition coalition appeared: the National Change Current. The front was headed by civil rights activist 'Ammar Qurabi and consisted largely of representatives of Syria's religious minorities. A prominent 'Alawi dissident became the front's vice chair.[98] Other founding figures hailed from the Turkmen, Druze, and Yazidi communities.

Weeks of relentless shelling culminated at the end of February in a large-scale ground assault on Baba 'Amru. Government forces gained control of the district in less than 36 hours after the Faruq Battalion carried out what it called a "tactical withdrawal" from the city.[99] At virtually the same time, the Hamza al-Khatib Battalion pulled out of al-Rastan. On March 10, armored units started shelling Idlib and entered the city after FSA units abandoned their positions the following day.[100] The capture of Idlib and subsequent advance on Ma'arah Nu'man set the stage for a major offensive that swept through Jabal al-Zawiyyah.[101] Thousands of local inhabitants fled to Aleppo and Hatay to escape the onslaught.

THE REGIME STRIKES BACK

March 14, 2012, saw the beginning of a renewed military assault on the towns and villages around Dir'a in the south, which took place immediately after residents of the province staged a wave of protests to mark the one-year anniversary of the outbreak of the uprising.[102] Four days later, troops cracked down on FSA fighters in the Damascus suburb of Mazzah. By March 20, FSA units and independent militias were pulling out of various parts of Jabal al-Zawiyyah, as well as from the environs of Dair al-Zur in the east.[103] Government forces then attacked the Bab Sba'ah district of Homs and launched a further offensive against Hamah and the towns of Saraqib and al-Qusair.[104] As regular army troops left Idlib for the front lines, the authorities turned the city over to shabbihah, who ransacked businesses and houses looking for FSA stragglers.[105] Tank and artillery fire targeted Hamah and A'zaz as the month drew to a close.

While opposition militias steadily gave ground to regime forces, Islamist militants turned to more indiscriminate tactics. Two large bombs exploded outside

Air Force Intelligence and police buildings in Damascus on March 17; a day later, an office of General Security in Aleppo was hit by a car bomb.[106] Leaders of the FSA immediately disavowed responsibility for the bombings and charged that they had been carried out by the regime in an attempt to "terrorize" the populations of the two metropolises.[107] On March 20, a shadowy group calling itself the Assistance Front for the People of Syria claimed to have ordered the bombings in Damascus.

In an effort to regroup, the SNC called for all components of the opposition to join it in Istanbul to forge a "national pact" that would lay out a unified strategy to combat the Ba'thi regime. The invitation was ignored by the SNC's primary rivals, the National Coordinating Committee of the Forces for Democratic Change and the Union of Coordinating Committees for the Syrian Revolution. Shortly after the congress opened, a handful of Kurdish parties that had agreed to attend in the hope of reconciling with the SNC walked out, complaining that the draft platform failed to envisage the establishment of a secular democratic order.[108] The National Change Current, whose representatives did attend the meeting, refused to sign the platform.[109] Discussion of the future of the Revolutionary Military Council was virtually absent, although the SNC announced that in future it would pay members of the FSA a regular salary out of funds provided by Qatar and Saudi Arabia.

While the SNC met in Istanbul, Syrian troops struck the Lebanese border town of Mashirah al-Qaa in hot pursuit of a formation of FSA fighters. Saraqib was retaken by government forces on March 28, and the fighting shifted to Qala'ah al-Madiq in western Hamah province. A particularly brutal attack was directed at the village of Taftanaz outside Idlib in early April, which left more than 90 residents dead.[110] Antiregime activists survived in al-Hasakah and al-Qamishli and organized sizable protests against the destruction that was being inflicted on the north-central provinces after Friday prayers on April 6, 2012.[111] That same day, 13 bodies were discovered in the streets of the Dair Ba'alba district of Homs; the victims had been shot with their hands bound behind their backs.[112]

President al-Asad accepted a ceasefire plan drawn up by UN special envoy Kofi Annan in the last week of March, which stipulated that Syrian troops would withdraw from urban areas by April 10 and that all shooting would end two days later. Colonel As'ad of the FSA pledged that his fighters would abide by the ceasefire if all government forces withdrew from the cities and towns and returned to their barracks.[113] Syrian officials quickly riposted that Damascus had not agreed to order the armed forces back to their barracks, that the agreement did not apply to police units, and that some form of military presence might still be necessary in order to deal with "terrorists" who ignored the truce. Little let-up in the tank and artillery barrages around Idlib and Homs could be discerned in the days leading up to the deadlines. On April 8, the foreign ministry announced that troops would only pull out of urban areas if all opposition forces promised in writing to lay down their weapons. In addition, it demanded that Annan obtain written guarantees that the FSA and independent militias would honor the cease-fire, along with pledges from foreign countries to stop funding the opposition.[114] The FSA high command rejected these terms out of hand. On the day before the ceasefire was due to begin, troops backed by helicopter gunships attacked towns on the northern edge of Aleppo, the outskirts of Hamah, and the area around Jisr al-Shughur.[115]

April 10 saw the imposition of tighter restrictions on movement between Damascus and its suburbs.[116] Soldiers remained deployed in the cities and towns, but actual shooting for the most part came to a stop. When SNC head Ghalioun called on the Syrian public to engage in peaceful protests after prayers on Friday the 13th, the Ministry of Interior warned that the police would only allow demonstrations that had been authorized in advance. " 'This is ridiculous,' said an activist called Musab from Hamah city," according to the Reuters news agency. " 'They will not give you permission and you will be taken to jail if you ask for it.' "[117] An uneasy calm nevertheless extended from al-Zabadani in the west to Dair al-Zur in the east.[118]

Tens of thousands of demonstrators took to the streets on April 13, 2012:

> Security forces fired live rounds, tear gas or beat protesters in some areas, but amateur videos showed large peaceful and seemingly cheerful anti-government rallies in other locations. In the Damascus suburbs of al-Zabadani and Duma and in the northern town of Idlib, large crowds linked arms and chanted anti-government slogans. In the southern city of Dir'a, birthplace of the uprising, several hundred people formed rows, holding hands and dancing to the beat of a drum while chanting "Come on, Bashshar, Leave!"[119]

The Syrian state news agency reported the next day that "armed terrorists" had killed a half-dozen soldiers outside Idlib and kidnapped an army colonel in Hamah. On April 15, shelling resumed at Homs, and security forces opened fire on a funeral procession in Aleppo, precipitating a firefight that raged through a residential neighborhood.[120] Fighting in Homs and Aleppo escalated further the next day and spread to Idlib and the southern town of Busra al-Harir.[121]

As the ceasefire disintegrated, the SNC debated whether or not to ask the United Nations to dispatch peacekeeping forces to Syria. Disgruntled fighters in the countryside around Idlib, meanwhile, turned to raiding 'Alawi and Isma'ili villages and kidnapping and murdering their inhabitants, a trend that provoked 'Alawis and Isma'ilis to retaliate against Sunni villagers, often in collaboration with shabbihah.[122] In the northeast, partisans of competing Kurdish parties started skirmishing with one another. Tanks and artillery bombarded Hamah on April 23, and troops clashed with FSA units along the border with Jordan the following day.[123] Fighting then resumed in the Damascus suburbs of Duma and Harasta, and whatever remained of the United Nations–sponsored ceasefire evaporated.

STALEMATE

Sporadic attacks by the FSA against military patrols accompanied occasional rounds of shelling on the part of the armed forces during the last week of April 2012. Residents slowly returned to devastated neighborhoods in Homs, Idlib, Hamah, and the environs of Damascus, only to pick their way through booby traps that had been left behind by one side or the other.[124] Colonel al-As'ad of the FSA and General al-Shaikh of the Revolutionary Military Council sparred with one another over the desirability of inviting foreign troops to set up a protected zone as a way of preventing further massacres.[125] On May 2, security forces accompanied by shabbihah raided the dormitory area of the University of Aleppo, shooting out windows, spraying tear gas, setting rooms on fire, and beating up anyone they caught. When the smoke cleared, four students lay dead. The incident galvanized the populace of the city into action, and antigovernment protests erupted in several neighborhoods. A group of attorneys marched to the Palace of Justice to demand that the perpetrators of the violence be punished.[126]

A series of bombings shook Damascus and Aleppo over the next two weeks. Government officials blamed the explosions on criminal gangs funded by Qatar and Saudi Arabia; opposition figures called the attacks the handiwork of the security forces; outside observers tended to point instead to the Assistance Front for the People of Syria. Every day some town or village was reported to be under attack by the armed forces.

On May 12, the SNC gathered in Rome to decide whether or not to allow Burhan Ghalioun to stand for reelection as head of the organization. Liberal representatives associated with the Damascus Declaration opposed any extension of his term in office on the grounds that he had not been very effective and other parties deserved a chance to lead the alliance.[127] Ghalioun's critics suggested that a Christian candidate should challenge the incumbent as a signal that the SNC represented all of Syria's religious communities and proposed that George Sabra's name be put forward. While the debate dragged on, signs of a massacre came to light in the village of Taman'ah outside Hamah; shabbihah and 'Alawis from an adjacent village were immediately accused of perpetrating the crime. State officials attempted to divert attention from the incident by releasing a list of al-Qa'idah cadres who had infiltrated into the country from Turkey.[128] The armed forces then launched simultaneous strikes against al-Qusair, Khan Shaikhun, al-Rastan, and Dair al-Zur.[129]

Ghalioun ended up being reelected as head of the SNC on May 15, thanks largely to support from three Kurdish parties.[130] He immediately announced that greater effort would be exerted to arm the fighters operating inside Syria, and evidence soon emerged that substantial quantities of new weaponry were indeed entering the country.[131] At the same time, simmering outrage over the attack at the University of Aleppo brought crowds into the streets of Aleppo,

Idlib, Homs, and Damascus.[132] In Dair al-Zur, antiregime protesters raised banners that read: "Burhan Ghalioun: The Syrian National Council is dying . . . We accept your resignation."[133] Demonstrations in al-Hasakah, al-Qamishli, and 'Amudah tended to voice "Support for the Kurds of Aleppo" rather than for the objectives proposed by the SNC.[134]

Tanks clattered through the streets of Aleppo for the first time on May 25, 2012, in the wake of massive marches in the impoverished neighborhoods of Kalasah and Bustan al-Qasr.[135] But attention quickly shifted to the district of al-Hulah in western Idlib province, where the mutilated bodies of more than 100 men, women, and children were discovered on May 26. A spokesperson for the foreign ministry was quick to assert that "This is not the hallmark of the heroic Syrian army" and put blame for the killings on the FSA; the opposition in turn accused shabbihah of instigating the massacre.[136] Popular revulsion over the incident led merchants in the central market of Damascus to take the unprecedented step of closing their shops in protest; when police ordered them to reopen their businesses, many sat outside and refused to deal with customers. The merchants' strike spread across the city over the ensuing week as evidence came to light of a second massacre of civilians at al-Sukar east of Dair al-Zur.[137] Such provocative actions on the part of the previously quiescent commercial elite of the capital reinvigorated the FSA, which set about rearming and preparing for a resumption of armed struggle.[138]

Confronted with widespread public anger, President al-Asad told the People's Assembly in a televised address that "Not even monsters would carry out what we have seen in al-Hulah. . . . There are no Arabic or even human words to describe it." He promised to continue the struggle against the Islamist extremists and foreign-backed terrorists who had engineered the ongoing violence in Syria. "When a surgeon in an operating room cuts and cleans and amputates, and the wound bleeds," he asked his audience, "do we say to him, 'Your hands are stained with blood?' Or do we thank him for saving the patient?"[139]

Fighting escalated sharply in the wake of the president's address. Shabbihah butchered more than 70 residents of the farming village of Mazra'ah al-Qubair in Hamah province; the armed forces bombarded Dir'a; and units of the FSA battled troops in the suburbs of Damascus for almost 12 hours on June 9, during which time tank shells struck the residential district of Qabun in the capital itself.[140] Government forces then launched an assault against the coastal town of Haffa and regained control of the area after an eight-day battle. The same day that Haffa fell to the army, a massive car bomb exploded outside the Shi'i shrine of al-Sayyidah Zainab on the southern edge of Damascus.[141] As heavy fighting continued at Homs, al-Rastan, and A'zaz, the separate militias of the FSA were reported to be merging into more coherent military formations.[142] The dramatic upsurge in violence convinced the head of the UN Supervisory Mission in Syria to suspend the mission's activities on June 16.[143] Attacks against

FSA strongholds in Homs, Duma, Dir'a, and Dair al-Zur intensified in the wake of the suspension.

Representatives to the SNC met in Istanbul on June 10 to choose a new leader after Burhan Ghalioun unexpectedly tendered his resignation. 'Abd al-Basit Sidah, a Kurdish teacher based in Sweden, emerged as the new head of the organization and immediately declared that "the regime is on its last legs."[144] In a final slap at Ghalioun, whose repeatedly renewed terms in office had stirred up grumbling inside the council, Sidah's term was limited to three months. Sidah went out of his way to remind an interviewer from *al-Jazeera* television that the SNC "is not a democratic institution, meaning that we do not hold elections; instead there is consensus and appointed officials. We said that we would derive our legitimacy through our accomplishments."[145]

Mid-June 2012 brought reports of large-scale clashes around Latakia, across the Jabal al-Akrad region southeast of Latakia, and in the towns north of Aleppo. Opposition forces killed dozens of government troops and proregime thugs, often in ambushes involving heavy machine guns and homemade explosive devices.[146] The escalation of violence around Aleppo propelled a large body of protesters toward the city's main square after Friday prayers on June 22, where they were met by tanks and snipers who opened fire on the march.[147] Troops backed by tanks and shabbihah launched a major offensive against Dair al-Zur and intercepted a guerrilla formation trying to cross into Latakia from Hatay. FSA units then attacked bases of the Republican Guard in the Damascus suburbs of Qadsayyah and al-Hama, resulting in the most intense round of fighting that had so far taken place in the immediate environs of the capital.[148] President al-Asad remarked to the newly appointed Council of Ministers on June 26 that "we live in a real state of war from all angles."[149]

BATTLE FOR THE NORTH

Fighting raged through the suburbs of the capital in early July after FSA commanders announced the initiation of Operation Damascus Volcano. FSA forces then launched a coordinated assault against crossing stations along the borders with Turkey and Iraq. By the third week of July, FSA units had advanced into the environs of Aleppo and engaged government troops in sustained combat in the districts of Salah al-Din, Sakhur, and Tariq al-Bab. Regular army units steadily regained control of the towns surrounding Damascus as the month went by, but the armed forces encountered considerably more difficulty in pushing FSA fighters out of areas around Aleppo. Artillery barrages and bombing runs by military aircraft failed to dislodge the rebels from Salah al-Din. Meanwhile, Kurdish activists formed the Salah al-Din Brigade to patrol predominantly Kurdish neighborhoods of the city, and Kurdish militants affiliated with the Democratic Union Party (PYD) took charge of the northeastern towns of Kobanah, 'Amudah and 'Afrin.

Government forces quickly pulled out of Jabal al-Zawiyyah and positions along the Turkish border to confront the FSA outside Aleppo. By the end of July, troops backed by tanks and helicopter gunships were engaged in constant battle with FSA guerrillas in Salah al-Din and Sakhur. Opposition forces attacked the military airfield at Managh between Aleppo and A'zaz on August 2 using a tank that had been captured from the armed forces, then seized a security complex at al-Mayadin outside Dair al-Zur.[150] As the fighting escalated across the northern provinces, activists of the Muslim Brothers organized a militia to operate alongside the FSA; Islamist militants outside Aleppo set up the Abu 'Imara Battalion as a rival to FSA units.[151] The proliferation of militias accompanied the gradual dispersion of large-scale skirmishing to neighborhoods close to the center of the city, including the southeastern district of Nairab and areas northwest of the thirteenth-century citadel. Notable among the new militia units were ones made up largely of foreign personnel that adopted an explicitly Islamist platform. Such formations included the Hawks of Syria in Jabal al-Zawiyyah, the Abu Bakr al-Sadiq Brigade in Aleppo, the Shaikh Hajjaj al-'Ajami Brigade at Al Bu Kamal, and the Banner of the Islamic Community (*Liwa al-Ummah*) Brigade around Homs.[152]

As fighting engulfed a greater number of neighborhoods of Aleppo, local FSA commanders joined guerrillas affiliated with the Local Coordinating Committees to form a unified Military Council under the leadership of former regular army colonel 'Abd al-Jabbar al-'Aqidi. The combined force designated itself the Unity (*al-Tawhid*) Brigade.[153] Elements of the Unity Brigade infiltrated the central districts of al-Tal, Jdaidah, and Sulaimaniyyah on August 18 but were repulsed after three days of intense combat with government troops.[154] As the month ended, the brigade launched a combined assault against military and security facilities around Aleppo called Operation Northern Volcano.[155] At the same time, FSA units struck military airfields around Idlib and Al Bu Kamal.[156] Government troops retaliated with a massive wave of artillery and aerial bombardment, accompanied by ground attacks against FSA-held neighborhoods all across Aleppo. The offensive cut off water supplies to wide areas of the city and prompted large numbers of residents to flee to the countryside.

In mid-September 2012, the FSA announced that it had transferred its headquarters from Turkey to an undisclosed location in northwestern Syria.[157] Meanwhile, foreign militants took an increasing role in the fighting in and around Aleppo. Units consisting of Chechens, Libyans, Iraqis, Afghans, and Tajiks played a crucial part in escalating the violence as the month passed, alienating rival FSA commanders and local residents alike.[158] Members of the Hawks of Syria on September 10 executed 20 soldiers who had been captured during the assault on the barracks in the Hananu district.[159]

Late September 2012 saw a resurgence of bombings against military and security targets around Damascus. The attacks were aimed not only at conventional installations, such as the headquarters of the general staff, but also at suspected strongholds of the shabbihah; responsibility for the bombings tended to be claimed by the Assistance Front for the People of Syria.[160] Such operations paled in comparison to the persistent fighting in the north. Commanders of the Unity Brigade announced the start of the "decisive battle" against the Ba'thi regime on September 27 and carried out coordinated attacks on several disparate districts of Aleppo, including the central neighborhood of al-Jamiliyyah, the area of Bab al-Hadid adjacent to the citadel and the largely Kurdish suburb of Shaikh Maqsud. Fierce fighting ensued and by September 29 the battle had reached the historic marketplace (*suq*) of the Old City. A brief but intense clash at Bab Antakya, the western entry to the suq, ignited a conflagration that burned down hundreds of nearby shops and threatened to destroy the entire covered market.[161] The blaze elicited outrage from supporters and opponents of the regime alike. One local resident told the Reuters news agency, "We all know that this is a criminal regime and it will do anything. That is why the fighters had no business being in the souk. Why did they go there?"[162]

NOTES

1. *Wall Street Journal*, January 31, 2011.
2. *Elaph*, January 28, 2011.
3. *al-Quds al-'Arabi*, March 7, 2011.
4. *al-Sharq al-Awsat*, March 8, 2011.
5. *al-Rai al-'Amm* (Kuwait), March 11, 2011.
6. *al-Watan* (Damascus), March 17, 2011.
7. *The National* (Abu Dhabi), March 30, 2012.
8. *al-Sharq al-Awsat*, March 24, 2011.
9. Syrian Arab News Agency (SANA), March 24, 2011.
10. Associated Press (AP), March 27, 2011; *al-Sharq al-Awsat*, March 27, 2011; *New York Times* (NYT), March, 27, 2011.
11. *Elaph*, March 28, 2011.
12. Institute for War and Peace Reporting (IWPR), March 29, 2011.
13. *Agence France Presse* (AFP), April 1, 2011.
14. *al-Quds al-'Arabi*, April 4, 2011.
15. *al-Quds al-'Arabi*, April 12, 2011.
16. *al-Hayah*, April 15, 2011.
17. British Broadcasting Corporation (BBC), April 19, 2011.
18. NYT, June 30, 2011.
19. *al-Akhbar*, October 1, 2011.
20. BBC, April 25, 2011.
21. David W. Lesch, *Syria: The Fall of the House of Assad* (New Haven: Yale University Press, 2012), 98.
22. BBC, May 4, 2011.
23. Reuters, May 10, 2011.
24. BBC, May 12, 2011.

25. BBC, May 14, 2011.

26. *Guardian*, May 30, 2011.

27. *al-Sharq al-Awsat*, May 30, 2011.

28. *al-Hayah*, May 31, 2011.

29. Jonathan Spyer, "The Syrian Opposition before and after the Outbreak of the 2011 Uprising," *Middle East Review of International Affairs* 15 (September 2011); Aron Lund, *Divided They Stand: An Overview of Syria's Political Opposition Factions* (Uppsala, Sweden: Foundation for European Progressive Studies, May 2012), 47–48.

30. *al-Akhbar*, May 31, 2011.

31. *Washington Post*, June 3, 2011; BBC, June 3, 2011.

32. BBC, June 7, 2011.

33. BBC, June 16, 2011.

34. Chris Zambelis, "The Turn to Armed Rebellion in Syria: The Rise of the Free Syrian Army," *Terrorism Monitor* 9 (December 16, 2011).

35. *al-Hayah*, June 7, 2011.

36. *al-Sharq al-Awsat*, June 16, 2011.

37. *al-Jazeera*, June 23, 2011.

38. NYT, June 24, 2011.

39. *al-Sharq al-Awsat*, June 28, 2011.

40. NYT, July 1, 2011.

41. *al-Quds al-'Arabi*, July 4, 2011.

42. *Los Angeles Times*, July 5, 2011.

43. IWPR, July 26, 2011.

44. *Syria Comment*, July 18, 2011, http://www.syriacomment.com.

45. *al-Jazeera*, July 31, 2011.

46. Joseph Holliday, *Syria's Armed Opposition*, Middle East Security Report No. 3, Institute for the Study of War, Washington, DC, March 2012, 15 and 22.

47. *al-Quds al-'Arabi*, August 5, 2011.

48. *Los Angeles Times*, August, 7, 2011.

49. BBC, August 16, 2011; *al-Ahram Weekly*, August 18–24, 2011.

50. NYT, August 17, 2011.

51. *Syria Comment*, August 31, 2011.

52. *al-Sharq al-Awsat*, August 27, 2011.

53. *Los Angeles Times*, September 6, 2011.

54. *al-Jazeera*, September 2, 2011.

55. *al-Sharq al-Awsat*, August 30, 2011.

56. AFP, September 2, 2011.

57. *Guardian*, September 15, 2011.

58. BBC, October 1, 2011.

59. See Holliday, *Syria's Armed Opposition*.

60. Lund, *Divided They Stand*, 36.

61. *al-Sharq al-Awsat*, October 2, 2011.

62. Reese Erlich, "In Syria, Kurds Split over Support for Assad Regime," pulitzercenter.org, October 27, 2011.

63. Joel Daniel Parker, "The Dilemma of Syria's Kurds," *Tel Aviv Notes* 5 (December 11, 2011), 2.

64. *al-Sharq al-Awsat*, October 17, 2011.

65. BBC, October 19, 2011; NYT, October 19, 2011.

66. NYT, October 26, 2011; BBC, October 29, 2011.

67. NYT, November 19, 2011.

68. NYT, November 7, 2011; *Washington Post*, November 7, 2011; *al-Sharq al-Awsat*, November 10, 2011.

69. AP, November 8, 2011.

70. NYT, November 15, 2011; Holliday, *Syria's Armed Opposition*, 24.

71. *al-Ahram Weekly*, November 17–23, 2011.

72. *al-Sharq al-Awsat*, November 18, 2011.

73. BBC, November 20, 2011.

74. *al-Quds al-'Arabi*, November 18, 2011.

75. International Crisis Group, "Uncharted Waters: Thinking through Syria's Dynamics," *Middle East Briefing*, no. 31 (November 24, 2011): 2.

76. *al-Sharq al-Awsat*, November 29, 2011.

77. NYT, December 8, 2011; BBC, December 9, 2011.

78. NYT, December 7, 2011.

79. *Washington Post*, December 12, 2011.

80. BBC, December 13–14, 2011.

81. BBC, December 21, 2011.

82. *al-Akhbar*, December 23, 2011.

83. BBC, December 29, 2011.

84. *al-Akhbar*, January 6, 2012.

85. *Christian Science Monitor*, January 9, 2012.

86. *al-Sharq al-Awsat*, January 18, 2012.

87. Reuters, January 21, 2012.

88. Reuters, January 29, 2012; *Washington Post*, January 29, 2012.

89. *al-Sharq al-Awsat*, January 31, 2012.

90. *al-Sharq al-Awsat*, February 1, 2012.

91. *al-Sharq al-Awsat*, February 7, 2012.

92. *al-Hayah*, February 16, 2012.

93. *al-Hayah*, February 21, 2012.

94. Reuters, February 3, 2012.

95. NYT, February 10, 2012.

96. Angry Arab News Service, March 4, 2012.

97. Lund, *Divided They Stand*, 53.

98. *Hurriyet*, February 22, 2012.

99. *Washington Post*, March 1, 2012; NYT, March 1, 2012.

100. *Los Angeles Times*, March 14, 2012.

101. IWPR, March 13, 2012; BBC, March 14, 2012.

102. *Daily Star*, March 15, 2012; *al-Sharq al-Awsat*, March 19, 2012.

103. IWPR, March 21, 2012; *Santa Rosa Press Democrat*, March 21, 2012; *Khalij Times*, March 12, 2012; *Washington Post*, March 12, 2012.

104. BBC, March 22, 2012; Human Rights Watch, March 22, 2012.

105. *Los Angeles Times*, March 24, 2012.

106. BBC, March 17–18, 2012.

107. *Daily Star*, March 19, 2012.

108. *al-Sharq al-Awsat*, March 29, 2012.

109. TASS (Moscow), March 2012; AFP, March 27, 2012.

110. *Washington Post*, April 6, 2012.

111. Reuters, April 6, 2012.

112. Reuters, April 7, 2012.

113. Reuters, April 6, 2012.

114. *Daily Telegraph*, April 8, 2012; BBC, April 9, 2012; *Los Angeles Times*, April 9, 2012; *al-Ahram Weekly*, April 12–18, 2012.

115. *al-Sharq al-Awsat*, April 9, 2012.

116. *al-Sharq al-Awsat*, April 10, 2012.

117. AP, April 12, 2012; Reuters, April 12, 2012.

118. *Guardian*, April 12, 2012.

119. *Guardian*, April 13, 2012.

120. Reuters, April 15, 2012.

121. AP, April 17, 2012.

122. *Los Angeles Times*, April 19, 2012.

123. *al-Hayah*, April 24, 2012.

124. AFP, May 3, 2012.

125. *al-Sharq al-Awsat*, May 1, 2012.

126. *Los Angeles Times*, May 4, 2012.

127. Reuters, May 12, 2012.

128. *al-Sharq al-Awsat*, May 13, 2012.

129. *Los Angeles Times*, May 15, 2012.

130. Reuters, May 15, 2012.

131. *Washington Post*, May 16, 2012.

132. BBC, May 18, 2012.

133. Reuters, May 21, 2012.

134. *Kurdwatch*, May 16, 2012.

135. *Le Monde*, April 26, 2012.

136. Reuters, May 27, 2012.

137. Reuters, May 28, 2012; *al-Akhbar*, May 29, 2012; AFP, May 31, 2012; *al-Sharq al-Awsat*, June 1, 2012; Reuters, June 5, 2012.

138. *Los Angeles Times*, May 31, 2012; *Daily Star*, June 5, 2012.

139. AP, June 3, 2012.

140. AP, June 9, 2012; *Guardian*, June 9, 2012.

141. AP, June 14, 2012.

142. AFP, June 16, 2012; BBC, June 17 and 25, 2012.

143. *Washington Post*, June 16, 2012.

144. *Los Angeles Times*, June 10, 2012.

145. *al-Jazeera Television*, June 13, 2012.

146. BBC, June, 25, 2012; *al-Sharq al-Awsat*, June 25, 2012.

147. Reuters, June 22, 2012.

148. *al-Sharq al-Awsat*, June 25, 2012; BBC, June 26, 2012.

149. BBC, June 26, 2012; NYT, June 26, 2012.

150. BBC, August 2, 2012; Reuters, August 3, 2012.

151. *Daily Telegraph*, August 3, 2012.

152. *al-Akhbar*, August 6, 2012.

153. *Los Angeles Times*, August 9, 2012.

154. *al-Akhbar*, August 23, 2012.

155. *Santa Rosa Press Democrat*, September 1, 2012; AP, September 1, 2012.

156. *al-Sharq al-Awsat*, September 2, 2012.

157. BBC, September 22, 2012; Reuters, September 22, 2012; NYT, September 22, 2012.

158. *Guardian*, September 23, 2012.

159. *Daily Star*, September 11, 2012.

160. Reuters, September 25, 2012; BBC, September 26, 2012; Reuters, September 28, 2012.

161. *Washington Post*, September 29, 2012; NYT, September 29, 2012.

162. Reuters, September 30, 2012.

FURTHER READING

Bassam Haddad. "Syria, the Arab Uprisings and the Political Economy of Authoritarian Resilience." *Interface* 4 (May 2012).

Raymond Hinnebusch. "Syria: From 'Authoritarian Upgrading' to Revolution?" *International Affairs* 88 (January 2012).

Joseph Holliday. *The Struggle for Syria in 2011*. Middle East Security Report No. 2, Institute for the Study of War, Washington, DC, December 2011.

Joseph Holliday. *Syria's Armed Opposition*. Middle East Security Report No. 3, Institute for the Study of War, Washington, DC, March 2012.

Aron Lund. *Divided They Stand: An Overview of Syria's Political Opposition Factions*. Uppsala: European Foundation for Progressive Studies, 2012.

Elizabeth O'Bagy. *Syria's Political Opposition*. Middle East Security Report No. 4, Institute for the Study of War, Washington, DC, April 2012.

CHAPTER 5

Syria's Relations with Israel, the Palestinians, and Lebanon

Syria's antagonism toward the Zionist movement took shape even before the Syrian and Israeli states came into existence. As early as May 1910, a group of Muslim notables from the region around Aleppo petitioned the Ottoman authorities to block a prominent Beirut landholder from selling large tracts of agricultural land to Zionist agents. At the end of the First World War, prominent Syrian nationalists expressed strong opposition to further Jewish immigration to Palestine, most notably in the Damascus Program that was presented to the King-Crane Commission in July 1919. Popular demonstrations erupted throughout the country at the news that Great Britain had been granted a separate mandate from the League of Nations to administer Palestine. During the 1936 Palestinian revolt against the British, anti-Zionist demonstrations were organized by the League of National Action as well as by the collection of Islamist associations that later coalesced into the Syrian Muslim Brothers. These organizations smuggled arms and recruits to guerrilla units operating inside Palestine, and in August 1936 a veteran of the 1925 Syrian revolt against the French, Fawzi al-Qawuqji, took command of a band of guerrillas in the name of the Arab Revolution in Southern Syria.

At an extraordinary Arab summit meeting in December 1947, Syria agreed to host the headquarters of the Arab Liberation Army (ALA), the assortment of guerrilla formations and popular militias that the Arab League's military committee entrusted with the task of carrying on the fight against the Zionists. Under the command of al-Qawuqji, ALA units initiated operations along the border in mid-December and moved into Palestine itself in January 1948. Strikes against Arab villages by the Zionist militia, the Haganah, in April 1948 generated public anger throughout Syria but failed to persuade the newly independent government in Damascus to order either the remainder of the ALA or regular Syrian troops to intervene in the fighting. When major hostilities broke out in May, elements of the ALA and the Syrian armed forces advanced toward the town of Samakh and Jewish settlements situated south of the Sea of Galilee. The offensive was beaten back with severe losses. More successful were military operations carried out in the north between the Sea of Galilee and Lake Hula, and to the east along the Yarmuk River. As a result of these operations, some 66 square kilometers of formerly Palestinian territory were occupied and held by Syrian troops.

Damascus accepted the terms of UN Security Council Resolution 801 on June 11, 1948, and ordered all of the forces under its command to cease firing. The Haganah then launched a counteroffensive between the Sea of Galilee and Lake Hula, and pushed northeastward from 'En Gev on the eastern shore of the Sea of Galilee. The advance prompted the Security Council to adopt a more comprehensive cease-fire resolution (902), which Syria immediately accepted. The ALA refused to accept the truce, however, and continued to fight in the Galilee hills throughout the summer. These activities were disowned by the Syrian authorities, who ignored al-Qawuqji's repeated pleas for assistance.

In November 1948, Syria's delegate on the UN Security Council affirmed that the Arab governments would only negotiate with Jewish representatives if the World Zionist Organization acknowledged the right of Palestinian Arabs to form an independent state. Damascus did not join the UN-sponsored mediation process until March 1949, and the Israel-Syrian Armistice Conference opened a month later. Syrian representatives at the meeting insisted that the talks deal exclusively with military matters, whereas the Israelis demanded that any agreement must cover political issues as well. After 13 sessions, the two parties signed a formal Armistice Agreement that set up four demilitarized zones along the border, backed by larger districts "in which defensive forces only shall be maintained." For practical reasons, but over Damascus's strenuous objections, these areas were patrolled by Israeli police units stationed at 'En Gev and Mishmar Ha-Yarden. The conclusion of the 1948 war therefore left a contested and unstable distribution of territory between the State of Israel and the Syrian Arab Republic, which created opportunities for subsequent military confrontations.

TWO WARS, TWO DEFEATS

Periodic skirmishes broke out along the Syrian-Israeli border during 1964 and 1965.[1] The Movement for the Liberation of Palestine (FATH) took advantage of the opportunity to launch a strike into Israel from Syrian territory in July 1965; in response, Syrian security forces arrested FATH officials in the country. Greater violence flared in the spring of 1966 when a number of armed incursions into

Israeli-held territory took place. The radical Ba'thi leadership that came to power in Damascus in February 1966 credited FATH guerrillas with carrying out most of these operations and openly provided the organization with supplies and training facilities.

Israeli aircraft retaliated by attacking construction equipment and farm machinery situated inside Syrian territory. The raids led the Syrian air force to target a pair of Israeli police boats operating in the Sea of Galilee on August 15, 1966. Radio Damascus declared on that occasion that Syria had decided "that she would not confine herself to defensive action but would attack defined targets and bases of aggression within the occupied area. Syria has waited for a suitable opportunity to carry out this new policy. That opportunity was presented today." Chief of staff General Ahmad al-Suwaidani concurred: "We have always been the defenders, but in this battle we were not resisting blows, but delivering blows."[2] In addition, the government set up its own Palestinian organization, the Palestine People's Liberation Front (*Jabhah al-Tahrir al-Sha'biyyah al-Filastiniyyah*), to support FATH's activities.

Throughout the spring of 1967, Damascus exhibited an increasingly belligerent posture toward Israel. In early April, when Israeli farmers once again moved armored tractors into the demilitarized zone north of the Sea of Galilee, Syrian units responded not only with artillery and mortar fire but also with tank and aircraft forays into the disputed area. Israeli armored and air force units counterattacked, bombarding villages across the border inside Syria and engaging Syrian warplanes in the skies over Damascus. In the wake of this air engagement, the Syrian government stepped up its support for military operations by Palestinian commandos based in Lebanon and Jordan. In addition, Damascus dispatched missions to Cairo to persuade Egypt to implement the mutual defense pact that the two governments had signed in November 1966. Persistent Syrian pressure, accompanied by Soviet reports that the Israel Defense Forces (IDF) had massed along the Syrian-Israeli border, convinced Egyptian President Gamal 'Abd al-Nasir to order the withdrawal of the UN Emergency Force from the Sinai and close the Straits of Tiran to Israeli shipping. War erupted on June 5, 1967.

Syrian bellicosity played a crucial role in escalating the confrontation of April–May 1967 into full-scale warfare between the Arab states and Israel. Nevertheless, when the fighting actually broke out, the Syrian high command proved inordinately cautious in joining the battle. Syrian artillery shelled Israeli settlements around the Sea of Galilee, and ground forces advanced across the border at two separate locations. But combat only escalated after the IDF turned its attention northward on the fifth day of the war. The Syrian city of al-Qunaitirah quickly fell, and Israeli troops occupied the surrounding Golan region. The two sides agreed to a cease-fire on June 10.

Embarrassed by the ease with which the IDF had captured the southwestern corner of Syria, Damascus flatly rejected Israeli calls to enter into direct negotiations after the war. Senior officials urged Palestinian guerrillas to continue the armed struggle and refused to endorse UN Security Council Resolution 242, which ordered the "withdrawal of Israel from territories occupied in the recent conflict" and the "acknowledgement of the sovereignty, territorial integrity and political independence of every state in the area." Military commanders remained careful, however, to prevent Palestinian fighters from striking across the Syrian border lest such action provoke Israeli retaliation. In December 1968, the Syrian government set up a Palestinian guerrilla formation of its own, called *al-Sa'iqah* (the Lightning Bolt), partly to counteract a growing rapprochement between FATH and Cairo and partly to offset the emergence of the more militant Popular Front for the Liberation of Palestine (PFLP). Al-Sa'iqah joined various Palestinian militias in undertaking raids into Israel and Israeli-occupied territory throughout 1969 and 1970.

November 1970 witnessed the downfall of the Ba'thi regime that had orchestrated the run-up to the 1967 war. The new government, headed by former Minister of Defense Hafiz al-Asad, continued to inveigh against Israel as forcefully as had its predecessor and remained unwilling to accept Resolution 242. But it gradually replaced the virulent anti-Zionist rhetoric of the mid-1960s with more nuanced condemnations of Israeli policy. Furthermore, the al-Asad regime adopted a more businesslike orientation toward the long-term struggle with Israel. New arms contracts were signed with the Soviet Union; greater efforts were made to coordinate military planning with Egypt and Jordan; and Palestinian guerrilla units were kept on a tighter leash. Military commanders loyal to al-Asad had already placed al-Sa'iqah under the strict control of the Ba'th Party.

Reining in the Palestinian guerrillas turned out to be more than Damascus could handle. Following the Jordanian civil war of September 1970, most Palestinian commando units decamped to bases in Syria and southern Lebanon. The activities, and often the mere presence, of these formations attracted repeated Israeli airstrikes. The IDF launched a major incursion into southern Lebanon in March 1972 and carried out a second offensive after the PFLP attacked Lydda Airport two months later. Yet a third Israeli operation followed the killing of Israeli athletes at the Munich Olympics that September. In February 1973, President al-Asad prohibited Palestinian militias from launching raids into Israel or Israeli-occupied land from Syrian territory. Constraints on guerrilla activity remained firmly in place during and after the October 1973 war, in the course of which Israel captured a small amount of additional territory in the Golan. Meanwhile, Damascus flatly rejected Egypt's March 1972 proposal to set up a Palestinian government-in-exile on the grounds that such a move would weaken the armed struggle against Israel and that the FATH-led Palestine Liberation Organization (PLO) constituted the only legitimate Palestinian authority.

Simmering hostility between Syria and Israel during the winter of 1973–1974, combined with the growing potential for American and Soviet military involvement in the Arab-Israeli conflict, persuaded U.S. Secretary of State Henry Kissinger to initiate eight months of concerted mediation. In an effort to encourage the authorities in Damascus to be flexible, Kissinger suggested to the Israeli government that it offer to pull back to the positions in the Golan that its troops had occupied immediately prior to the outbreak of the October war. After initially rejecting this suggestion, Israeli officials eventually conceded, and in May 1974 a disengagement agreement was signed. It provided for the withdrawal of Israel troops from al-Qunaitirah, the creation of a buffer zone patrolled by UN peacekeeping forces, strict limitations on the number and composition of Israeli and Syrian units deployed on each side of the buffer zone, and procedures for exchanging prisoners of war. At the same time, Damascus resisted Egypt's efforts to convene a general peace conference in Geneva, as well as Cairo's insistence that the PLO be designated the sole representative of the Palestinian people. On the other hand, al-Sa'iqah joined FATH in approving the so-called "phased political program" that was adopted by the Palestine National Council (PNC) in June 1974.

CONFLICT SPREADS TO LEBANON

Syria's relations with Israel remained frigid despite the 1974 disengagement agreement. Damascus expressed sharp criticism of Egypt's accelerating rapprochement with Israel, and the IDF launched strikes against Palestinian bases in southern Lebanon in January, May, and August 1975. As fighting intensified both among rival Lebanese militias and between Lebanese forces and the PLO during the fall and winter of 1975–1976, Syrian officials moderated their vituperation against Cairo and made overtures to Washington. Israeli commanders responded by funneling military supplies to the militia of the Maronite Christian Phalangist (*Kataib*) Party, which stepped up attacks against Palestinian refugee camps inside Lebanon in early 1976. These moves set the stage for Syria's large-scale military intervention in Lebanon that spring, as well as for U.S. officials to exert pressure on Israel to refrain from attacking Syrian ground and air forces operating north of a line stretching from Saidah to Jazzin (the so-called Red Line). In return, Damascus refrained from interfering in the area south of the Zaharani River.

President al-Asad subsequently stated on several occasions that he stood ready to negotiate a peace agreement with Israel if Israel pulled out of the lands that it had seized in 1967 and recognized the Palestinians' right to set up an independent, sovereign state. Such statements encouraged U.S. Secretary of State Cyrus Vance to make a series of trips to Damascus, and President al-Asad conferred directly with U.S. President Jimmy Carter in Geneva in May 1977. Whatever potential there might have been for a thaw in Syrian-Israeli relations disappeared when the Likud Bloc, led by the former Revisionist Zionist Menachem Begin, gained control of the Israeli parliament that same month. Nevertheless, Damascus prevented Palestinian guerrillas from crossing into Israel and Israeli-occupied territory from Syria and restrained its regular armed forces from interfering when the IDF launched a large-scale incursion against PLO bases in southern Lebanon in March 1978. Syrian military commanders meanwhile cultivated political and military links to the Shi'i movement AMAL (*Afwaj al-Muqawamah al-Lubnaniyyah*, or Lebanese Resistance Battalions), which became Damascus's primary ally inside Lebanon.

Egyptian President Anwar al-Sadat's dramatic peace initiatives toward Israel in 1977 and 1978 convinced Damascus that Cairo was preparing to abandon its Arab allies and pursue a bilateral peace treaty. President al-Asad riposted by trying to persuade the leaders of Jordan and Saudi Arabia to join him in issuing a public condemnation of Egypt's policy. An Arab summit meeting in December 1977 produced little more than vague pronouncements regarding the continuing importance of Arab unity, although the PLO ended up endorsing Syria's position to a greater extent than one might have expected, given the defeats in Lebanon that the organization had suffered at Syrian hands. Syria and the PLO embarked on a gradual rapprochement during 1978, which culminated in the January 1979 PNC congress taking place in Damascus. At that meeting, President al-Asad won PLO support for his assertion that Syria's ongoing military involvement in Lebanon constituted an extension of the struggle against Zionism.

Because Damascus refused to put aside its long-standing differences with Baghdad, it found itself unable to do anything more than voice strenuous opposition to the steadily accelerating Egyptian-Israeli peace process and the treaty that the two governments signed in March 1979. Determined that it would never again be left hanging by a major strategic partner, the Syrian leadership set out to achieve "strategic parity" with Israel by enlarging and upgrading its armed forces and signing a Treaty of Friendship and Cooperation with the Soviet Union. Damascus also adopted a more belligerent posture toward the IDF in Lebanon, scrambling warplanes in June 1979 to intercept Israeli aircraft that were bombing PLO camps. Eight months later, Syrian troops pulled out of coastal Lebanon and took up positions in the central Biqa' Valley.

During the first months of 1981, Israel complained that the Syrian military presence in Lebanon, along with its alliance with AMAL and encouragement of PLO guerrillas, posed a threat to its northern border. Prime Minister Begin unleashed a succession of fulminations and hinted that the IDF might come to the rescue of Lebanon's Maronite community, which he claimed was suffering as a result of the Syrian presence. Israeli warplanes shot down a pair of Syrian military helicopters at the end of April, prompting Syrian commanders to move anti-aircraft missile batteries into the Biqa'. Fears that the confrontation between Israel and Syria was about to escalate to war brought U.S. special envoy Philip

Habib to the region. Habib's mediation efforts defused the so-called missile crisis of May 1981 and at the same time ended the protracted battle for Zahlah between Syrian troops and the Maronite Lebanese Forces. At the end of June, the Lebanese forces finally pulled out of Zahlah, leaving the Biqa' Valley firmly in Syrian hands.

In December 1981, the Likud government imposed Israeli civil law on the occupied Golan, and a month later Israel's Minister of Defense Ariel Sharon traveled secretly to Beirut to confer with the commanders of the Lebanese Forces. Israeli troops subsequently moved into positions along the Lebanese border and advanced en masse into southern Lebanon in June 1982. Syrian units held their fire for the first two days of the offensive but finally engaged the IDF in defense of the strategic town of Jazzin. Israeli aircraft and artillery then attacked Syrian positions all across the Biqa' Valley, while IDF and Syrian warplanes clashed in the skies overhead. Further battles occurred when Israeli units rolled into the southern suburbs of Beirut. After the fighting came to an end, Damascus's relations with the PLO collapsed, with the two parties blaming one another for their evident lack of battlefield coordination. Syrian agents even encouraged dissidents inside the PLO to challenge the organization's historic leader, Yasir 'Arafat, who afterwards distanced himself from Damascus.

For the next three years, the focus of Syrian-Israeli antagonism stayed firmly fixed on Lebanon. Relations between Syria and the PLO went from bad to worse, leading to the November 1983 expulsion of the last contingents of PLO commandos from Nahr al-Barid and al-Badawi camps outside Tripoli by fighters from al-Sa'iqah, the PFLP, the Popular Front for the Liberation of Palestine—General Command (PFLP-GC), and the Democratic Front for the Liberation of Palestine. Damascus at the same time facilitated efforts by the Islamic Republic of Iran to arm and train AMAL militants who had defected from the movement to form the more radical Party of God (*Hizbullah*); the new organization joined Islamic Jihad, al-Sa'iqah, and the PFLP in prosecuting a war of attrition against the IDF that ended up pushing Israeli troops south of the Litani River.

In November 1985, a pair of Syrian warplanes buzzed an Israeli reconnaissance aircraft operating in Lebanese airspace, only to be shot down by IDF interceptors. Syrian commanders responded by moving anti-aircraft missile batteries back into the Biqa' Valley and deploying surface-to-air missiles along the Golan front. AMAL's militia unleashed a series of large-scale rocket attacks against Israeli border towns in January 1986. A month later, Israeli military aircraft forced a Libyan jet carrying the speaker of the Syrian People's Assembly to land in Israel and only permitted it to resume its flight after Syria lodged a formal complaint with the UN Security Council. Skirmishing with Israel accompanied an all-out offensive against the PLO, carried out largely by AMAL. The fighting that erupted across Lebanon led to occasional clashes between Syrian forces and Hizbullah fighters, which set the stage for the return of Syrian troops to West Beirut in February 1987.

Military operations on the part of Iranian- and Syrian-backed militias in southern Lebanon persisted throughout the remainder of the year. These activities sharpened Israeli hostility toward the Ba'thi regime in Damascus. As a result, a February 1988 peace initiative undertaken by U.S. Secretary of State George Shultz elicited no more than an offhand dismissal from Israeli Prime Minister Yitzhak Shamir. Any further attempt to reconcile the conflicting interests of Syria and Israel was derailed by the outbreak of severe fighting between AMAL and Hizbullah, which pulled additional Syrian soldiers into the southern suburbs of Beirut as the spring went by. That November, the PNC meeting in Algiers officially accepted UN Security Council Resolutions 242 and 338, thereby opening the door to negotiations with Israel. Damascus and its allies in the Palestinian national movement immediately denounced the action: Abu Musa of the dissident FATH Uprising organization told reporters that " 'Arafat has become an enemy of the [Palestinian] revolution, and should be treated as such."[3]

MEDIATION INITIATIVES

1989 saw a subtle but significant shift in Damascus's stance toward Israel. Senior Syrian officials, perhaps encouraged by indications that the new administration in Washington intended to adhere to a more even-handed approach to the Middle East, signaled a willingness to take part in negotiations on the basis of the principles that had been codified in UN Security Council Resolutions 242 and 338. More important, Damascus took steps to reconcile with Cairo and raised no public objection to the PLO's own overtures to Israel. During the course of a July 1990 summit meeting with Egypt's President Husni Mubarak, President al-Asad told reporters that his government was fully prepared to sign a formal treaty with Israel on the basis of an exchange of territory for peace.

Yet Damascus showed a marked reluctance to jump onto the U.S.-sponsored bandwagon to convene an international conference to deal with the Arab-Israeli conflict in the immediate aftermath of the 1990–1991 Gulf War. Following a meeting with U.S. Secretary of State James Baker in early April 1991, Foreign Minister Faruq al-Shar' reaffirmed Damascus's position that the United Nations should play "a significant role" in such a conference and that the results of any negotiations had to be "based on Resolutions 242 and 338."[4] Although Syrian officials later retreated from their insistence that the talks be sponsored by the United Nations, they persisted in demanding that the two Security Council resolutions serve as the basis for deliberations. On the eve of the initial meeting in Madrid, Damascus announced that it would take no part in follow-up sessions concerning economic and environmental issues unless there were clear progress in resolving the problem of the occupied territories.

Syria boycotted the January 1992 Moscow round of talks on the grounds that any discussion of long-term regional security matters was premature so long as Israeli troops remained in control of the Golan, the West Bank, and Gaza. Bilateral negotiations in Washington two months later produced virtual deadlock between Syria and Israel. Damascus tried to focus attention on the occupied territories while the Israelis remonstrated against purported Syrian threats to Israeli security. When negotiations resumed in August, Syrian delegates expressed optimism that the Labor Party–led government in Israel would adopt a more conciliatory posture. Damascus reiterated its demand for the complete return of the Golan, rebuffing Israeli hints that unspecified territorial concessions might follow—rather than precede—the signing of a peace treaty. But at the same time, the Syrians hinted that the Golan could end up being demilitarized or placed under international supervision. Israel responded by stating for the first time that it considered the Golan to be covered under the terms of Resolution 242. Such reciprocal flexibility resulted in a dramatic improvement in the atmosphere surrounding the talks, and in September the Syrian delegation circulated a draft Declaration of Principles that outlined the general terms of a comprehensive peace agreement.

Nevertheless, the seventh round of discussions in October 1992 evidenced none of the optimism that had pervaded the preceding session. Syria denounced Israel's rejection of a complete withdrawal from the Golan as well as the IDF's escalating air and artillery strikes in southern Lebanon. When Israeli delegates declared that they had decided to go home early, the head of the Syrian team called the talks "frustrating." Syria's position became even more intransigent during the early November recess. When the talks resumed, Syria reaffirmed its demand that a full Israeli withdrawal from the occupied territories must take place before any other issues could be discussed.

Even as the talks foundered, President al-Asad softened Syria's hard line. He told reporters that it was conceivable, even likely, that some aspects of the conflict might be settled in advance of others, so long as the ultimate objective of comprehensive peace were kept firmly in mind. When a reporter asked whether Syria would be willing to sign an agreement that did not turn over all of the West Bank to the Palestinians, al-Asad replied that he "did not want to go into details," but that the notion of comprehensiveness referred to the range of topics under consideration, not to the amount of real estate involved. He then repeated that so long as all of the Arab delegations retained their confidence in one another, "it would be possible for one side to progress more speedily than the others."[5] In mid-March, however, al-Asad reverted to a much less conciliatory position. He told an audience in Damascus that any separate Syrian-Israeli settlement would be rejected out of hand. He went on to assert that Syria would under no circumstances abandon its Arab partners but could instead be counted on to treat matters that were vital to the Palestinians, Lebanese, and Jordanians as vital to itself.

Syrian delegates reasserted President al-Asad's hard line just prior to the ninth round of negotiations at the end of April 1993. The head of the negotiating team told the Lebanese newspaper *al-Diyar* that Damascus had no intention of making a separate deal with Israel but instead remained "committed to a comprehensive peace and solving the Arab-Israeli conflict on all fronts."[6] A week later, Vice President 'Abd al-Halim Khaddam noted that "peace requires withdrawal from all the occupied Arab territories and recognition of the national rights of the Palestinian people," both of which were presently blocked by Israel.

Damascus was by all accounts caught completely off guard by the August 1993 Oslo accords between Israel and the PLO. Syrian officials immediately branded the agreement a "partial solution" that undermined the overall prospects for an honorable settlement. They also invited a variety of radical Palestinian organizations, which were equally upset with the PLO, to set up offices in the Syrian capital. These included the PFLP, the PFLP-GC, Palestinian Islamic Jihad, and the Islamic Resistance Movement (*Harakah al-Muqawamah al-Islamiyyah*, or HAMAS). At the same time, Damascus solicited more active U.S. mediation.

U.S. Secretary of State Warren Christopher then presented al-Asad with a secret offer from Israeli Prime Minister Yitzhak Rabin to pull out of the Golan in exchange for explicit security guarantees and the establishment of normal diplomatic relations. The Syrian president asked whether such a withdrawal would be to the border that had existed as of June 4, 1967, and was eventually informed that Rabin intended to use the boundary that had been laid down by British and French authorities in 1923, which put the entirety of the Jordan River and Sea of Galilee inside Israeli territory.[7] President al-Asad therefore turned down the proposal but agreed to meet U.S. President William J. Clinton in Geneva in January 1994. During the course of the meeting, al-Asad expressed a commitment to "establish normal relations in the area."[8] Clinton inferred from this that Syria was willing to complement correct diplomatic ties with broader economic and social connections. Israeli officials, on the other hand, read into the statement an intention on Syria's part to hold back until a comprehensive agreement was reached concerning the West Bank and Gaza. Talks once again stalemated.

In January 1995, al-Asad sent a letter to Clinton outlining the fundamental guidelines that might govern future security in the Golan. The letter was reworked by U.S. officials into a one-page Statement of Aims and Principles that was formally presented to Syria and Israel in May. Prime Minister Rabin refused to accept a written version of the principles, prompting al-Asad to doubt that he was serious about the oral pledges that he had already made. Before such misgivings could be assuaged, Rabin was assassinated. It was left to U.S. diplomats to pass along the details of Rabin's secret proposal to his successor, Shimon Peres.

President al-Asad found Prime Minister Peres to be an enigma. Whereas al-Asad understood diplomacy to involve precise language and firm commitments, Peres employed vague formulations and broad visions. Furthermore,

Peres's conception of a "New Middle East," in which state borders were irrelevant and mutual prosperity trumped political differences, left the Syrian president cold. On the contrary, such a utopia appeared to Damascus to be simply a façade for Israel's unlimited exploitation of the water resources of the Golan and domination of the regional economy. Syria joined a new round of bilateral talks beginning in December 1995. But in February 1996, Peres called for parliamentary elections and then suspended negotiations a month later in the wake of a string of suicide bombings inside Israel.

For two weeks that April, the IDF and Hizbullah engaged in an intense military clash in southern Lebanon. Prime Minister Peres placed the blame for Hizbullah's belligerence squarely on Iran and hinted only vaguely at Syria's ongoing support for the movement. Damascus in turn kept its distance from the confrontation but defended Hizbullah as acting in a defensive fashion to liberate "occupied land."[9] The Syrian government cooperated with the governments of Israel and Lebanon in setting up the UN monitoring group that deployed along the border when the fighting came to an end and assisted in enforcing the terms of the ceasefire agreement. Israel's inability to crush Hizbullah contributed to Peres's electoral defeat that May and the Likud Bloc's return to power. Faced with a more uncompromising Israeli leadership, Syrian troops moved back into forward positions in central Lebanon in August, a move that Israel considered to be aggressive.

Binyamin Netanyahu's government abandoned the "land for peace" formula that had long been associated with UN Security Council Resolution 242 and insisted instead upon the less tangible concept of "peace with security." The new Israeli prime minister pledged that he would never give back the Golan and announced that any talks with Damascus would have to proceed "without preconditions," that is, taking no account of his predecessors' proposals and actions. Syrian officials demanded that any further talks be resumed at the point where they had been broken off by Peres. Any other procedure would imply that "the negotiations could last another century . . . since every time there is a new Israeli government we have to return to point zero."[10] U.S. representatives managed to elicit support from Damascus for resurrecting negotiations but received no reciprocal signals from the Israeli government. Syrian-Israeli relations remained frozen so long as Netanyahu served as prime minister.

Syrian officials welcomed the May 1999 electoral victory of Ehud Barak. The incoming Israeli prime minister signaled that he was willing to negotiate on the basis of the Golan boundary that existed on June 4, 1967, although he added that any final agreement might require "very marginal border adjustments" to ensure Israel's security and access to vital water supplies. The apparent thaw in Syrian-Israeli relations prompted the PFLP to distance itself from Damascus and reconcile with the mainstream PLO. That December, President al-Asad informed U.S. Secretary of State Madeleine Albright that Syria was prepared to restart negotiations "where they had left off." Washington immediately organized a new round of bilateral talks and put together a draft peace treaty that might provide a basis for discussion. The Syrian delegation quickly discovered, however, that the Israelis were once again basing their proposals on the 1923 border rather than the one of 1967. Furthermore, Israel now demanded unrestricted access to the water resources of the Golan, including various tributaries of the Jordan River. The Syrians riposted that future water rights would conform to conventional international standards. After three months of sparring, the Israeli government pulled out of the talks.

NO WAR, NO PEACE

President Hafiz al-Asad died unexpectedly in June 2000. His successor, Bashshar al-Asad, hinted on a number of occasions over the course of the summer that he hoped that negotiations with Israel would resume in short order. Before the two sides could work out a mutually agreeable starting point, however, Hizbullah launched a series of attacks against Israeli positions around the disputed Shib'a farms, and the second (al-Aqsa) Palestinian uprising erupted.[11] At the end of October, the Israeli government started building 1,500 new houses for Jewish settlers in the Golan. February 2001 brought the electoral defeat of Prime Minister Barak and his replacement with the hardliner Ariel Sharon. The Sharon government immediately stepped up Israeli military operations in southern Lebanon and in April attacked a Syrian radar post in retaliation for Hizbullah activities along the Lebanese border.

Despite these setbacks, Damascus again signaled that it would be interested in reopening bilateral discussions. Such signals were rebuffed, to the growing irritation of the Syrian president, who in turn escalated his own anti-Israel rhetoric. More important, al-Asad revived the notion that any Syrian-Israeli peace must be predicated upon a just resolution of the Israel-Palestinian conflict. Such sentiments led Washington to exclude Syria from the initial stages of the so-called Road Map to Peace that was drawn up in the fall of 2002 by the United States, the United Nations, the European Union, and Russia.

The March 2003 U.S. military offensive in Iraq accompanied renewed signs that Damascus was interested in resuming bilateral talks with Israel. Prime Minister Sharon seemed receptive to the idea so long as any discussions took place "without conditions." But the Israeli government linked the resumption of negotiations with Syria to an end to all strikes against Israeli targets by Hizbullah and other guerrilla organizations. Taking the hint, HAMAS and Palestinian Islamic Jihad closed their Syrian offices, while the PFLP reduced its activities to a bare minimum. In October 2003, the IDF bombed an alleged Palestinian commando training camp on the northern outskirts of Damascus. The year closed with the announcement that Israel planned to double the number of Jewish settlers in the Golan. Nevertheless, President al-Asad took advantage of a December interview with the *New York Times* to reiterate his willingness to pick up talks where they had left off in January 2000.

U.S. and Israeli demands that Syria eject all radical Palestinian organizations from its territory raised tensions all around as 2004 went by. In September, Israel uncharacteristically claimed responsibility for the killing of an influential member of HAMAS outside his house in the Syrian capital. The attack derailed Damascus's clandestine overtures to the Sharon government, which were being passed along through the good offices of former U.S. ambassador to Israel Martin Indyk. Further initiatives proved impossible in the wake of the February 2005 assassination of former Lebanese prime minister Rafiq al-Hariri, which sparked a severe crisis in Syria's relations not only with Lebanon but also with the United States, France, and Israel. Syrian troops pulled out of Lebanon two months later, and shortly after that Islamist militants infiltrated the country from Iraq, taking the name al-Qa'idah in the Lands of Syria (*al-Qa'idah fi Bilad al-Sham*) and vowing to resume the fight against Israel where Hizbullah had left off.[12] The IDF struck Hizbullah positions at the end of May, prompting Hizbullah fighters to raid Israeli positions around the disputed village of Ghajar and channel greater financial assistance to the al-'Aqsa Martyrs' Brigade in the West Bank.[13] President al-Asad's unprecedented greeting to Israeli President Katsav at the funeral for Pope John Paul II did little to reverse the downward spiral.

Following the July 2006 Israel-Hizbullah war in southern Lebanon, President al-Asad gave a series of interviews to international journalists in which he signaled his government's willingness to resume talks with Israel. He even hinted that new negotiations need not take account of previous understandings. Such intimations were firmly rejected by Israeli Prime Minister Ehud Olmert, who was reported to have remarked, "As long as I am prime minister, the Golan Heights will remain in our hands forever, because it is an inseparable part of Israel."[14] Olmert further charged that Damascus was supplying Hizbullah with missiles and other heavy weapons and had to stop doing so before any bilateral negotiations could begin. A squadron of Israeli warplanes bombed an alleged nuclear facility outside Dair al-Zur in September. Exasperated and angry, Syrian officials stopped making overtures to Israel and turned to Washington to persuade the Israeli government to show greater flexibility.

But it was Turkey rather than the United States that seized the initiative in brokering an agreement between Syria and Israel. Turkish Foreign Minister Ali Babacan and Special Adviser to the Prime Minister Ahmet Davutoglu arranged and coordinated a series of indirect talks during the course of 2007 and 2008, which laid the foundation for a proposed trilateral meeting that was scheduled to take place in Istanbul at the end of December. The green light to announce the conference was to come in a telephone call on December 27, 2008, from Prime Minister Olmert to Prime Minister Recep Tayyip Erdogan. One half-hour before the call was to be placed, Israeli troops and tanks advanced into Gaza, initiating a three-week war between the IDF and HAMAS.[15] Turkish officials found the carpet pulled out from under them, and Syrian representatives abruptly terminated the negotiations. President al-Asad expressed his outrage during an Arab summit meeting in Qatar in January 2009, asserting that the Gaza war demonstrated that the Israeli government only understood "the language of blood."[16] He demanded that the Arab states impose a comprehensive boycott against Israel, shut down all Israeli embassies, and cut off all "direct and indirect ties with Israel."

Nevertheless, al-Asad soon afterwards sent messages to prominent journalists that talks with Israel might get underway once again as soon as the dust had settled. His willingness to try yet again to engage the Israelis was heartily encouraged by Qatar and reinforced by the arrival of a new administration in Washington. The Syrian president welcomed the chairman of the Foreign Relations Committee of the U.S. Senate to Damascus in February 2009, telling him that Syria was ready to "have direct discussions with Israel over the Golan Heights—with the Americans at the table."[17] Before any concrete proposals could be drawn up, however, Binyamin Netanyahu regained the prime ministership of Israel at the head of an exceptionally hardline government. French President Nicolas Sarkozy tried in November to revive the talks, but Netanyahu insisted that they resume with no preconditions; al-Asad told Sarkozy that he would come back to the table only after the Israeli government "guarantees the full return of land and rights."[18] The Syrian president then called on U.S. President Barack Obama to "draw up an action plan" to deal with the dispute. Meanwhile, IDF warships seized a German freighter off the coast of Cyprus and charged that it was bound for Latakia to offload thousands of Iranian rockets and other weapons for delivery to Hizbullah.[19]

In February 2010, Israeli Minister of Defense Ehud Barak told senior military commanders that "in the absence of an arrangement with Syria, we are liable to enter a belligerent clash with it that could reach the point of an all-out, regional war." Damascus interpreted this as a thinly veiled threat and riposted that the Israelis were "acting like thugs." "Do not test the determination of Syria," Foreign Minister Walid al-Mu'allim warned. "You know that war this time would move to your cities." He then cautioned Israel that the Syrian armed forces would intervene if the Israeli army attacked southern Lebanon. Raising the ante, Israeli Foreign Minister Avigdor Lieberman remarked that "Asad should know that in the next war, he will lose. Neither he nor the Asad family will remain in power." Liberberman went on to say that Damascus may as well "relinquish its demand for the Golan Heights."[20] Two months later, Israeli President Shimon Peres and Minister of Defense Barak both charged that Syria had begun to supply intermediate-range SCUD rockets to Hizbullah fighters in southern Lebanon.[21]

U.S. officials failed to dismiss the allegation out of hand and instead summoned Syria's ambassador to Washington to the State Department to warn him of the consequences of such a transfer. The incident burst any hopes on Damascus's part that the Obama administration might take a different tack from the one pursued by its predecessor, and Damascus turned back to Turkey to act as mediator vis-à-vis Israel.[22] Shortly after this, Peres sent a proposal to al-Asad by way of Russian President Dimitry Medvedev to return the Golan in exchange for Damascus's severing all ties to Hizbullah, the Palestinian resistance movement, and the Islamic Republic of Iran; the Syrian president flatly rejected the proposal.[23] He then told the Italian newspaper *La Repubblica* that any agreement must include the long-standing demands of the Palestinians and not be limited to the Golan alone.[24]

On May 15, 2011, the anniversary of the establishment of the State of Israel, hundreds of Palestinian refugees residing in Syria rushed Israeli border posts along the Golan. The protest was organized by a group of young refugees that called itself the Youth Initiative for Palestinian Return.[25] A handful of marchers made it across the frontier and into the town of Majdal Shams, where they were met by Israeli troops who shot into the crowd.[26] At least one protester succeeded in getting past Majdal Shams and made it all the way back to his family's home in Jaffa.[27] The protest was repeated on the anniversary of the June 1967 war, but this time Israeli border guards were prepared and opened fire right away, killing a larger number of participants.

Funeral ceremonies for those who had been killed in the June march exploded into violence as the militia of the PFLP-GC resorted to force in an attempt to keep the mourners in line. Infuriated Palestinian activists subsequently surrounded the PFLP-GC's headquarters in Damascus and set it on fire.[28] The incidents of May and June 2011 were widely interpreted as hamfisted signals to the Israeli government that the al-Asad regime could rapidly generate an armed confrontation along the Golan border if it chose to do so.

NOTES

Portions of Chapter 5 first appeared in Fred H. Lawson, "Syria and the Israel-Palestinian Conflict," in *The Encyclopedia of the Israel-Palestinian Conflict*, ed. Cheryl Rubenberg (Boulder, CO: Lynne Rienner Publishers, 2010). Used by permission.

1. Asher Kaufman, " 'Let Sleeping Dogs Lie': On Ghajar and Other Anomalies in the Syria-Lebanon-Israel Tri-Border Region," *Middle East Journal* 63 (Autumn 2009): 55.

2. Avner Yaniv, "Syria and Israel: The Politics of Escalation," in *Syria under Assad*, eds. Moshe Ma'oz and Avner Yaniv (New York: St. Martin's Press, 1986), 166–67; Moshe Ma'oz, *Syria and Israel: From War to Peace-making* (Oxford, UK: Clarendon Press, 1995), 93–94; Fred H. Lawson, *Why Syria Goes to War* (Ithaca, NY: Cornell University Press, 1996), 20–22.

3. *al-Nahar*, November 13, 1988.

4. Fred H. Lawson, "Domestic Pressures and the Peace Process," in *Contemporary Syria*, ed. Eberhard Kienle (London: British Academic Press, 1994), 141; Helena Cobban,

The Israeli-Syrian Peace Talks: 1991–96 and Beyond (Washington, DC: United States Institute of Peace Press, 1999), 17.

5. Lawson, "Domestic Pressures," 142.

6. Ibid., 143.

7. See Frederic C. Hof, *Mapping Peace between Syria and Israel*, Special Report No. 219, United States Institute of Peace, Washington, DC, March 2009.

8. Cobban, *Israeli-Syrian Peace Talks*, 61.

9. Syrian Arab Television, April 17, 1996, as reported in Foreign Broadcast Information Service, "Daily Report: Near East and South Asia," April 18, 1996.

10. Sami G. Hajjar, "The Stalled Peace Process: Israeli-Syrian Track," in *Mediterranean Security in the Coming Millennium*, ed. Stephen J. Blank (Carlisle, PA: U.S. Army War College, 1999), 336.

11. Asher Kaufman, "Who Owns the Shebaa Farms? Chronicle of a Territorial Dispute," *Middle East Journal* 56 (Autumn 2002): 577.

12. Reinoud Leenders, " 'Regional Conflict Formations': Is the Middle East Next?" *Third World Quarterly* 28 (May 2007): 963.

13. Sune Haugbolle, *The Alliance between Iran, Syria and Hizbollah*, DIIS Report No. 2006:10, Danish Institute for International Studies, Copenhagen, November 2006, 25; Kaufman, " 'Let Sleeping Dogs Lie,' " 558; International Crisis Group, "Syria after Lebanon, Lebanon after Syria," *Middle East Report*, no. 39 (April 12, 2005): 4.

14. International Crisis Group, "Restarting Israeli-Syrian Negotiations," *Middle East Report*, no. 63 (April 10, 2007): 3.

15. Thomas Seibert, "Israel-Syria Talks 'Were a Phone Call Away,' " *The National* (Abu Dhabi), November 13, 2010.

16. Seymour M. Hersh, "Syria Calling," *The New Yorker*, April 6, 2009.

17. Ibid.

18. *Haaretz*, November 21, 2009.

19. *Middle East International* (MEI), November 20, 2009.

20. MEI, February 19, 2010.

21. *al-Safir*, April 16, 2010.

22. Reuters, May 8, 2010.

23. *al-Safir*, May 1, 2010.

24. *La Repubblica*, May 8, 2010.

25. *al-Jazeera*, March 12, 2011.

26. *New York Times*, May 15, 2011.

27. Anaheed al-Hardan, "A Year On: The Palestinians in Syria," *Syrian Studies Association Newsletter* 17 (2012).

28. Ibid.

FURTHER READING

Helena Cobban. *The Israeli-Syrian Peace Talks: 1991–96 and Beyond*. Washington, DC: United States Institute of Peace Press, 1999.

Alasdair Drysdale and Raymond Hinnebusch. *Syria and the Middle East Peace Process*. New York: Council on Foreign Relations Press, 1991.

Philip S. Khoury. "Divided Loyalties? Syria and the Question of Palestine, 1919–39." *Middle Eastern Studies* 21 (July 1985).

Moshe Ma'oz. *Syria and Israel*. Oxford, UK: Clarendon Press, 1995.

Itamar Rabinovich. *The Brink of Peace: The Israeli-Syrian Negotiations*. Princeton, NJ: Princeton University Press, 1998.

Patrick Seale. *Asad: The Struggle for the Middle East*. Berkeley: University of California Press, 1988.

Arye Shalev. *Israel and Syria: Peace and Security on the Golan*. Boulder, CO: Westview Press, 1994.

Avner Yaniv. "Syria and Israel: The Politics of Escalation." In *Syria under Asad*, edited by Moshe Ma'oz and Avner Yaniv. New York: St. Martin's Press, 1986.

CHAPTER 6

Syria's Relations with Iran, Turkey, and Iraq

Syria's relations with surrounding states involve a complex interplay of rivalry and cooperation. Damascus's primary regional adversary remains the State of Israel, although for most of the last half-century Turkey and Iraq have been important strategic rivals as well.[1] Since the late 1970s, Syria has cultivated a close strategic alliance with the Islamic Republic of Iran.[2] How Damascus deals with its adversaries is intimately connected with the way that it deals with its allies, and vice versa.

GENERAL PRINCIPLES

Syria's strategic partnership with Iran entails what Glenn Snyder calls an "alliance dilemma." Whenever Damascus takes firm steps to confront one of its adversaries, Tehran can be expected to grow more confident and assertive. The Iranian leadership is then likely to carry out risky foreign-policy initiatives that have the potential to draw Syria into conflicts in which it has no intrinsic interest. Snyder calls this dynamic "entrapment."[3] On the other hand, whenever Damascus moves to conciliate one of its major adversaries, Tehran worries that Syria is preparing to abandon it. The Iranian leadership can then be expected to refrain from pursuing dangerous foreign-policy initiatives and may even make overtures of its own toward the adversary, a move that Snyder labels "pre-emptive realignment."[4] Syria's policies toward adversaries therefore have a significant impact on relations with allies, and the consequences often turn out to be detrimental to Damascus's underlying security interests.

Faced with this pervasive dilemma, Syria has for the most part kept its commitments to Iran loose and fluid. This posture has enabled Damascus to avoid being dragged into long-standing conflicts in the Gulf, although it has left Syria vulnerable to being abandoned by Tehran.[5] Still, Syria's comparatively loose ties to the Islamic Republic have not eliminated the possibility that it will get entrapped in unwanted conflicts. For example, as the 1980s drew to a close, Syria and Turkey adopted more belligerent postures toward one another. Ankara expressed great irritation over Damascus's failure to rein in Kurdish and Armenian militants and stop them from carrying out armed attacks against Turkish targets.[6] In October 1989, a pair of Syrian MiG-21 interceptors crossed into Turkish airspace east of Iskandarun and shot down a Turkish survey plane, killing the five civilians on board.[7] Turkey responded by announcing that it planned to shut off the southward flow of the Euphrates River for an entire month, purportedly to fill the massive reservoir behind the newly completed Ataturk Dam.

Escalating tensions between Syria and Turkey prompted Iran to undertake a provocative foreign-policy initiative of its own. The Islamic Revolutionary Guards Corps (IRGC) stepped up its material and moral support for the Lebanese Islamist organization Hizbullah, precipitating a series of armed clashes during the spring of 1988 between that organization and its primary rival for leadership among the Lebanese Shi'ah, the Battalions of the Lebanese Resistance (*Afwaj al-Muqawamah al-Lubnaniyyah*, or AMAL).[8] Iran's foreign minister played a pivotal role in persuading the two parties to accept a truce in February 1989 but nevertheless insisted that Hizbullah guerrillas be permitted to return to strongpoints in southern Lebanon from which they had been ousted by AMAL nine months earlier.[9] A week after Syrian warplanes violated Turkish airspace, Iran's foreign minister arrived in Damascus to coordinate efforts on the part of a collection of radical Lebanese groupings to undermine the peace agreement for Lebanon that had been drawn up under Arab League auspices in the Saudi resort city of Taif.[10] The foreign minister was joined by Iran's influential, and strongly pro-Hizbullah, former ambassador to Damascus, Hujjah al-Islam 'Ali Akbar Mohtashemi, who went on to Lebanon's Biqa' Valley to rally the organization's cadres and supporters to do all they could to resist the implementation of the Taif accords.

This Iranian initiative threatened to drag Syria deeper into two whirlpools that it had a clear interest in avoiding. One was a resumption of large-scale fighting in Lebanon, not only between Hizbullah and AMAL militants but also between Christian forces commanded by the dissident General Michel 'Awn and army units loyal to the Lebanese central government; the other was a military confrontation with Israeli troops stationed in southern Lebanon. No sooner had Mohtashemi arrived in the Biqa' than fighting erupted between the militias of Hizbullah and AMAL.[11] So even though observers at the time tended to interpret the situation as one in which Syria's "unnatural alliance with Iran" was teetering on the brink of dissolution,[12] it is more insightful to see relations between the two states in terms of an Iran that steadily became emboldened—as a direct result of greater Syrian firmness vis-à-vis Turkey—to carry out risky initiatives that threatened to entrap Syria in renewed warfare in Lebanon.

In much the same way, Syria immediately condemned Iraq's invasion of Kuwait in August 1990 and then joined Egypt and Saudi Arabia in orchestrating the emergency summit meeting at which the Arab League Council voted to resist the Iraqi occupation by force. Damascus justified the organization's active collaboration with U.S., British, and French military units on two main grounds: first, that Arab governments should not hand over responsibility for dealing with inter-Arab conflicts onto outside powers; and second, that Baghdad's aggression against Kuwait weakened the Arab nation as a whole in its ongoing struggle against Israel.[13] As President Hafiz al-Asad told the summit, "If we want the foreigners to leave [the Gulf] quickly, then let us quickly resolve the problem so as to remove any pretext for their stay, especially if there are hidden motives for their presence."[14] Units of the Syrian armed forces, including an armored division that was pulled out of its forward position on the Golan front, began to arrive on Saudi territory on August 20, 1990.

Syria's overt hostility toward Iraq led Iran to distance itself from Damascus and even to make guarded overtures to Baghdad. Following a visit to Tehran by Iraqi Foreign Minister Tariq 'Aziz in late August, Iranian officials announced that formal diplomatic relations would soon be restored between the two states.[15] The Syrian president's subsequent trip to Tehran did little to diminish the rift between the two partners: in the wake of his trip, "Iranian and Syrian experts agreed that President Asad's visit to Iran did more harm than good to Iranian-Syrian relations. It weakened their 'strategic alliance' instead of strengthening it, as the two sides stood by [initial] their positions" and refused to compromise.[16] An Iraqi mission returned to Tehran in mid-October to negotiate outstanding boundary disputes and a timetable for exchanging prisoners left over from the First Gulf War of 1980 through 1988.[17]

Pronounced Syrian belligerence toward Iraq also accompanied a marked reduction in Iran's assertiveness in Lebanon. Throughout the fall of 1990, Syrian and Iranian officials engaged in a series of discussions concerning both the future of the Lebanese political system and the fate of Western hostages held by Iranian-sponsored organizations. These talks resulted in Tehran's adopting a much more conciliatory posture with regard to Lebanese affairs, culminating in a four-party summit in Damascus that November which produced an agreement whereby Hizbullah and AMAL promised to lay down their arms and recognize the authority of Lebanon's regular armed forces.[18] Equally important, Syria's decision to play an active role in the anti-Iraq military campaign left Iran with little choice but to adopt a posture of strict neutrality as the conflict in the Gulf intensified. Following President al-Asad's visit to Tehran, the Iranian authorities at last agreed to honor the terms of the UN embargo on trade with Iraq.[19]

REFORGING THE SYRIA-IRAN ALLIANCE

Syria took a sharp turn away from belligerence in its relations with Turkey after the serious crisis between the two states that erupted in October 1998.[20] On that occasion, Syrian officials backed down in the face of Turkish saber-rattling and promised to terminate its support for the militant Kurdistan Workers' Party (PKK), set up links between the two countries' internal security services, and take steps to reduce barriers to bilateral economic activity. A year later, Syria's chief of staff, General Hikmat al-Shihabi, signed a mutual security pact that committed Damascus to increase the general level of surveillance along the Syrian-Turkish border. Not even persistent disagreements over the distribution of Euphrates River water dampened the steady improvement in relations between the two governments.[21]

Tehran responded to Damascus's marked rapprochement with Ankara by keeping successive Turkish governments at arm's length.[22] In July 1999, Turkish aircraft bombed districts around the Iranian city of Piranshahr, leading Iranian officials to charge that Turkey was carrying out an "invasion" of the Islamic Republic.[23] Relations plummeted in October when Turkish police arrested 92 members of a clandestine Iranian-trained organization called Hizbullah.[24] Another militant group with connections to Iran's Revolutionary Guards was broken up seven months later.[25] At the same time, however, the Iranian government refrained from pushing Lebanon's Hizbullah to take advantage of the resignation of Lebanese Prime Minister Rafiq al-Hariri to enhance its domestic political position.[26] Iran's President Muhammad Khatami visited Damascus in May 1999 and reaffirmed his country's commitment to the Syria-Iran alliance, along with concluding agreements to implement a variety of bilateral economic projects.[27]

Improvements in relations between Syria and Turkey accelerated during the months surrounding the death of President Hafiz al-Asad. A delegation of 100 prominent Turkish businesspeople, led by Minister of Economy Recep Önal, traveled to Damascus in early May 2000 to revive the long-dormant Joint Economic Commission.[28] The two countries' foreign ministers met in Qatar that November and hinted that they were putting the finishing touches on a "memorandum of understanding" that would consolidate closer ties between them.[29] Senior Syrian military officers traveled to Ankara in January 2001 to propose that relations become fully normalized.[30] Two months later, Syria's minister of electricity announced that large portions of the country's electrical grid were going to be integrated with Turkey's grid by the end of the year.[31] On September 10, the two ministers of the interior signed a wide-ranging security cooperation agreement, according to whose terms their respective governments would work together to fight terrorism, organized crime, smuggling, the drugs trade, and illegal immigration.[32] Plans to inaugurate a variety of cultural exchanges quickly followed.[33]

By the spring of 2002, there were clear signs that the Syrian and Turkish armed forces were preparing to carry out joint military exercises.[34] Syria's new chief of staff, General Hasan al-Turkmani, journeyed to Ankara in June to meet with his Turkish counterpart; the two commanders initialed an agreement that provided for combined maneuvers and closer cooperation with regard to military manufacturing. Other agreements laid the foundation for greater bilateral trade and investment.[35] In January 2003, Turkey's Prime Minister Abdullah Gül held discussions in Damascus with President Bashshar al-Asad concerning the imminent war in Iraq; these talks culminated in the signing of an unprecedented crisis-management pact. The two governments also collaborated in organizing a regional conference in Istanbul to boost foreign policy coordination among six Middle Eastern states (Turkey, Syria, Egypt, Jordan, Saudi Arabia, and Iran) in light of escalating U.S. threats to launch offensive military operations against Iraq.[36]

Burgeoning Syrian-Turkish cooperation accompanied a virtual freeze in Tehran's relations with Ankara.[37] Tensions between the latter two states rose steadily during the course of 2000 and 2001 as Turkey strengthened ties to both Azerbaijan and Israel; Turkey and Iran narrowly avoided an armed confrontation in the Caspian Sea in July 2001.[38] Iranian Foreign Minister Kamal Kharrazi's participation in the January 2003 Istanbul conference and his subsequent visit to Ankara both appeared to be no more than pro forma and resulted in no new agreements between the two governments.[39] Meanwhile, Iran refrained from carrying out destabilizing initiatives in Lebanon. The authorities in Tehran watched passively, for instance, as Damascus bolstered the influence of AMAL at Hizbullah's expense in early 2002.[40] Kharrazi visited Beirut that April and reportedly warned Hizbullah and other Lebanese militant organizations to restrain themselves lest they give Israel an excuse to crack down on radical Palestinian groups.[41]

On the other hand, the government in Tehran took concrete steps to reinvigorate the alliance with Syria. Iranian officials proposed a bilateral industrial cooperation agreement, which was signed in April 2002, and then set up a US$50 million fund to finance joint ventures with Syrian private manufacturers;[42] that September, a delegation of Iranian industrialists arrived in Damascus to discuss a wide range of prospective investments. Iran's Minister of Security 'Ali Yunesi visited the Syrian capital in October to explain his government's position regarding the future of Iraq to President al-Asad.[43]

At the same time that Damascus was undertaking an extensive rapprochement with Ankara, the Syrian government made increasingly friendly overtures to Baghdad. Relations between the two Ba'thi rivals warmed up steadily during the late 1990s[44] and improved dramatically in 2000 and 2001. Syrian Prime Minister Muhammad Mustafa Miru welcomed a delegation headed by Iraq's minister of trade to Damascus in August 2000, which eventuated in the resumption of railroad traffic from the northern Iraqi city of Musil to the Syrian port of Tartus on the Mediterranean Sea.[45] An agreement to phase out duties on trade between the two countries was signed in January 2001, and some 150,000 barrels of oil per day started to flow through the long-abandoned pipeline linking northern Iraq to the docks at Banyas.[46] Miru led a group of state officials, economic advisers, and businesspeople to Baghdad in mid-August. The trip resulted in a mutual defense pact along with treaties to expand bilateral commercial and technical exchanges.[47]

Syria's concerted opening to Iraq sparked no attempt on Tehran's part to realign preemptively with Baghdad. On the contrary, knowledgeable observers speculated that the Islamic Republic planned to provide tacit support for the United States' campaign to overturn the Ba'th Party–led regime in Baghdad, just as it had done in the case of the Taliban in neighboring Afghanistan.[48] The authorities in Tehran hosted a delegation of leading figures of the Iraq-based Kurdistan Democratic Party (KDP) in September 2002 and quietly arranged for the Iran-sponsored Supreme Council for the Islamic Revolution in Iraq (SCIRI) to co-ordinate its future activities with the KDP.[49] SCIRI representatives joined a number of other organizations working to combat the Iraqi regime at a general congress in London that December. The organization's presence at the meeting prompted the leader of the Patriotic Union of Kurdistan (PUK), Jalal Talabani, to remark that "Iran is a great neighbour which has always supported the Iraqi opposition, and some sort of understanding between Iran and the United States, direct or indirect, would be a great help in the liberation of Iraq."[50]

Iranian overtures to the two most influential Kurdish organizations in Iraq led Syria to undertake discussions with these same two parties. Officials in Damascus hosted a meeting with Talabani in October 2002, while the head of KDP, Mas'ud Barzani, arrived in the Syrian capital a month later.[51] More important, Iran's redoubled efforts to undermine the Iraqi regime forced Syria to make the unpalatable decision to vote in favor of UN Security Council Resolution 1441, which required the Iraqi government to open all suspected chemical, biological, and nuclear production and storage facilities to UN weapons inspectors. To have abstained on this issue, as most observers expected Damascus to do, would have alienated Syria not only from Egypt and Saudi Arabia but from the Islamic Republic as well.[52] Damascus then tried to obtain assurances that Washington would do everything it could to block the emergence of a fully autonomous Kurdish entity in the event that war ensued, an interest that Syria shared with both Turkey and Iran.[53]

Consequently, by the time the United States initiated the March 2003 military campaign that overthrew Saddam Hussein, Syria's strategic alliance with Iran had been buttressed rather than undermined by Damascus's conciliatory moves toward Ankara and Baghdad. Not even Syria's deep-seated suspicions that the

Islamic Republic was predisposed to coordinate its Iraq policy with the United States proved sufficient to disrupt the partnership.[54] At the same time, ties between Syria and Hizbullah, Iran's primary client in Lebanon, strengthened markedly.[55]

POSTWAR COMPLICATIONS

Shortly after the Ba'thi regime in Baghdad was overthrown, Iran embarked on a campaign of guarded conciliation toward the new Iraq.[56] The change in posture was foreshadowed by comments on the part of former president Akbar Hashemi Rafsanjani, who told reporters in April 2003 that

> the dissolution of the Baath regime per se was neither good nor bad; it all depended on the kind of regime that replaced it. If the United States succeeded in establishing a client state in Iraq, that would be extremely detrimental to Iran's national security. On the other hand, if elections were held and an independent government emerged, that would be in Iran's interests because it was bound to be dominated by a Shiite majority.[57]

Such sentiments lay behind Tehran's expressed overtures to the Iraqi Interim Government that took office in June 2004; SCIRI members accepted ministerial positions in the new cabinet, including the post of minister of finance.[58] Iranian officials subsequently convened a high-level workshop on Opportunities for Iran and Iraq Economic Cooperation, during the course of which it was announced that the Islamic Republic had set up an Office for Iraq's Reconstruction and had authorized US$300 million for reconstruction projects.[59]

Tehran's guarded steps to conciliate its long-time regional adversary triggered parallel efforts on Damascus's part to resuscitate relations with Baghdad. Syrian officials welcomed successive delegations of Iraqi notables as 2003 passed and did their best to reestablish commercial and transportation links to postwar Iraq.[60] President al-Asad told reporters in January 2004 that some US$200 million that had been deposited in Syrian banks by high-ranking figures in Iraq's Ba'thi regime would soon be repatriated.[61] That July, the president welcomed Iraq's prime minister and deputy prime minister for national security affairs, laying the groundwork for a substantial improvement in bilateral relations.[62] The two governments then signed a deal whereby Syria agreed to provide Iraq with a wide range of refined petroleum products in exchange for shipments of crude oil.[63] In July 2003, Syrian commanders ordered a large-scale withdrawal of troops from southern Lebanon; immediately after Syrian forces left the area, however, Hizbullah guerrillas launched a cluster of attacks on Israeli military outposts around the Shib'a Farms.[64]

As Iran's rapprochement with Iraq gained momentum, Syria undertook riskier initiatives. Over widespread opposition, both inside and outside Lebanon, Damascus in September 2004 orchestrated a three-year extension of the term in office of pro-Syrian President Emile Lahoud.[65] The move elicited sharp criticism from a broad range of Lebanese politicians and community leaders, which in turn prompted several of Hizbullah's elected representatives to speak out "to support Lahoud and to reject the policies of the American administration." Moreover, Hizbullah's Secretary General Hasan Nasrallah publicly denounced a draft UN Security Council resolution that had been introduced by the United States and France, which demanded that Syria pull all of its armed forces out of Lebanon and refrain from interfering in the election of the president.[66]

Such moves complemented strenuous efforts on Damascus's part to reinvigorate the strategic alliance with Tehran. A memorandum of understanding concerning the possibility of creating a free-trade area between the two countries was signed during Khatami's visit to Damascus in May 2003.[67] Vice President 'Abd al-Halim Khaddam traveled to Iran in September and attempted to hammer out a mutually agreeable policy toward Iraq with Khatami, Rafsanjani, and Supreme Leader 'Ali Khamene'i.[68] Additional economic projects were discussed over the course of the following months.[69] Syria's chief client in Lebanon, Nabih Berri of AMAL, invited the speaker of the Iranian parliament, Mehdi Karrubi, to come to Beirut to meet with senior government officials there in April 2004.[70] Then in July, President al-Asad, Vice President Khaddam, and Foreign Minister Faruq al-Shar' journeyed to Tehran to confer with President Khatami and Supreme Leader Khamene'i; the visit was reciprocated by Khatami and Kharrazi three months later.[71] Plans to set up a high committee to promote bilateral trade and investment were announced in September.[72]

Iran's engagement with Iraq peaked following the January 2005 elections for the Iraqi Transitional Government. In the wake of the balloting, "consolidating the Shiite-dominated government of Ibrahim al-Jafari became Iran's chief goal. If pro-Iranian Shiite groups could be kept in power," observed Kamran Taremi, "Tehran could then rightly claim to have won Iraq over without firing a shot or sustaining a single casualty."[73] A succession of bilateral agreements was signed and implemented during the spring and summer of 2005. These included "a memorandum of understanding on security cooperation to guarantee border security to prevent terrorists from entering Iraq from Iranian territory, to cooperate in locating the remains of the victims of the Iran-Iraq War, and to establish a joint commission to exchange maps and information on minefields planted on both sides of the border."[74] A further agreement committed the Islamic Republic to supply refined petroleum products to Iraq on concessionary terms.

Damascus responded to the blossoming of Iran-Iraq ties by redoubling its efforts to revivify the alliance with Tehran. Prime Minister Muhammad Naji' al-'Utri announced in February 2005 that his government intended to implement plans to set up a free trade zone in order to encourage greater bilateral trade;[75] al-'Utri then traveled to the Iranian capital to confer with senior officials on ways to counter charges that Syria was responsible for the assassination of former Lebanese prime minister Rafiq al-Hariri. The visit ended with the Syrian prime minister and Iranian Vice President Muhammad Reza Aref declaring that the two countries had concluded a mutual defense pact.[76] That the announcement was instigated by the Syrian delegation is evident from Iranian Foreign Minister Kharrazi's quick disavowal that any sort of formal agreement had been reached.[77]

President Bashshar al-Asad was the first foreign head of state to visit newly elected President Mahmud Ahmadi-Nejad, prompting the host to remark that "Syria represents the front line of the Muslim nation; shared threats bring us together and make our co-operation even more necessary."[78] The influential head of Syrian Military Intelligence made a quick trip to Iran that October to meet with the commanders of the IRGC.[79] And when the UN Security Council insisted that officials in Damascus cooperate fully with the commission that was investigating al-Hariri's assassination, President al-Asad is reported to have requested that President Ahmadi-Nejad "activate the 'strategic pact' between the two nations."[80]

More important, Damascus openly and unreservedly endorsed Tehran's decision to resume its nuclear research program despite widespread international condemnation of the program. Deputy Prime Minister for Economic Affairs 'Abdullah al-Dardari praised the uranium enrichment project in September 2005 and expressed the hope that the two countries would be able to work out innovative ways to strengthen their economic cooperation.[81] Syria at the same time encouraged Hizbullah to reinforce its direct connections to Iran. The authorities in Damascus made a concerted effort to convince Secretary General Nasrallah to work out new ways to obtain financial and material assistance from the Islamic Republic after Syrian troops pulled out of Lebanon.[82] In addition, Damascus acted as intermediary between high-ranking Iranian officials and the leaderships of the Popular Front for the Liberation of Palestine—General Command and the Democratic Front for the Liberation of Palestine.[83]

2006 consequently opened with Damascus and Tehran more closely tied to one another than at any time since the late 1980s. President Ahmadi-Nejad visited Syria in January and elicited an unconditional pledge of support from President al-Asad for Iran's nuclear research program as well as a firm commitment to work toward greater mutual cooperation with Hizbullah and other radical organizations.[84] To cement the partnership, Hizbullah's Nasrallah and AMAL's Nabih Birri made unexpected trips to the Syrian capital to confer with the two heads of state.[85] No doubt worried that the evident strengthening of the Syria-Iran alliance might come at the expense of the Islamic Republic's relations with radical forces in Iraq, the militant Iraqi Shi'i leader Muqtada al-Sadr showed up in Damascus for consultations with Syrian officials in early February.[86] Syria and Iran subsequently announced plans to construct a petroleum pipeline linking the oil fields of Khuzestan to the Mediterranean coast, crossing southern Iraq; a number of other development projects followed.[87] In June, the two countries' defense ministers announced that they had drawn up a military cooperation agreement, which the Syrian minister called "purely defensive and pre-emptive" in character; the Iranian minister remarked that his government "considers Syria's security its own security, and we consider our defense capabilities to be those of Syria."[88]

Iran reacted to the surge in hostility between Syria and Israel that took place in the summer of 2006 by threatening to inflict a "crushing response" on Israel if the Israel Defense Forces (IDF) attacked Syria.[89] President Ahmadi-Nejad reportedly telephoned President al-Asad on the second day of the war between Hizbullah and the IDF to reassure Damascus of his government's support, and the Iranian armed forces were put on high alert.[90] Yet the chief of the Iranian general staff told reporters that the Islamic Republic would "never militarily" take part in the conflict that was raging in southern Lebanon.[91] More tellingly, the commander of the paramilitary Basij called rumors that Iranians had volunteered to fight in Lebanon mere "propaganda" and suggested that "there no doubt exist better ways to defend the Islamic resistance" than throwing untrained volunteers into battle against Israeli troops.[92] Iran's foreign minister traveled to both Istanbul and Cairo in early August to discuss ways that the carnage might be brought to an end.[93] The most remarkable aspect of Tehran's behavior, though, was the fact that throughout the war Iranian officials "sought to remain aloof from Hezbollah, pointedly striving not to do or say anything that could serve as a pretext for widening the conflict."[94] Supreme Leader Khamene'i urged the country's most senior religious figures not to issue a religious ruling (*fatwa*) that would have made it incumbent upon Muslims to take part in the fighting. And it was only after the August 14 cease-fire that the Iranian armed forces resumed large-scale exercises, which were concentrated in the country's far northern and southeastern provinces.[95]

WRESTLING WITH TURKEY

Steady improvements in Syria's relations with Iran coincided with a period of stagnation in Syrian-Turkish relations. Turkish President Sezer sent a dramatic signal to Washington in April 2005 by paying an official visit to Damascus despite U.S. warnings to cancel the trip.[96] But no new bilateral agreements resulted from the visit. That same month, some 55 Syrian textile and food enterprises engaged in marathon talks with 87 Turkish companies, but the negotiations led to no more than a half-dozen new contracts to export Syrian products to Turkey and purchase Turkish industrial machinery.[97] Although Syria's deputy prime minister for economic affairs, 'Abdullah al-Dardari, told reporters in October that the two governments had agreed to work together in the area of oil exploration and production, he also remarked to reporters that serious obstacles stood in the way of new investments. Moreover, the draft bilateral free-trade agreement remained unratified.[98]

Political relations took an equally chilly turn. Foreign Minister Abdullah Gül pointedly admonished his Syrian counterpart that "the international community has concrete expectations from you [regarding the February 2005 assassination of the former Lebanese prime minister, Rafiq al-Hariri]. We, as a friendly country, advise you to heed the international community's warning. You should take solid steps to prove that you take them into account. Otherwise, you will be unable to find any support to defend you."[99] More ominously, Foreign Minister Walid Mu'allim met with his Armenian counterpart in Damascus in early April 2006 to discuss a number of regional issues, including the prospects for Syria's relations with Turkey.[100] The government in Yerevan had long complained that Ankara's imposition of sanctions on Armenia to force it to give up its claim to Nagorno-Karabakh damaged not only the country's domestic economy but also the prospects for expanded commercial relations between Armenia and Syria.[101]

In May 2006, a newly organized Syrian Islamist opposition party, the Movement for Justice and Construction (*Harakah al-'Adalah wal-Bina*), intimated that it enjoyed loose ties to Turkey's ruling Justice and Development Party (*Adalet ve Kalkinma Partisi*, or AKP).[102] Shortly thereafter, the Turkish government welcomed Lebanese Prime Minister Fuad al-Sanyurah to Ankara and concluded a bilateral protocol on educational and technical exchange.[103] And in a less-than-tactful moment, Prime Minister Recep Tayyip Erdogan commented that he had sent a special envoy to President al-Asad to ensure that escalating tensions in the region would be defused without resorting to what he called "an emotional approach. We have to try," he went on, "to reach a [stable] point through a reasonable approach" instead.[104] A month later, Erdogan presided over the groundbreaking ceremony for a massive new dam across one of the major tributaries of the Tigris River.[105] Relations reached a nadir of sorts in August 2006 when Ankara proposed to deploy a contingent of Turkish troops to southern Lebanon to secure the area in the aftermath of the Israeli invasion.[106]

Meanwhile, Turkey significantly reduced its involvement in the Kurdish-controlled areas of northern Iraq. Turkish restraint derived in the first place from deference to the United States, whose government warned that military operations against the PKK would precipitate violence across the region. In addition, the authorities in Ankara appear to have expected U.S. military commanders to take steps to uproot the PKK from its Iraqi strongholds, perhaps with the assistance of the mainstream Kurdish militias. Only after Iranian troops carried out military operations in northeastern Iraq did the Turkish high command order a resumption of air and artillery strikes against PKK targets.[107] By this time, Kurdish unrest had erupted inside Syria, making it much harder for the Ba'thi regime in Damascus to manipulate Kurdish discontent as a retaliatory weapon against Turkey.

Taking advantage of its strengthened position, Ankara exerted pressure on Syria to remain on the sidelines as tensions between Israel and the Palestinians heated up during the summer of 2006. In early July, Prime Minister Erdogan dispatched a senior adviser to Damascus to urge President al-Asad to refrain from taking part in the escalating crisis.[108] President al-Asad in turn appealed to Erdogan to restrain Israel when it became apparent that the IDF was about to advance across the border into Lebanon.[109] Turkish efforts to keep Syria from intervening in the fighting continued into August.[110] When it looked as if Damascus might be working with Tehran to supply weapons to Hizbullah, Ankara resorted to firmer measures: On at least four different occasions, Turkish warplanes forced aircraft suspected of carrying armaments to land at Diyarbakir to be searched.[111] Such bullying put a damper on cooperation between the two governments.

RENEWED COOPERATION WITH TURKEY

Not until the last weeks of 2006 did Syrian-Turkish rapprochement regain momentum. At the close of the Joint Economic Committee meeting in late November, Deputy Prime Minister al-Dardari and Turkey's Deputy Prime Minister Abdullatif Sener signed a collection of agreements aimed at boosting bilateral trade and investment. The agreements also initiated cooperation between the Central Bank of Syria and Turkey's Banking Supervisory Commission.[112] A week later, Prime Minister al-'Utri convened the inaugural congress of Syrian-Turkish Local Authorities, noting that "The aims of this conference constitute a progressive step and specific move for further cementing the ever-growing relations of co-operation between Syria and Turkey in economic, commercial, cultural and social domains."[113] More important, Syria's interior minister, General Bassam 'Abd al-Majid, was simultaneously conferring with his Turkish counterpart on a wide range of security issues. The two ministers agreed to set up joint coordination committees to implement the antiterrorism protocols that had previously been signed. Furthermore, the Turkish team invited Syrian cadets to enroll in Turkey's well-equipped police academies.[114]

At the beginning of February 2007, Foreign Minister al-Mu'allim traveled to Ankara as part of a drive "to revive tripartite co-ordination" among Syria, Turkey, and Iran.[115] His agenda included the promotion of economic relations with the coming into force of the bilateral free-trade agreement on January 1, developments in Iraq, and "the situation in the Palestinian territories." To facilitate his mission, the Turkish government announced that it "has decided to lessen its role in Lebanon after its attempts in the period following the Israeli aggression, because of its realization that the Lebanese issue is too complicated and because it is aware that there is a rejection among certain Lebanese factions for such a role." In early April, Minister of Defense al-Turkmani and Chief of the General Staff 'Ali Habib welcomed the commander of the Turkish air force to Damascus;

the generals reviewed ways to enhance bilateral military cooperation.[116] Meanwhile, in Aleppo, President al-Asad met with Prime Minister Erdogan to coordinate energy-production and oil-transportation policies. The two leaders capped the summit by attending a football match between Syria's al-Ittihad and Turkey's Fenerbahce, with al-Asad telling reporters that he planned to cheer for Fenerbahce and Erdogan had promised to root for al-Ittihad. Residents of Hatay who wished to attend the match were permitted to cross the border without passports, "thanks to co-ordination by the foreign and interior ministries of the two countries."[117]

President al-Asad paid a return visit to Ankara in mid-October 2007, "placing yet another brick in the edifice of special relations between the two countries."[118] Turkish officials let it be known that they intended to help their guest to "understand" the reasons behind any future military incursion into northern Iraq.[119] While he was in the Turkish capital, al-Asad signed a broad-ranging memorandum of understanding, according to whose terms the two governments pledged to promote investments and expand joint projects in border districts, improve transportation links, accelerate Turkish technical assistance to Syrian financial institutions, and rehabilitate the obsolete oil pipeline between Killis and Homs, the site of Syria's primary oil refinery.[120] Syria's new minister of economy and trade, 'Amr Husni Lutfi, attended the first meeting of the Syrian-Turkish Partnership Council in Mersin in mid-November and announced plans to open a free trade zone "in one of Syria's main industrial centres for Turkish investors."[121] He also announced that an additional commercial passageway would shortly be opened at al-Qamishli.

The thorny question of water distribution at last received concerted attention as 2008 opened. The water and environment ministers of Syria, Turkey, and Iraq gathered in Damascus in January and agreed to set up technical committees to investigate the "most rational" and sustainable means to exploit regional water resources.[122] In the wake of the conference, the Syrian Ministry of Agriculture released plans to bring 50,000 hectares of newly reclaimed land into production in al-Hasakah province, using water drawn from the Tigris River.[123] Brighter prospects for cooperation over water set the stage for a joint economic forum in Damascus, in which some 700 Syrian and Turkish businesspeople discussed items of mutual interest.[124] Meanwhile, across town, Syria's finance minister, Muhammad al-Husain, was discussing strategies to increase efficiency at the border crossings with Turkey's minister of state for foreign trade, Kursad Tuzman.[125] Two weeks later, the Syrian government revised its official maps so as to remove the district around Iskandarun from Syrian territory.[126] In June, Syrian Minister of Petroleum Sufyah al-Alaw attended the Third Turkish-Arab Economic Forum in Istanbul and announced that the two governments planned to form a joint company to explore for oil in Syria; he went on to remark that "in the future we could found joint nuclear power plants for electricity production."[127] And in July, the Syria-Turkey Inter-Regional Cooperation Program launched 18 additional development projects in the contiguous provinces of Aleppo, Killis, Gaziantep, and Onkobinar Gate.[128]

President al-Asad's return to Ankara in early August 2008 underscored the accelerating pace of Syrian-Turkish cooperation. The Syrian president was reported to have brought with him a confidential report detailing Iran's nuclear research program as well as thoughts on how best to deal with current trends in Iraq and Palestine.[129] He was followed to the Turkish capital by Deputy Prime Minister al-Dardari, who initialed an agreement to build a jointly run pipeline to transport natural gas, and by Minister of the Interior 'Abd al-Majid, who worked with Turkish officials to formulate common policies on a variety of internal and border security matters.[130]

Closer relations between Damascus and Ankara took shape in the context of clear signs that Turkey intended to resume direct intervention in northern Iraq. As 2007 opened, Prime Minister Erdogan called U.S.-led efforts to collaborate in suppressing radical Kurdish organizations "a failure" and hinted that he would order the Turkish armed forces to supply arms to the Turkmen population of Kirkuk and Musil if the situation continued to deteriorate.[131] Turkish troops took up forward positions along the border at the end of May and chased Kurdish guerrillas back into Iraqi territory on several occasions. Commanders on the ground were reported to be pushing the government to authorize more extensive operations.[132] The potential for a large-scale offensive remained high throughout the summer and fall despite the signing of a Turkish-Iraqi security pact in late September that pointedly omitted a provision that would have allowed Turkish troops to engage in "hot pursuit" of Kurdish fighters.[133] Matters came to a head in mid-October when Turkish forces launched artillery and aerial assaults against PKK positions. The offensive continued into the spring of 2008.[134]

THE GRAND ALLIANCE

Syria enjoyed close relations with both Iran and Turkey from 2007 to 2010. Damascus's strategic partnerships with these two powerful neighbors paid dividends in the military and economic arenas alike. The Islamic Republic announced in July 2007 that it was going to provide Damascus with US$1 billion in military assistance, and in January 2008 an Iranian freighter carrying artillery shells, high-explosive charges, and other armaments was intercepted by the authorities of Cyprus.[135] April 2009 saw the first joint exercises take place between the Syrian and Turkish armed forces,[136] and a set of undisclosed mutual security agreements was signed that December.[137]

Economic relations expanded even more pronouncedly. In August 2008, Iran's minister of industries and mines claimed that the Islamic Republic was engaged in some US$1.3 billion worth of investment projects inside Syria and was considering embarking on an additional US$1 billion worth.[138] A year later, the Iranian-Venezuelan petroleum consortium VENIROGC announced that it intended to construct a modern oil refinery at Banyas to supplement the aging facility at Homs.[139] More than 30 Turkish investment projects got underway in Syria between 2005 and 2007, valued at over US$150 million. Bilateral trade jumped from under US$500 million in 2002 to around US$1.5 billion in 2007, reaching US$4 billion two years later.[140] The potential for commerce between Aleppo and Gaziantep increased even further at the end of 2009 when the long-dormant railway line connecting the two cities was reopened.[141] Ankara and Damascus inaugurated a bilateral free-trade zone in 2008; two years later, President al-Asad and Iran's First Vice President Muhammad Reza Rahimi laid out plans to create a mutual free-trade zone as well.[142]

Relations between Syria and Turkey soared after Israeli forces attacked a flotilla of Turkish vessels headed for Gaza with food and medical supplies. Ankara's furious response to the attack convinced Damascus that Turkey had seen the folly of its collaboration with Israel and had taken a giant step toward joining the Palestinian cause. For its part, Iran welcomed Turkey's apparent change of heart as well. Supreme Leader Khamene'i's liaison officer to the naval forces of the Revolutionary Guards Corps announced that the IRGC stood fully prepared "to escort freedom and peace caravans transporting humanitarian aid from the entire world to Gaza," and urged Turkish activists to make a second run.[143]

Nevertheless, Ankara's frenetic diplomatic activism during 2009 and 2010 raised major obstacles in the path of the Syria-Turkey-Iran grand alliance. Turkish officials engaged in a campaign to normalize relations with Armenia during the summer and fall of 2009;[144] at the same time, Ankara made serious overtures to the Abkhazia region of Georgia.[145] These initiatives directly infringed on Iran's efforts to cultivate ties with the states of the south Caucasus.[146] Moreover, Turkey's signals that it might recognize the breakaway republic of Abkhazia clashed with Iran's diplomatic and economic commitments to the central government in Tbilisi. Friction in the Caucasus was aggravated by Ankara's willingness to allow the North Atlantic Treaty Organization to install sophisticated anti–ballistic missile radar stations on Turkish territory; a senior Iranian commander warned that if Turkey went ahead with the construction of such tracking stations, the Islamic Republic might launch a retaliatory strike.[147]

Confronted with mounting challenges from Ankara, Tehran stepped up its ties to Damascus. In May 2010, Iranian Vice President Muhammad Rida Rahimi responded to U.S. allegations that Syria was arming Hizbullah with rockets by warning that the Islamic Republic would "stand alongside Syria against any threat" and would in fact "cut off Israel's feet" if it carried out an assault against Syria;[148] at the same time, the two governments announced the establishment of a joint Syrian-Iranian bank, capitalized at US$30 million.[149] A month later,

Iran was reported to be providing Syria with a "sophisticated radar system" that could detect airborne strikes against targets located inside either country.[150] The October meeting between Syrian Foreign Minister al-Mu'allim and U.S. Secretary of State Hillary Clinton prompted Tehran to invite President al-Asad for discussions on a wide range of topics.[151] In the wake of the summit, Iran's deputy minister of defense and head of state-sponsored Sa-Iran Electronic Industries traveled to Damascus to discuss the application of advanced technology to security matters of mutual concern.[152]

Not to be outdone by Tehran, Ankara redoubled its own efforts to consolidate strategic and economic links to Damascus. Turkey's Defense Minister Vecdi Gonul welcomed Vice President al-Turkmani to Ankara at the end of September 2010 to work out ways to enhance "security and defense co-ordination between Syria and Turkey and the exchange of information to serve both the Syrian and Turkish armies";[153] the meeting set the stage for the second meeting of the Turkish-Syrian Strategic Council, whose agenda included a wide range of internal security matters and plans to expand the Syrian ports at Latakia and Tartus so that they could handle greater imports of Turkish goods.[154] More important, Prime Minister Erdogan arrived in Damascus in mid-October to coordinate the two countries' policies toward the PKK.[155] The end of the year brought news of a marked increase in Syrian exports of frogs to Turkey for re-export to European buyers.[156]

Damascus's relations with Baghdad meanwhile fluctuated wildly. Bilateral trade recovered after 2008 and was expected to jump with the completion of a highway connecting Baghdad to the port at Tartus and a cluster of new railroad lines.[157] Prime Minister Nuri al-Maliki paid an official visit to Damascus that August, which resulted in a handful of economic agreements and the reanimation of the joint committee charged with overseeing security along the Syrian-Iraqi border. The day after al-Maliki departed, however, a cluster of bombings shook Baghdad, and Iraqi officials immediately placed blame for the attacks on remnants of the Ba'th Party based in Syria. The Iraqi government demanded the extradition of two individuals who were alleged to have planned the bombings and pulled its ambassador out of Syria pending their delivery; "the Syrians," observes Sami Moubayed, "were infuriated by the accusations, responding immediately by recalling their own diplomat, Nawwaf al-Fares, from Baghdad."[158] The Turkish foreign minister hurried to the two capitals in an attempt to mediate the dispute but failed to talk Baghdad out of augmenting its military forces along the border with Syria.[159] A second wave of bombings in early December elicited another round of charges and denials between the two capitals.[160]

Yet Iraqi officials asked to take part in the Arab-Turkish Forum that was scheduled for mid-December in Damascus and hinted that Syria and Iraq had a shared interest in resisting moves by Turkey and Iran to divert greater amounts of water from the Euphrates and Tigris Rivers.[161] Iraqi Vice President Tariq al-Hashimi traveled to the Syrian capital in early March 2010 and remarked that the visit was intended to settle "disagreements among members of one family."[162] Syrian officials welcomed the overture and pointed out that new investments in infrastructure taking place around Dair al-Zur were intended to facilitate trade between the two countries. Relations cooled in late April when Iraqi commanders put troops along the border on high alert and Iraq's ministry of water resources charged that a Syrian irrigation project funded by Kuwait was going to pull too much water out of the Tigris River.[163]

But in mid-September, the two governments agreed to resume shipments of Iraqi oil across Syria and started work on a major pipeline that would transport Iranian natural gas across Iraqi territory to Syria.[164] Full diplomatic relations were restored at the end of September. Prime Minister al-'Utri went to Baghdad in January 2011 to open talks on a wide range of bilateral projects, including oil exploration, electricity sharing, border security, and the elimination of visas for citizens moving from one country to the other.[165]

INTERNAL REVOLT AND REGIONAL RELATIONS

When popular unrest exploded into violence in southern Syria in March 2011, Tehran, Ankara, and Baghdad all fell in line behind the regime in Damascus. Prime Minister al-'Utri arrived in Tehran on March 11 and was told by President Ahmadi-Nejad that "the two countries should smartly take further steps to expand their relations and co-operation, especially in the economic and social arenas."[166] Five new pacts concerning trade and housing were signed during the visit. 'Ali Larijani, the speaker of the Iranian parliament, pointed out that the uprisings in Tunisia, Egypt, Bahrain, and Yemen "highlighted the strategic importance of co-operation between Iran, Syria, Turkey and Iraq." Although Ankara had sided with the protesters in Tunisia and Egypt, an astute observer noted that "for Turkey, all these countries are on one hand, and the new situation in Syria is on another hand."[167] Prime Minister Erdogan advised President al-Asad to carry out fundamental political reforms, and the Syrian president responded positively; as a result, Ankara saw no reason to abandon the Ba'th Party–led government.

As the protests escalated, however, Turkey and Iran distanced themselves from the actions of the Syrian authorities. A senior Turkish official told reporters in mid-April that "the current events [in Syria] cannot possibly be managed in the manner that is currently being employed. President Bashshar al-Asad must be a leader for change and not against it."[168] A spokesperson for the Iranian foreign ministry told the press that "we respect the demands of [Syria's] people. We consider the use of violence against the people of any country unacceptable. We call on all regional regimes to address the demands of their people."[169] Officials in Ankara postponed indefinitely a high-level meeting to launch a free-trade area covering Turkey, Syria, Lebanon, and Jordan that was scheduled for early May "because of Syrian developments."[170] Shortly afterwards, Prime Minister Erdogan telephoned President al-Asad to urge him to permit "the Syrian street to express its views freely and without additional bloodshed."[171] Rather than accepting the advice, the Syrian president and his advisers became annoyed with Turkey's attempt to interfere in domestic affairs and expressed their displeasure over the freedom of action and expression that was being accorded to senior members of the Muslim Brothers inside Turkey.[172]

By late spring, Tehran and Ankara had diverged sharply in their dealings with the embattled Syrian regime. Repeated, but unconfirmed, reports claimed that contingents of the IRGC had deployed to Syria to assist in combating opposition fighters with the blessing of Supreme Leader Khamene'i.[173] Syria and Iran agreed to set up a preferential trading area in July as a way to stimulate bilateral trade.[174] In contrast, Turkey hosted a succession of conferences of opposition groups and the so-called Friends of Syria states, and Syria's official news agency spit venom when Erdogan publicly criticized the Syrian regime for its handling of the crisis in early June.[175] Foreign Minister Ahmet Davutoglu traveled to Damascus in early August and warned that his government would stop trying to mediate between Syria and outside powers unless the authorities immediately changed their tactics; when the warning was rebuffed, Ankara stated that it had "lost confidence" in the Ba'thi regime.[176] As tensions between Turkey and Syria heightened, the Syrian armed forces set up two dozen anti-aircraft batteries around the town of Kassab to interdict any incursion from the north.[177] Iran, meanwhile, took steps to open a large-scale facility at Latakia airport to receive "military hardware" supplied by the Revolutionary Guard Corps.[178]

As Turkey offered increased material and moral support for the Free Syrian Army that fall, elements of the PKK started to mobilize along Syria's northeastern frontier.[179] Turkish warships seized a Syrian-flagged vessel in late September and reported that it was transporting arms.[180] A week later, the Turkish armed forces carried out military maneuvers along the border.[181] The evident shift in Ankara's policy toward Syria prompted shopkeepers in Aleppo to begin stocking their shelves with locally made goods in place of imports from Turkey.[182]

Deteriorating relations with Turkey accompanied a steady improvement in relations with Iraq. Under pressure from Tehran, the government in Baghdad earmarked US$10 billion for assistance to the al-Asad regime.[183] Prime Minister al-Maliki remarked that the overthrow of the government by externally spon- sored opponents "will lead to a new Sykes-Picot," dividing the Middle East into weak, vulnerable statelets.[184] Syrian and Iraqi officials met in mid-October to work out plans to create a pair of new free-trade zones along the border near Al Bu Kamal.[185] Iraqi representatives abstained from voting when the Arab League imposed economic sanctions on Syria in November and instead reduced fees on Syrian imports and dispatched a delegation of businesspeople to explore trade and investment opportunities in the besieged country.[186] Senior officials in the Syrian Ministry of Interior and security forces met with their Iraqi counterparts in Baghdad in early 2011 to coordinate their efforts to combat radical Islamist movements.[187]

Spreading chaos inside Syria posed a threat to the interests of both Turkey and Iran. In November, a convoy of buses transporting Turkish pilgrims home from Mecca was raked by gunfire on the highway north of Homs.[188] A month later, five Iranian engineers working on a power station near Homs were kidnapped by opposition fighters.[189] By the spring of 2012, trade between Turkey and Syria had all but dried up, and Turkish businesspeople no longer ventured across the border.[190] Iranian commercial companies stepped up their presence as international sanctions took hold: a joint trading promotion company was formed in January 2012 to promote bilateral exchange.[191] Measures to expand cooperation in agriculture soon followed,[192] and at the end of April 2012, Syria and Iran announced the inauguration of a bilateral free-trade area.[193]

Turkey's tolerance for disorder inside Syria all but exhausted itself by the spring of 2012. Prime Minister Erdogan pointedly warned that Ankara would "implement steps" to deal with the ongoing violence if UN efforts to end the fighting failed.[194] A day after the prime minister's warning, Syrian troops shot across the border into a refugee camp outside Kilis; Erdogan, on a trip to China, hinted that the Turkish armed forces would set up a safe haven along the border to protect refugees.[195] The Turkish navy then seized a German cargo ship bound for Syria and inspected it for weapons.[196] The Turkish government ratcheted down the belligerence of its rhetoric and actions in the weeks after the border incident but expelled Syria's ambassador to Ankara in the aftermath of the massacre at al-Hulah.[197]

Tensions redoubled after Syrian gunners shot down a Turkish RF-4E Phantom reconnaissance plane on June 22 and then fired at one of the rescue aircraft that was engaged in searching for the downed plane.[198] Prime Minister Erdogan told the National Assembly four days after the incident that from that point on, "every military element approaching Turkey from the Syrian border and representing a security risk and danger will be assessed as a military threat and will be treated as a military target."[199] Turkish commanders deployed large numbers of additional troops and anti-aircraft missile batteries along the border east of Iskandarun and south of 'Urfa over the next few days.[200] When Syrian helicopters approached the borders of Hatay and Mardin province on June 30, Turkish F-16 fighters scrambled in response, an action that was repeated on July 1.[201] The following day, President al-Asad was quoted in the Turkish daily *Cumhuriyet* as stating that "the [RF-4E] was using a corridor which Israeli planes have used three times before. Soldiers shot it down because we did not see it on our radar and because information was not given." Nevertheless, he went on to "say 100 per cent: 'If only we had not shot it down.' "[202]

Turkey sent additional ground-to-air missile batteries to the border with Syria in mid-July, as FSA fighters attacked crossing stations at Jarabalus, Bab al-Hawa, and al-Salamah. The governor of Kilis province took the unprecedented step of walking into Syrian territory in early August to shake hands with members of the FSA who were garrisoning the post across from Oncupinar station.[203] Large-scale ground and air exercises took place adjacent to the border a week later, after Kurdish fighters took control of several towns in northern Syria, and on August 19 Turkish officials distributed food, sleeping bags and other supplies to a group of refugees huddling on Syrian territory outside the Turkish town of Reyhanli.[204] A day later, a bomb detonated outside a police station in Gaziantep, killing eight persons. Foreign Minister Davutoglu then warned that Turkey would take steps to establish a buffer zone inside Syria if the total number of Syrian refugees in Turkey exceeded 100,000.[205]

Baghdad too pulled away from Damascus as the spring of 2012 went by. The Iraqi government endorsed the UN peace plan that was adopted in April and voiced support for the mediation mission led by Kofi Annan. The inability of the Annan mission to bring an end to the fighting prompted Foreign Minister Hushyar Zibari to declare that Iraq could "no longer remain neutral" with regard to the conflict, a clear signal that Baghdad was adopting a more hostile posture.[206] Zibari told a group of Syrian opposition figures gathered in Cairo in early July that the Ba'thi regime should be held fully responsible for "destroying the cities and killing the innocent people" of Syria. At the same time, however, Prime Minister Nuri al-Maliki "stressed that his country is following neutral policies vis-à-vis the situation in Syria," while Minister of Transportation Hadi al-Amiri of the Badr Brigade "had threatened Turkey and the Gulf states by saying that Iraq will not stand still in the face of any threat against Syria."[207]

This left Iran as Syria's only remaining regional partner. After international sanctions made it almost impossible for Syria to market its oil openly and directly to the outside world, Iranian oil companies devised clandestine ways to inject Syrian petroleum into the global marketplace. One scheme involved Iranian oil tankers that loaded up at Tartus and Banyas, then raised the Bolivian flag and turned off their electronic tracking devices as they passed through the Red Sea. The vessels ended up delivering their shipments of crude oil to the Iranian terminus at Bandar Abbas, where the Syrian oil got blended together with local output before being offered to international buyers.[208] Reports that the Islamic Republic was supplying Damascus with armaments became increasingly frequent and detailed as the summer of 2012 went by.[209]

NOTES

Portions of Chapter 6 first appeared in Fred H. Lawson, "Syria's Relations with Iran: Managing the Dilemmas of Alliance," *Middle East Journal* 61 (Winter 2007). Used by permission.

1. David Kushner, "Conflict and Accommodation in Turkish-Syrian Relations," in *Syria under Assad*, eds. Moshe Ma'oz and Avner Yaniv (New York: St. Martin's Press, 1986); Muhammad Muslih, "Syria and Turkey: Uneasy Relations," in *Reluctant Neighbor: Turkey's Role in the Middle East*, ed. Henri J. Barkey (Washington, DC: United States Institute of Peace Press, 1996); Robert Olson, "Turkey-Syria Relations since the Gulf War: Kurds and Water," *Middle East Policy* 5 (May 1997); Robert Olson, "Turkey-Syria Relations, 1997 to 2000," *Orient* 42 (March 2001); O. Zeynep Oktav Alantar, "The October 1998 Crisis: A Change of Turkish Foreign Policy towards Syria?" *Cahiers d'Etudes sur la Mediterranee Orientale et le Monde Turco-Iranien*, no. 31 (2001); Erik L. Knudsen, "Syria, Turkey and the Changing Power Configuration in the Middle East," in *Turkey's Foreign Policy in the 21st Century*, eds. Tareq Y. Ismael and Mustafa Aydin (Aldershot, UK: Ashgate, 2003); Meliha Benli Altunisik and Ozlem Tur, "From Distant Neighbors to Partners? Changing Syrian-Turkish Relations," *Security Dialogue* 37 (June 2006); Amazia Baram, "Ideology and Power Politics in Syrian-Iraqi Relations 1968–1984," in Ma'oz and Yaniv, *Syria under Assad*; Eberhard Kienle, *Ba'th v. Ba'th: The Conflict between Syria and Iraq 1968–1989* (London: I. B. Tauris, 1990).

2. Yair Hirschfeld, "The Odd Couple: Ba'athist Syria and Khomeini's Iran," in Ma'oz and Yaniv, *Syria under Assad*; Elie Chalala, "Syria's Support of Iran in the Gulf War," *Journal of Arab Affairs* 7 (Fall 1988); Yosef Olmert, "Iranian-Syrian Relations: Between Islam and Realpolitik," in *The Iranian Revolution and the Muslim World*, ed. David Menashri (Boulder, CO: Westview, 1990); Christin Marschall, "Syria-Iran: A Strategic Alliance, 1979–1991," *Orient* 33 (September 1992); Shireen T. Hunter, "Iran and Syria: From Hostility to Limited Alliance," in *Iran and the Arab World*, eds. Hooshang Amirahmadi and Nader Entessar (New York: St. Martin's, 1993); Hussein J. Agha and Ahmad S. Khalidi, *Syria and Iran* (London: Pinter, 1995); Anoushiravan Ehteshami and Raymond A. Hinnebusch, *Syria and Iran* (London: Routledge, 1997); Jubin M. Goodarzi, *Syria and Iran* (London: Tauris Academic, 2006).

3. Glenn H. Snyder, "The Security Dilemma in Alliance Politics," *World Politics* 36 (July 1984), 467; Glenn H. Snyder, *Alliance Politics* (Ithaca, NY: Cornell University Press, 1997), 182–83.

4. Snyder, "The Security Dilemma in Alliance Politics," 467; Snyder, *Alliance Politics*, 195.

5. Bruce Stanley, "Drawing from the Well: Syria in the Persian Gulf," *Journal of South Asian and Middle Eastern Studies* 14 (Winter 1990); Rosemary Hollis, " 'Whatever Happened to the Damascus Declaration?': Evolving Security Structures in the Gulf," in *Politics and International Relations in the Middle East*, ed. M. Jane Davis (Aldershot, UK: Edward Elgar, 1995).

6. Suha Bolukbasi, "Ankara, Damascus, Baghdad and the Regionalization of Turkey's Kurdish Secessionism," *Journal of South Asian and Middle Eastern Studies* 14 (Summer 1991).

7. *Maghreb/Machrek*, no. 127 (January–March 1990), 181; *Middle East Contemporary Survey 1989*, 642–43; Ken Mackenzie, "Turkey: Terrorism and Water," *Middle East International* (MEI), December 15, 1989.

8. Olmert, "Iranian-Syrian Relations," 183–84.

9. Jim Muir, "Lebanon's Shi'ites Forced to Call a Truce," MEI, February 3, 1989.

10. *New York Times* (NYT), December 29, 1989; *Maghreb/Machrek*, no. 127 (January–March 1990), 173; Godfrey Jansen, "Syria and Iran: The Glue Is Thinning," MEI,

November 17, 1989; Graham E. Fuller, *The "Center of the Universe:" The Geopolitics of Iran* (Boulder, CO: Westview Press, 1991), 131.

11. *Maghreb/Machrek*, no. 127 (January–March 1990), 174; Jim Muir, "Lebanon Faces Partition or War," MEI, January 19, 1990.

12. Jansen, "The Glue is Thinning;" Fida Nasrallah, "Factors behind the Amal-Hizbullah War," MEI, March 2, 1990; Olmert, "Iranian-Syrian Relations," 185.

13. Gerald Butt, "Seizing the Opportunity," MEI, August 31, 1990; Ann Mosely Lesch, "Contrasting Reactions to the Persian Gulf Crisis," *Middle East Journal* 45 (Winter 1991). Eyal Zisser observes that "Syria's ardent stand was all the more blatant against the background of the hesitant and dithering attitudes taken by most other Arab countries in the first stages of the crisis." Zisser, "Syria and the Gulf Crisis: Stepping on a New Path," *Orient* 34 (December 1993), 567.

14. Quoted in Ghayth N. Armanazi, "Syrian Foreign Policy at the Crossroads," in *State and Society in Syria and Lebanon*, ed. Youssef M. Choueiri (New York: St. Martin's Press, 1993), 115.

15. Safa Haeri, "Iran and Iraq: Mending Fences," MEI, September 14, 1990.

16. Safa Haeri, "Iran and Syria: Fruitless Visit," MEI, September 28, 1990.

17. MEI, October 26, 1990, 15; Shahram Chubin, "Iran and the Gulf Crisis," *Middle East Insight*, December 1990.

18. Safa Haeri, "Iran and Syria: Axis Revived," MEI, November 9, 1990.

19. *International Herald Tribune*, September 26, 1990.

20. Mahmut Bali Aykan, "The Turkish-Syrian Crisis of October 1998: A Turkish View," *Middle East Policy* 6 (June 1999); Yuksel Sezgin, "The October 1998 Crisis in Turkish-Syrian Relations: A Prospect Theory Approach," *Turkish Studies* 3 (Autumn 2002).

21. Patrick Seale, "Turkey and Syria: The War over Water," MEI, June 4, 1999.

22. Robert Olson, *Turkey's Relations with Iran, Syria, Israel and Russia, 1991–2000* (Costa Mesa, CA: Mazda, 2001), 21–43; Nader Entessar, "Whither Iranian-Turkish Relations?" *Journal of Iranian Research and Analysis* 16 (2000).

23. Olson, *Turkey's Relations with Iran, Syria, Israel and Russia*, 56.

24. Ibid., 59–60; Robert Olson, *Turkey-Iran Relations, 1979–2004* (Costa Mesa, CA: Mazda, 2005), 56–69.

25. Olson, *Turkey's Relations with Iran, Syria, Israel and Russia*, 64; Nicole Pope, "Turkey: Iran Crisis Cools," MEI, June 2, 2000.

26. Reinoud Leenders, "Lebanon's Democratic Coup," MEI, December 11, 1998.

27. British Broadcasting Corporation (BBC), May 17, 1999; Saeed Barzin, "Evolving New Axis?" MEI, May 21, 1999; Jubin Goodarzi, "Behind Iran's Middle East Diplomacy," MEI, September 17, 1999.

28. Turkish Press Review, May 8, 2000; Middle East News Line, May 9, 2000.

29. *Daily Star* (Beirut), November 13, 2000.

30. "Syria: Onward March," MEI, February 9, 2001.

31. "Syria: Foreign Ventures," MEI, March 23, 2001.

32. BBC, September 11, 2001; *Turkish Daily News*, September 12 and 16, 2001.

33. *Turkish Daily News*, December 26, 2001.

34. *al-Hayah*, March 1, 2002.

35. *al-Mustaqbal* (Beirut), July 24, 2002; Malik Mufti, "Turkish-Syrian Rapprochement: Causes and Consequences," *Policywatch*, no. 30, June 21, 2002.

36. *al-Safir*, January 23, 2003; Oxford Business Group, "Syria: Weekly Briefing," January 26, 2003.

37. Robert Olson, "Turkey-Iran Relations, 2000–2001," *Middle East Policy* 9 (June 2002), 111–14.

38. Ibid., 114–19.

39. *al-Safir*, April 8, 2003.

40. Jim Quilty, "Duelling Triumvirs," MEI, January 11, 2002.

41. Jim Muir, "Iran: Focus on Palestine," MEI, April 19, 2002; Anders Strindberg, "USA Hardens Stance against Syria," *Jane's Intelligence Review*, July 2002.

42. *al-Wifaq*, April 27, 2002.

43. *al-Safir*, October 29, 2002; *al-Hayah*, November 7, 2002.

44. Murhaf Jouejati, "The Syrian-Iraqi Rapprochement," *Middle East Insight*, November–December 1997; Ahmad S. Moussalli, "The Geopolitics of Syrian-Iraqi Relations," *Middle East Policy* 7 (October 2000); Ed Blanche, "Syria and Iraq Find Common Cause," *Jane's Intelligence Review*, October 1, 2001.

45. *Tishrin*, August 7, 2000; BBC, September 27, 2000.

46. *Daily Star*, November 13, 2000; BBC, January 29, 2001; Gary C. Gambill, "Syria's Foreign Relations: Iraq," *Middle East Intelligence Bulletin* 3 (March 2001).

47. Agence France Presse (AFP), August 12, 2001; *al-Ahram Weekly*, August 16–22, 2001; *al-Ittihad* (Abu Dhabi), August 21, 2001.

48. *al-Hayah*, November 7, 2002.

49. Jim Muir, "Iran: Challenges on Two Fronts," MEI, September 27, 2002; *al-Hayah*, January 29, 2003.

50. Jim Muir, "Opposition Gathers," MEI, December 20, 2002.

51. "Syria: Bashar's Manoeuvres," MEI, November 22, 2002.

52. *al-Hayah*, November 12, 2002; Najm Jarrah, "Arabs' Brave Face," MEI, November 22, 2002.

53. "Syria: Fear of the US," MEI, December 6, 2002; Robert Olson, *Turkey's Relations with Iran, Syria, Israel and Russia, 1991–2000* (Costa Mesa, CA: Mazda, 2001); Robert Olson, "Turkey-Iran Relations, 1979–2004: Accommodation and Competition," *Journal of South Asian and Middle Eastern Studies* 28 (Winter 2005).

54. *al-Nahar*, March 20, 2003.

55. Anders Strindberg and Mats Waern, "Syria, Hizbullah and the Iraqi Dimension," MEI, June 13, 2003.

56. Anoushiravan Ehteshami, "Iran-Iraq Relations after Saddam," *The Washington Quarterly* 26 (April 2003).

57. Kamran Taremi, "Iranian Foreign Policy towards Occupied Iraq, 2003–05," *Middle East Policy* 12 (Winter 2005): 35–36.

58. Ibid., 39.

59. Ibid.; Dow Jones Newswires, August 2, 2004.

60. *al-Hayah*, December 12, 2003.

61. *Bloomberg News*, January 9, 2004.

62. *al-Rai al-'Amm* (Kuwait), July 23, 2004; Associated Press (AP), July 24, 2004; *Daily Star*, July 26, 2004.

63. AFP, July 25, 2004.

64. Jim Quilty, "Lebanon: More Syrians Out," MEI, August 8, 2003; Jim Quilty, "Lebanon: Border Tensions," MEI, August 22, 2003.

65. Jim Quilty, "Lebanon and Syria against the World," MEI, September 10, 2004.

66. Ibid.

67. BBC, May 14, 2003.

68. *al-Hayah*, October 1, 2003.

69. BBC, October 13, 2003; February 18, 2004; May 5, 2004; and May 10, 2004.

70. *Daily Star*, April 22, 2004.

71. AFP, July 6, 2004; Islamic Republic News Agency, October 7 and 8, 2004.

72. Islamic Republic News Agency, September 16, 2004; October 27, 2004; and December 30, 2004.

73. Taremi, "Iranian Foreign Policy towards Occupied Iraq," 42.

74. Ibid., 43; *Financial Times*, July 7, 2005.

75. Xinhua News Agency (Beijing), February 15, 2005.

76. *Financial Times*, February 16, 2005; *Guardian*, February 16, 2005.

77. Bishara Sharbel, "Syria-Iran: Firm Relations with Varied Considerations," Emirates Center for Strategic Studies and Research, April 24, 2005.

78. AFP, August 7, 2005; *Gulf News* (Bahrain), August 12, 2005.

79. *Intelligence Online*, November 11, 2005.

80. Ibid.

81. Islamic Republic News Agency, September 27, 2005.

82. *al-Safir*, August 9, 2005; NYT, March 13, 2006.

83. Deutsche Presse-Agentur, October 2, 2005.

84. AFP, January 19, 2006; *Daily Star*, January 20, 2006.

85. *Daily Star*, January 21, 2006.

86. *Daily Star*, February 7, 2006.

87. Xinhua, February 24, 2006; MENAFN.com, March 12, 2006.

88. *al-Hayah*, June 16, 2006; AFP, June 15, 2006; *Daily Star*, July 4, 2006.

89. AP, July 14, 2006.

90. Kamal Nazer Yasin, "Iran Maneuvers for Geopolitical Advantage," Eurasianet.org, July 18, 2006.

91. BBC, July 24, 2006.

92. Radio Free Europe/Radio Liberty (RFE/RL), July 24, 2006.

93. *Daily Star*, August 12, 2006.

94. Kamal Nazer Yasin, "For Iranian Radicals, the Fighting in Lebanon was an Exercise in Self-Restraint," Eurasianet.org, August 14, 2006.

95. RFE/RL, August 17, 2006.

96. AFP, April 14, 2005; Philip Robins, "Turkish Foreign Policy since 2002," *International Affairs* 83 (March 2007): 296.

97. *Syria Report*, second quarter 2005.

98. Anatolia News Agency, October 6, 2005; ArabicNews.com, October 8, 2005.

99. *Millyet*, July 23, 2005; United Press International, January 12, 2006.

100. Noyan Tapan News Agency, April 10, 2006 (BBC Monitoring Trans-Caucasus Unit).

101. *Arminfo* (Yerevan), March 5, 2002 (BBC Monitoring Trans-Caucasus Unit).

102. *al-Quds al-'Arabi*, May 10, 2006.

103. Anatolia News Agency, June 7, 2006.

104. Turkish TRT 2 Television, July 3, 2006.

105. Anatolia News Agency, August 5, 2006.

106. Anatolia News Agency, August 16, 2006.

107. AP, May 10, 2006; *Christian Science Monitor*, August 29, 2006.

108. Anatolia News Agency, July 4, 2006; *Jerusalem Post*, July 7, 2006.

109. Syrian Arab News Agency (SANA), July 19, 2006; Anatolia News Agency, July 19, 2006.

110. SANA, August 4, 2006.

111. *Hurriyet*, August 19, 2006.

112. SANA, November 30, 2006.

113. SANA, December 9, 2006.

114. SANA, December 10, 2006.

115. *al-Hayah*, January 31, 2007.

116. SANA, April 3, 2007.

117. *Turkish Weekly*, April 4, 2007.

118. *Tishrin*, October 16, 2007.

119. *al-Hayah*, October 17, 2007.

120. *al-Thawrah*, October 17, 2007.

121. Oxford Business Group, "Syria: Turkish Delight," November 19, 2007.

122. SANA, January 11, 2008.

123. *al-Hayah*, March 12, 2008.

124. Xinhua, April 27, 2008.

125. SANA, April 28, 2008.

126. Institute for War and Peace Reporting, "Syria Media Report," May 23, 2008, http://www.iwpr.net.

127. Gareth Jenkins, "Syria Proposes Nuclear Cooperation with Turkey," *Eurasia Daily Monitor*, June 16, 2008.

128. *Syria Today*, July 16, 2008.

129. SANA, August 6, 2008.

130. SANA, August 20, 2008.

131. *Financial Times*, January 31, 2007.

132. *Daily Star*, May 31, 2007; *Guardian*, June 1, 2007; Yigal Schleifer, "Turkish Military Presses for Offensive against Militant Bases in Iraq," Eurasianet.org, June 5, 2007; *Christian Science Monitor*, June 8, 2007; *Guardian*, June 30, 2007; AP, July 9, 2007.

133. BBC, September 28, 2007.

134. AP, October 10, 2007; *Guardian*, October 22, 2007; *Washington Post*, October 24, 2007; NYT, October 29, 2007; *al-Ahram Weekly*, December 6–12, 2007; *Washington Post*, December 27, 2007; Reuters, January 11, 2008; *Washington Post*, February 5, 2008; AFP, March 20, 2008; *Guardian*, May 2, 2008.

135. AFP, March 11, 2009.

136. *Jane's Foreign Report*, May 6, 2009.

137. *al-Hayah*, December 22, 2009.

138. Fars New Agency, August 19, 2008.

139. Press TV (Tehran), September 22, 2009.

140. NYT, December 15, 2009.

141. SANA, December 31, 2009.

142. IRIB.ir, April 30, 2010.

143. *Christian Science Monitor*, June 8, 2010.

144. *Central Asia-Caucasus Analyst*, September 16, 2009.

145. Eurasianet.org, October 8, 2009.

146. Haley Edwards, "Iran's Near Abroad," Foreign Policy (September 2010).
147. Eurasianet.org, February 23, 2012.
148. AFP, May 1, 2010.
149. Press TV (Tehran), May 25, 2010.
150. *Wall Street Journal*, June 30, 2010.
151. *Los Angeles Times*, October 3, 2010; *al-Quds al-'Arabi*, October 4, 2010.
152. *al-Quds al-'Arabi*, October 11, 2010.
153. *al-Quds al-'Arabi*, September 28, 2010.
154. *al-Hayah*, September 6, 2010.
155. *al-Akhbar*, October 14, 2010.
156. *Hurriyet*, December 19, 2010.
157. *Syria Today*, February 2009.
158. *Asia Times*, August 27, 2009.
159. RFE/RL, August 31, 2009; *Guardian*, September 9, 2009.
160. *Guardian*, December 9, 2009.
161. *al-Safir*, December 9, 2009; *al-Hayah*, December 9, 2009.
162. AP, March 2, 2010.
163. *al-Akhbar*, April 28, 2010; *al-Quds al-'Arabi*, May 28, 2010.
164. *al-Watan* (Damascus), September 14, 2010.
165. AP, January 15, 2011.
166. *Tehran Times*, March 12, 2011.
167. *al-Safir*, March 28, 2011.
168. *al-Safir*, April 18, 2011.
169. *Los Angeles Times*, April 27, 2011.
170. *al-Akhbar*, April 21, 2011.
171. *al-Sharq al-Awsat*, April 27–28, 2011.
172. *al-Safir*, May 4, 2011.
173. *al-Sharq al-Awsat*, May 14, 2011; *Washington Post*, May 28, 2011.
174. *Syria Report*, August 21, 2011.
175. *al-Watan*, June 12, 2011; *Los Angeles Times*, June 17, 2011.
176. *al-Quds al-'Arabi*, August 11, 2011; *Christian Science Monitor*, August 26, 2011.
177. *al-Quds al-'Arabi*, August 22, 2011.
178. *Daily Telegraph*, August 12, 2011.
179. *al-Hayah*, August 30, 2011.
180. BBC, September 23, 2011.
181. *al-Safir*, October 8, 2011.
182. *al-Watan*, October 25, 2011.
183. *al-Sharq al-Awsat*, August 2, 2011.
184. *al-Ahram Weekly*, August 25–31, 2011.
185. *Day Press*, October, 23, 2011.
186. *al-Akhbar*, November 25, 2011; *Financial Times*, December 4, 2011.
187. *al-Mustaqbal*, January 11, 2012.
188. *Financial Times*, November 21, 2011.
189. AP, December 21, 2011.
190. *Hurriyet*, March 28, 2012.
191. *al-Watan*, January 16, 2012.
192. *Day Press*, April 1, 2012.

193. *Tehran Times*, April 29, 2012.

194. AFP, April 8, 2012.

195. *Guardian*, April 9, 2012; AFP, April 11, 2012.

196. BBC, April 18, 2012.

197. *al-Safir*, May 8, 2012; RFE/RL, May 30, 2012.

198. BBC, June 25, 2012; *al-Sharq al-Awsat*, June 26, 2012.

199. BBC, June 26, 2012; NYT, June 26, 2012.

200. *Washington Post*, June 28, 2012; *al-Akhbar*, June 28, 2012.

201. BBC, July 1, 2012; *Los Angeles Times*, July 2, 2012.

202. Reuters, July 3, 2012.

203. al-Monitor.com, August 3, 2012.

204. Eurasianet.org, August 3, 2012; AFP, August 19, 2012.

205. *al-Safir*, August 24, 2012.

206. *The National* (Abu Dhabi), March 30, 2012.

207. *al-Safir*, July 4, 2012.

208. *Financial Times*, May 18, 2012.

209. NYT, September 4, 2012; Reuters, September 19, 2012.

FURTHER READING

Hussein J. Agha and Ahmad S. Khalidi. *Syria and Iran*. London: Pinter, 1995.

Anoushiravan Ehteshami and Raymond A. Hinnebusch. *Syria and Iran*. London: Routledge, 1997.

Jubin M. Goodarzi. *Syria and Iran*. London: Tauris Academic, 2006.

Eberhard Kienle. *Ba'th v. Ba'th: The Conflict between Syria and Iraq 1968–1989*. London: I. B. Tauris, 1990.

Fred H. Lawson. "The Beginning of a Beautiful Friendship: Syrian-Turkish Relations since 1998." In *Demystifying Syria*, ed. Fred H. Lawson. London: Saqi Books, 2009.

Christin Marschall. "Syria-Iran: A Strategic Alliance, 1979–1991." *Orient* 33 (September 1992).

Malik Mufti. *Sovereign Creations*. Ithaca, NY: Cornell University Press, 1996.

CHAPTER 7

Syria's Relations with the United States, the Soviet Union, and Russia

Syria's strategic location and active involvement in the Arab-Israeli conflict have attracted the attention of external powers since before the country's independence in April 1946. From the beginning, Damascus has attempted to juggle its relations with the world's major states in ways that further its own strategic objectives in the struggle against Israel and in rivalries with surrounding governments. The United States and Soviet Union represented the crucial players in this juggling act throughout the twentieth century, and Russia has continued to be a key Syrian ally in the first decades of the twenty-first century. Expanding economic ties to the People's Republic of China and recent diplomatic overtures to Brazil and the other countries of Latin America may well complicate Damascus's future interactions with Washington and Moscow but are unlikely to push these two great powers from center stage.

SYRIA AND THE UNITED STATES BEFORE 2001

Relations between Syria and the United States have vacillated wildly over the decades. As early as September 1944, the nationalist leadership in Damascus appealed to Washington to take the lead in recognizing Syria's independence. Shortly after French forces evacuated the country in April 1946, the authorities in Damascus approached U.S. officials with a request to provide modern equipment and professional training for the country's infant armed forces. More important, throughout the summer of 1949, senior figures in the Truman administration attempted to convince the military government led by Colonel Husni al-Za'im to permit some 200,000 Palestinian refugees to settle permanently in Syria in return for a substantial infusion of American economic assistance.[1]

Negotiations between Washington and Damascus resumed after Colonel 'Adib al-Shishakli seized power in December 1949 despite an explicit warning from the new minister of national economy that Syria would have great difficulty agreeing to any plan that was predicated upon the resettlement, rather than the repatriation, of displaced Palestinians. Washington ignored such misgivings, however, and allocated funds both to pay for the relocation of Palestinian refugees to Syria and to upgrade the Syrian military establishment.

Damascus firmly rejected the initial U.S. proposal to relocate Palestinian refugees but nevertheless hinted that it would welcome American economic and military assistance. These intimations grew more insistent as al-Shishakli's opponents became bolder and the Iraqi monarchy pushed more forcefully for the implementation of Fertile Crescent unity during the winter and spring of 1952. That April, the Syrian government offered to accept 500,000 Palestinian refugees in exchange for US$400 million in aid, but the offer was quietly withdrawn in the face of the upsurge in Arab nationalist sentiment that followed the July revolution in Egypt. Meanwhile, the advent of the Eisenhower administration in January 1953 marked a hardening of U.S. attitudes in opposition to any political movement that appeared to be radical or leftist in character, including several organizations that were gaining strength inside Syria, most notably the Syrian Communist Party and the Arab Socialist Party.

As U.S.-Soviet rivalry escalated during 1953 and 1954, Syria found itself increasingly at odds with Washington's plans for Middle Eastern defense. U.S. efforts to coerce the Syrian government to fall in line with the anti-Soviet alliance were actively supported by Turkey, the one state in the region that was a member of the U.S.-led North Atlantic Treaty Organization. At the beginning of 1955, Turkish representatives in Damascus cultivated ties to dissident Syrian military officers in an unsuccessful attempt to blunt the sitting government's opposition to the U.S.-supported Baghdad Pact. A year later, as tensions mounted over the final disposition of Egypt's Suez Canal, Turkey once again encouraged high-ranking Syrian commanders to overthrow the government, which both Ankara and Washington saw as leading Damascus toward an overt alliance with Moscow.

By the summer of 1956, Turkish and Syrian troops were engaged in routine skirmishes along the border. Officials in Ankara warned in August 1957 that Syria stood on the brink of joining the Communist Bloc; Washington responded by sending American military advisers to Turkey and by offering support to any of Syria's neighbors that mobilized to defend themselves against Damascus under the terms of the UN Charter. Finally, the Syrian government complained to the UN Security Council that Turkish military activities posed an immediate danger to the security of the country, a charge that was seconded by Moscow. Faced with the threat of Soviet intervention, U.S. officials convinced Ankara to back down, and the crisis dissipated.

These events left a legacy of animosity and mistrust that continues to haunt relations between Damascus and Washington. Successive U.S. administrations during the 1960s dismissed Syria as an implacable adversary. Only in the aftermath of the October 1973 war did the two governments reestablish official contact. Several months of "shuttle diplomacy" on the part of U.S. Secretary of State Henry Kissinger set the stage for President Richard M. Nixon's unprecedented visit to the Syrian capital in June 1974. The trip resulted in the restoration of full diplomatic ties, which were to be reinforced by a resumption of large-scale economic assistance. Unrelenting Syrian resistance to Egypt's dogged conciliation of Israel steadily undermined this brief rapprochement with the United States despite a moment of renewed contact in the fall of 1977. By the fall of 1983, U.S. troops and the Syrian military units based in Lebanon found themselves standing on the brink of war with one another.

Not until the Iraqi invasion of Kuwait in August 1990 did the freeze in Syrian-U.S. relations start to thaw. The Syrian government was the first party to accept Washington's invitation to take part in multilateral peace talks in Madrid in October 1991. Even after this particular initiative collapsed, U.S. diplomats continued to carry on bilateral discussions with their Syrian counterparts on a wide range of issues. Washington's repeated efforts to act as intermediary between Syria and Israel, however, failed to overcome the deep-seated antagonism that existed between the two bitter adversaries.

Consequently, U.S. officials turned their attention elsewhere in the region during the last years of the George H. W. Bush administration and first years of the William J. Clinton administration. This posture changed dramatically in January 1994, when President Clinton met President Hafiz al-Asad in Geneva. The two leaders appeared at that point to be in agreement on the general outlines and conditions of a possible settlement with Israel. But when they met again in Damascus nine months later, the U.S. president came away convinced that he had been profoundly misled by al-Asad's earlier statements, and relations went back into the deep freeze.

In the twilight of his second term in office, President Clinton made one last attempt to act as mediator between Syria and Israel. Following a series of talks among high-level American, Syrian, and Israeli representatives, he invited President al-Asad to meet him once again in Geneva at the end of March 2000. The meeting did not go well: Clinton presented little more than the standard Israeli bargaining position, while al-Asad insisted that the entirety of the Golan as it was on June 4, 1967, must be returned to Syria. The Syrian president's death three months later put any further negotiations on hold.

Meanwhile, the U.S. Congress grew increasingly agitated over the long-standing Syrian military presence in Lebanon. Criticism of Syria's direct involvement in Lebanese internal affairs took root among influential right-wing political activists, many of whom gravitated toward the Republican Party's candidate in the 2000 U.S. presidential elections, Texas Governor George W. Bush. Damascus's diplomatic and economic overtures to Iraq, combined with its steadfast support for the Lebanese Islamist movement Hizbullah and a wide range of radical Palestinian organizations, all but guaranteed that relations would deteriorate after Bush assumed the presidency in January 2001.

SYRIA AND THE UNITED STATES AFTER 2001

In the George W. Bush administration's first encounter with the leadership in Damascus, Secretary of State Colin Powell did his best in February 2001 to convince President Bashshar al-Asad to incorporate the oil distribution network that linked Syria and Iraq into the UN Oil-for-Food program. The Syrian president agreed to integrate a planned new pipeline into the UN scheme but said nothing about revising Damascus's existing arrangements with Baghdad. Believing that he had obtained al-Asad's assent to have all oil shipped through Syrian territory abide by the dictates of the UN oil regime, Powell proclaimed that he had accomplished a major U.S. objective. When he discovered that this was not the case, in the words of Flynt Leverett, "he interpreted this episode as one in which the president of Syria had lied to him."[2]

Syria's quick condemnation of the September 2001 attacks on the World Trade Center in New York and the Pentagon in northern Virginia, along with its willingness to cooperate with U.S. intelligence agencies in monitoring and rounding up suspected Islamist militants inside Syria, postponed the collapse of bilateral relations. Syria's expressed opposition to the U.S. military offensive against Iraq during the winter of 2002–2003 nevertheless widened the rift once again. Secretary of State Powell returned to Damascus in May 2003 and pointedly warned Syrian officials to take no steps that might endanger U.S. forces inside Iraq. He also pushed his hosts to shut down the Damascus offices of the Popular Front for the Liberation of Palestine—General Command, the Palestinian Islamic Jihad, and the Movement of Islamic Resistance (*Harakah al-Muqawamah al-Islamiyyah*, or HAMAS), as well as to dismantle Hizbullah's militia in southern Lebanon. Syria ignored the advice, and a month later a U.S. special operations unit in Iraq crossed the border into Syria in pursuit of a convoy that was rumored to be transporting members of the Iraqi political elite. Officials in Damascus held their tongues in response to the incident, in which a handful of Syrian civilians lost their lives and several Syrian troops received serious injuries, but immediately suspended all intelligence sharing with Washington concerning Islamist militants.

From then on, relations plummeted. U.S. officials expressed sympathy for Israel's October 2003 air strike against a purported Palestinian training camp on the outskirts of Damascus. Two months later, President Bush signed the

Syrian Accountability and Lebanese Sovereignty Restoration Act, which threatened to impose a wide range of economic sanctions on Syria if it did not repudiate its ties to Hizbullah and Palestinian radicals, give up its unconventional weapons programs, and take immediate steps to withdraw its forces from Lebanon. President Bush in May 2004 ordered the implementation of the first set of sanctions under the terms of the act, prohibiting U.S. companies from shipping goods to Syria, cutting all links between U.S. financial institutions and the state-run Commercial Bank of Syria, and freezing the overseas investments and bank accounts of a handful of officials and agencies.[3]

Syrian authorities bristled at the accusation that they engaged in or sponsored any form of international terrorism and argued that a clear distinction needed to be drawn between armed struggle against aggression and occupation on the one hand and wanton acts of individual and collective violence on the other. Such a nuanced distinction was lost on the Bush administration, which insisted that all countries and governments must choose to align themselves with Washington or else accept the sobriquets of "evil-doer" or "rogue state." The belligerent U.S. posture toward Syria converged with that of France during the fall of 2004: Washington and Paris joined forces to convince the UN Security Council to adopt Resolution 1559 that September, which ordered all foreign troops to leave Lebanon. President Bashshar al-Asad responded to this UN initiative by sharply condemning U.S. and French interference in Lebanon's internal affairs.

At the same time, U.S. officials warned repeatedly that Syria might be developing or harboring weapons of mass destruction. Persistent reports from U.S. commanders on the ground in Iraq that they could find no evidence of insurgents moving across the border, nor any indication that Syrian weaponry and war materiel were being used in attacks on the American armed forces, did little to dampen the rising wave of anti-Syria rhetoric that emanated from Washington in the weeks following the November 2004 presidential election.

U.S. officials blamed Syria and its allies for the February 2005 bombing that killed former Lebanese Prime Minister Rafiq al-Hariri and called the popular protests that erupted in the wake of the assassination the "Cedar Revolution."[4] Secretary of State Condoleezza Rice joined French Foreign Minister Michel Barnier to reiterate the terms of Security Council Resolution 1559, and Washington and Paris continued to exert pressure on Damascus to refrain from meddling in subsequent developments inside Lebanon. Despite the withdrawal of Syrian troops in the weeks following al-Hariri's death, President Bush renewed economic sanctions against Syria in May 2005, citing alleged Syrian activities in Iraq and unspecified support for international terrorism. The U.S. Department of the Treasury on June 30, 2005, took the unprecedented step of labeling Syria's two top-ranking military and security officers in Lebanon as "specially designated nationals"; this designation authorized officials in the treasury department "to freeze their [individual] assets on the grounds that they pose a threat to US national security."[5]

Washington persisted in its campaign to isolate and punish Syria during the course of 2006 and 2007, even as Germany, the United Kingdom, Spain, and other European governments tried to engage with Damascus in the wake of the Israel-Hizbullah war in Lebanon. From the perspective of the Bush administration, these overtures simply encouraged the Syrian government to stand firm with regard to such troublesome matters as negotiations with Israel and backing for Hizbullah.[6] After Damascus sent only a junior diplomat to the highly anticipated November 2007 Arab-Israeli conference at Annapolis, President Bush on December 4 invited a delegation of Syrian dissidents to the White House, infuriating the Syrian government.

U.S. officials grudgingly acknowledged the importance of the Israel-Syria talks that took place in the spring of 2008 thanks to Turkish mediation and expressed even less enthusiasm for France's efforts to work with Syria to restore stability to Lebanon. So as not to be outflanked completely by the United States' strategic partners, Secretary of State Rice held a low-key meeting with Syrian Foreign Minister Walid al-Mu'allim at the United Nations in September 2008. "But time was short," observed the International Crisis Group, "and Syrian goodwill (after years of U.S. pressure) in even shorter supply. A Syrian official asked, 'Why should we do them any favours? They did nothing but try to destabilize us for years; they should not expect anything from us in return. We'll do what we can with the next administration.' "[7] In the waning weeks of the Bush administration, U.S. troops based in Iraq carried out a raid on a farming community near the eastern town of Al Bu Kamal, claiming to be hunting a leader of the Iraqi resistance.

President al-Asad welcomed the election of Barack Obama to the presidency of the United States, telling reporters: "We have the impression that this administration will be different, and we have seen the signals. But we have to wait for the reality and the results."[8] Foreign Minister al-Mu'allim's initial meeting with acting Assistant Secretary of State for Near Eastern Affairs Jeffrey Feltman turned out to be disappointing, however, and Syrian officials signaled afterwards that Damascus would not sacrifice its strategic partnerships with Iran, Hizbullah, and HAMAS in order to placate Washington. Damascus then called on the Obama administration to remove Syria from the U.S. list of governments that sponsor international terrorism and repeal the legislation that imposed stringent U.S. economic sanctions on Syria.[9] But instead of reevaluating U.S. policy regarding sanctions, President Obama renewed the strictures that had been imposed by his predecessor, claiming that Syria had not done enough to reduce its connections to global and regional terrorist organizations.

In February 2010, the United States named Robert Ford to be ambassador to Syria, filling a vacancy that had stood since February 2005. At the same time,

Undersecretary of State William Burns traveled to Damascus to confer with President al-Asad. Yet the two countries remained wary of one another: When Israeli leaders claimed two months later that Damascus had shipped bulky, intermediate-range SCUD missiles to Hizbullah, U.S. officials expressed skepticism that such a delivery had actually taken place but could not refrain from commenting that "the intent [to do so] is there."[10] The chief spokesperson for the Syrian foreign ministry, Bushra Kanafani, replied that "the American behavior over this matter was provocative and unacceptable."[11] Secretary of State Hillary Clinton then put a steely edge on the episode, pointing out the assignment of a U.S. ambassador to Damascus was neither "a reward or [a] concession," but instead "a tool that can give us added leverage and insight and a greater ability to convey strong and unmistakably clear messages aimed at Syria's leadership."[12]

More tellingly, Secretary Clinton situated Syria's policy regarding Hizbullah squarely in the context of Damascus's relations with the Islamic Republic of Iran. "We know," she asserted, that President al-Asad "is hearing from Iran, Hizbullah and HAMAS. It is crucial that he also hear directly from us, so that the potential consequences of his actions are clear."[13] Allegations that Syria was assisting Iran in supplying Hizbullah with armaments nevertheless prevented the U.S. Congress from confirming Ford's appointment, and in early May President Obama once again renewed wide-ranging economic sanctions against Syria.[14]

By the summer of 2010, Syrian officials had become more strident in voicing complaints about the sanctions regime that had been constructed by the Bush administration and sustained by the Obama administration. Minister of Transportation Yarub Badr told the newspaper *al-Quds al-'Arabi* that "the American embargo on [commercial aircraft to Syria] is similar to the Israeli blockade imposed on Gaza" in light of the political motivations underlying both policies.[15] President al-Asad led a delegation of economic advisers to South America to discuss the possibility of purchasing Brazilian-made Embraer airliners, but the mission ended up being stymied by the fact that U.S. investors owned more than 10 percent of the company, making its products subject to the sanctions regime.[16]

U.S. sanctions were stepped up after popular unrest inside Syria flared into violence in March 2011. President Obama issued an executive order that froze the assets of three prominent figures: the commander of the Fourth Armored Division, the head of the national intelligence directorate, and the former head of Political Security for Dir'a province. "I have determined," the president announced at the end of April, "that the government of Syria's human rights abuses constitute an unusual and extraordinary threat to the national security, foreign policy and economy of the United States, and warrant the imposition of additional sanctions."[17] Punitive measures against President al-Asad and a handful of his relatives were introduced by the U.S. ambassador to the

UN Security Council in August, only to be watered down in the face of Russian and Chinese objections.[18]

Unable to convince the Security Council to adopt a resolution that inflicted serious penalties on the Syrian government, the Obama administration ordered a U.S. Navy aircraft carrier task force to take up positions in the eastern Mediterranean in late November 2011.[19] Washington subsequently cracked down on shipping insurance companies when it came to light that Iranian vessels were helping Syria move oil onto international markets.[20] By March 2012, U.S. military commanders had drawn up plans to send troops to Syria to restore order, and Secretary of Defense Leon Panetta told the U.S. Congress "that preparations [had] been made to supply communications and other 'non-lethal' equipment to Syrian opposition forces."[21] Secretary of State Clinton announced a month later that the United States was going to supply the umbrella opposition organization, the Syrian National Council (SNC), with sophisticated communications equipment. In mid-June, it was reported that the Central Intelligence Agency had started to work directly with units of the SNC's military arm, the Free Syrian Army (FSA), and was laying the groundwork to share operational intelligence with FSA commanders.[22]

SYRIA AND THE SOVIET UNION

Syria's nationalist leadership invited official representatives of the Soviet Union to come to Damascus in June 1944 to discuss the possibility of establishing formal diplomatic relations between the two countries. Following a banquet for the Soviet delegation on July 24, the leaders of the primary nationalist movement (the National Bloc) released a communiqué stating that "the recognition by the Soviet Union of the Syrian Republic as an independent and sovereign State is a full recognition, unvitiated by any reservation."[23] The nationalists appealed to Moscow once again that September at the height of tensions with France over the future of the Syrian armed forces: "The Syrian government considers the [League of Nations] Mandate to have been terminated both de jure and de facto since the establishment in Syria of liberal, democratic and independent institutions and also since the recognition by Great Britain, the Soviet Union and the United States and other countries of Syria's independence."[24] A permanent Soviet diplomatic representative was posted to the Syrian capital in the wake of the July 1944 mission; the envoy helped Syria's prime minister escape to Lebanon when French troops shelled Damascus in May 1945.[25] Moscow agreed in February 1946 to assist the Syrian nationalists to strengthen the local armed forces.[26] Soviet prestige plummeted in May 1948, however, after Moscow recognized the State of Israel.

Syrian politicians looked again to the Soviet Union in the spring of 1950 when rumors spread that the United States and Britain were trying to push the Arab states into accepting Israel's legitimacy. The head of Syria's Muslim Brothers expressed the sentiments of many when he declared that his movement would even align itself with the Soviet Union in order to combat Zionism: "We are resolved to turn towards the eastern camp if the Democracies do not give us justice. . . . To those who say that this eastern camp is our enemy, we would answer: when has the western camp been our friend? . . . We will bind ourselves to Russia were she the very devil."[27] Ma'ruf al-Dawalibi of the liberal People's Party echoed this viewpoint shortly after the outbreak of the Korean War that June.

Moscow welcomed the ouster of Colonel Adib al-Shishakli as military ruler of Syria in February 1954 and urged the parliamentary order that took shape to resist U.S. and British efforts to create an anti-Soviet alliance in the Middle East.[28] The restored civilian government reciprocated and moved quickly to align itself with the world's most important anti-imperialist power. Foreign Minister Khalid al-'Azm explained that Syria found itself in a vulnerable position and "needed the support of a group of nations which had no preconceived notions on the Israeli issue and which could give us their backing at the United Nations. This," he went on, "was the reason we became pro-Soviet, deriving great moral and material support from the eastern bloc."[29] Damascus purchased tanks and military equipment from Czechoslovakia and the other Warsaw Pact countries and in March 1955 accepted Soviet pledges of protection when hostilities appeared to be imminent along the border with Turkey. The unwillingness of the United States, Britain, and France to provide Syria with heavy weapons in the face of Israeli incursions into Gaza and Jordan led the authorities in Damascus to make a series of arms deals with the Soviet Union during 1955 through 1957. Patrick Seale notes that the successful conclusion of these agreements prompted a "rapprochement" between the Syrian Communist Party and the Ba'th Party, which had prior to this time been bitter rivals.[30]

August 1955 saw the assignment of a Soviet military attaché to the permanent mission in Damascus, and three months later the mission was upgraded to a fully functioning embassy.[31] Seale remarks that

> by the spring of 1956 Syrian contacts with the Communist bloc were so numerous as to make enumeration tedious: trade was under way with all the European satellites; invitations by the dozen flowed in from Moscow addressed to municipal councillors, trade unionists, lawyers, footballers, students, [religious scholars]; Czechoslovakia offered to build an oil refinery and each day brought news of the visit of a Communist dance ensemble or of scholarship places for young Syrians in Eastern Europe. A Syrian [religious notable], Muhammad al-Ashmar, was awarded a Stalin Peace Prize.[32]

Meanwhile, armaments and military advisers flooded into the country, cementing the political alliance between the Syrian Communist Party and the Ba'th. Even the liberal National Bloc committed itself to a foreign policy of strict neutralism, deliberately refusing to take sides in the global Cold War.

Soviet Foreign Minister Dmitri Shepilov showed up in Damascus in June 1956, bringing with him funding for development projects, greater access to armaments, and a variety of cultural initiatives. As soon as Shepilov departed, the Syrian government recognized the People's Republic of China.[33] Moscow and Damascus signed a comprehensive cultural agreement that August, the first such pact between the Soviet Union and any Arab country.[34] President Shukri al-Quwwatli led a high-level delegation to Moscow to discuss a common response to the British-French-Israeli assault on the Suez Canal that September; the trip was rewarded with a further influx of Soviet arms and military equipment along with "blanket assurances" that the Soviet Union would come to Syria's aid in the event that Israel launched an attack northward.[35]

As tensions between pro-Western and neutralist governments across the Middle East heated up in the summer of 1957, Foreign Minister al-'Azm went to Moscow, where he signed a major economic and technical assistance pact in early August. Officials in Moscow later that month warned that the United States was attempting to encircle Syria by constructing a regional partnership with Turkey, Jordan, and Iraq. The Soviet government then accused Turkey of building up its military presence along the Syrian border preparatory to a strike southward. Foreign Minister Salah al-Din Bitar rushed to New York to complain to the United Nations, while two Soviet warships anchored at Latakia.[36] In late October, Syria requested that the United Nations send a fact-finding mission to investigate Turkey's actions; the request enjoyed the firm support of the Soviet Union.

Closer ties to Moscow accompanied growing popular sympathy for the Syrian Communist Party, which set off alarm bells among the leaders of the Ba'th Party in Damascus. Military officers close to the Ba'th convinced Egyptian President Gamal 'Abd al-Nasir to agree to a merger between Syria and Egypt as a way to counteract the rise of the communists. Immediately after the formation of the United Arab Republic in February 1958, the leader of the Syrian Communist Party decamped for an Eastern European capital, and the organization went into hibernation.[37] Soviet influence diminished as well and only started to recover when the union started to dissolve in the fall of 1960 and the flow of industrial and agricultural assistance resumed.[38]

Syria's relations with the Soviet Union blossomed after the radical wing of the Ba'th Party consolidated its hold over the central administration in 1965 and 1966. The coup d'état that brought Salah Jadid to power set the stage for substantially augmented economic and diplomatic links, along with the return to Syria of the historic leader of the Syrian Communist Party.[39] The peak of bilateral cooperation was reached in March 1968 when Soviet officials supervised the initial stage of construction of the high dam at Tabqa on the Euphrates River. Relations withered that fall, however, when Minister of Defense Hafiz al-Asad shouldered aside two of Moscow's key allies, Prime Minister Yusif al-Zu'ayyin and Foreign Minister Ibrahim Makhus. As it became clear that al-Asad intended to push the radicals out of pivotal positions in the state apparatus, Soviet Ambassador Nuridin Mukhidinov hurried back from vacation on the Black Sea to tell the defense minister "that his complete seizure of power might lead to the withdrawal of Soviet aid and experts from Syria."[40] al-Asad riposted by blaming the Soviets for the diplomatic and economic problems that plagued his country, although he held out the possibility of retaining ties to the Soviet Union if it agreed to stop interfering in Syria's internal affairs.

Soviet officials stood aside as the struggle between radical and pragmatic Ba'this played itself out during the course of 1969 and 1970. The authorities in Moscow then welcomed Hafiz al-Asad to the Soviet capital three months after he consolidated power in November 1970. Syria's new leader presented an olive branch to his hosts in the form of an agreement that permitted the Soviet navy to use the port of Tartus as a refueling and maintenance facility. Arms shipments to the Syrian military accelerated, and in March 1971, Soviet General Secretary Leonid Brezhnev referred to Syria using the same terms that he applied to Egypt, "which at that time still ranked as the USSR's most prominent Third World ally."[41] A succession of major weapons deals was concluded during 1972 and 1973, and Damascus took advantage of the steady deterioration of Soviet-Egyptian relations to forge a strategic partnership with Moscow. As a token of their trust in the new alliance, Syrian officials granted the Soviet air force permission to operate TU-16 reconnaissance planes out of airfields on Syrian territory.[42]

Ties between the two countries stagnated in the months surrounding the October 1973 Arab-Israeli war. Moscow pointedly refused to replace Syria's aging MiG-21 fighters with newer MiG-23s. Galia Golan points out that "some friction apparently existed between the two [governments] in the month prior to the war—some ten Soviet specialists in Syria were declared persona non grata, and there were rumors of Syrian complaints in the wake of the embarrassing loss of thirteen Syrian MIGs to the Israeli Air Force in a battle which took place September 13, 1973."[43] Although Moscow quickly replaced the military hardware that was destroyed during the fighting, relations did not regain momentum until the following April, when General Secretary Brezhnev, Prime Minister Alexei Kosygin, and Foreign Minister Nikolai Podgorny all turned out to greet President al-Asad at Moscow airport.[44] As part of the package of military and economic agreements that was negotiated during the visit, the Syrian air force won the first shipment of advanced MiG-23 interceptors to be delivered outside the Soviet Union. A Soviet naval flotilla called at Latakia in November 1974.[45]

Immediately following the signing of the Interim Agreement in Sinai between Egypt and Israel, President al-Asad paid a surprise visit to the Soviet capital. His hosts made an attempt to persuade him to draw up a treaty of friendship between Damascus and Moscow, but the Syrian president rejected the proposal.[46]

Differences between the two governments over whether to join the U.S.-sponsored effort to restart Arab-Israeli peace talks in Geneva (which the Soviets preferred) or come up with some way to negotiate under the auspices of the United Nations (which the Syrians favored) hampered any improvement in relations over the subsequent months.[47]

Relations cooled further in the spring of 1976 as Syria gave strong indications that it intended to send its armed forces into Lebanon, but warmed up after the United States fell in with Israel's insistence on retaining "defensible borders" a year later.[48] Egyptian President Anwar al-Sadat's unexpected peace initiative to Israel in November 1977 pushed Damascus and Moscow into one another's arms, and weapons agreements concluded in February 1978, March 1979, and October 1979 culminated in the signing of a bilateral Treaty of Friendship and Cooperation in October 1980. Moscow did its best to manipulate the terms of the pact to restrain Damascus during the November 1980 crisis with Jordan and the Lebanese missile crisis of May 1981, and tried to deter Israel from escalating the conflict in Lebanon by carrying out joint military maneuvers with the Syrian army and navy in July 1981.[49] Nevertheless, the Soviet leadership resisted Syria's requests for enhanced weaponry in the wake of the November 1981 U.S.-Israel Memorandum of Strategic Understanding and backed away from giving unquestioned backing for Damascus during the winter and spring of 1981–1982.

Syria ended up preventing Israeli forces from gaining a strategic advantage when war broke out in Lebanon in June 1982 and in the aftermath of the fighting reconciled with the Soviet Union. President al-Asad requested, and received, two Red Army brigades equipped with advanced SAM-5 anti-aircraft missiles, and Moscow stepped up delivery of a wide range of other armaments including SS-21 intermediate-range ballistic missiles.[50] When he returned to Moscow in October 1984, however, the Syrian president received a much chillier welcome. General Secretary Konstantin Chernenko refused to delay repayment of Syria's rapidly compounding military debts and informed his guest that the two Red Army brigades would be withdrawn from Syria, although their SAM-5 batteries could remain in place.[51] In response, the Syrian government made overtures to Washington and Paris and hinted that it might take steps to replace Soviet weaponry with arms from the West.

Syria therefore found itself alienated from the Soviet Union when it fell into conflict with Israel over the deployment of missiles along the Lebanese border in the final weeks of 1985. General Secretary Mikhail Gorbachev at first refused to supply the Syrian air force with advanced MiG-29 warplanes and only agreed in April 1987 to reschedule Damascus's burgeoning military debt and provide funding for a long-planned high dam across the Euphrates River. In exchange for these concrete benefits, Gorbachev made it clear that he expected the Syrian government to patch up relations with the Palestine Liberation Organization, refrain from using force against Israel, and scale back its support for the Islamic Republic of Iran.[52] Moscow increasingly criticized Syria's campaign to achieve "strategic parity" with Israel and embarked on a rapprochement of its own with Israel. By 1988 and 1989, Soviet officials were talking about the need to work out some sort of balance between the security interests of Israel and those of the Arab states.

SYRIA AND RUSSIA

Immediately after the collapse of the Soviet Union at the end of 1991, Russia shifted its attention away from the Arab world and toward Iran and Turkey, both of which had embarked on campaigns to extend their influence throughout the former Soviet republics of the Caucasus and Central Eurasia.[53] At the same time, the leadership in Moscow took steps to boost its relations with Israel, which had become Russia's single largest Middle Eastern trading partner. More important, President Boris Yeltsin and Foreign Minister Andrei Kozyrev pursued a policy of rapprochement with the West in general and the United States in particular. Russia sent a pair of warships to help enforce the UN sanctions regime against Iraq; it became a supporter of economic sanctions against Libya; and it took an active part in the drawn-out, U.S.-sponsored Arab-Israeli peace process that got underway immediately following the 1990–1991 Gulf War.

Meanwhile, Syria drifted in the direction of Western Europe and the United States. Damascus joined the U.S.-led alliance that pushed the Iraqi armed forces out of Kuwait in early 1991, then solicited investment funds from the Arab Gulf states and favorable commercial arrangements from the European Union. Syrian hostility toward Iraq persisted throughout the 1990s, even as Russia switched toward a more accommodative posture vis-à-vis the Ba'thi regime in Baghdad. And the marked decline of the Russian economy left the authorities in Damascus with little incentive to cultivate economic or military connections with Moscow during the first decade of the post-Soviet era.

President Hafiz al-Asad traveled to the Russian capital in July 1999, seeking relief from the crushing debt obligations that survived the collapse of the Soviet Union. He was also reported to be looking for upgraded weapons, particularly anti-aircraft missile systems, for which the Syrian government was prepared to pay cash.[54] Before a major deal could be struck, however, President Yeltsin stepped down and President al-Asad died. Russian Foreign Minister Igor Ivanov traveled to the Syrian capital to meet President Bashshar al-Asad three months after he had been confirmed in office, initiating a series of high-level visits back and forth between the two countries over the next seven months.

Damascus and Moscow worked together to block U.S. efforts to win UN backing for a military offensive against Iraq during 2002 and 2003, and both governments openly opposed the March 2003 invasion when it at last took place.

Nevertheless, the Russian authorities refused to sell the advanced S-300 anti-aircraft missile system to Syria and carefully avoided committing themselves to come to the defense of Syria in the event of an attack by the United States.[55]

Relations brightened dramatically in January 2005 when President al-Asad met with President Vladimir Putin in Moscow. Putin agreed to forgive almost three-quarters of Syria's outstanding military debts and revised repayment terms on the remaining 25 percent in ways that were highly advantageous to Syria. Furthermore, Syria obtained the Strelets mobile anti-aircraft missile system as well as a contract with the Russian state hydrocarbons company Tatneft to start exploring for oil and natural gas in the desert east of Homs. The Russian enterprise Stroytansgaz subsequently agreed to construct a new gas pipeline and processing facility in the same region.[56] Damascus acknowledged Moscow's generosity by inviting the Russian-sponsored President of Chechnya, Alu Alkhanov, for an official visit that September.[57]

Russian representatives blocked the world's largest industrial countries, the so-called Group of 8 (G-8), from imposing economic sanctions against Syria for transferring missiles that had been purchased from Russia to Hizbullah fighters during the July 2006 Israel-Hizbullah war.[58] When Israeli Prime Minister Ehud Olmert arrived in Moscow to complain about Syria's actions, President Putin deftly parried the criticism, calling the entire episode a "closed topic."[59] President al-Asad reciprocated by expressing support for Russia's August 2008 offensive against Georgia; he then met President Dmitry Medvedev at Sochi on the Black Sea, where he overplayed his hand by suggesting that Israel's military assistance program to Georgia made it imperative for Moscow to supply the Syrian armed forces with state-of-the-art S-300 anti-aircraft batteries, MiG-31 warplanes, and Iskander-E short-range ballistic missiles. Foreign Minister Sergei Lavrov replied noncommittally that his government would "consider" the Syrian proposal. That September, a delegation of Syrian naval commanders visited Moscow and laid out plans to renovate the largely abandoned Russian staging facility at Tartus. Negotiations over the sale of MiG-31s dragged into the fall of 2009.[60]

President Medvedev paid a visit to Damascus in May 2010 and agreed to sell the Syrian armed forces upgraded MiG-29 warplanes, 36 mobile Pantsir S-1 anti-aircraft missile batteries, a pair of K-300 Bastion coastal defense batteries, and a variety of antitank weapons.[61] He also intimated that Russia might supplement its growing involvement in oil and gas exploration by assisting Syria with the development of nuclear power. Four months later, Minister of Defense Anatoly Serdyukov told officials in Washington that Russia intended to follow through in supplying the Syrian navy with P-800 antiship missiles.[62]

Moscow responded to the outbreak of popular disorder in Syria in the spring of 2011 by advising opponents of the Ba'thi regime to engage in dialogue with the authorities and refrain from taking up arms. Foreign Minister Lavrov asserted in September that President al-Asad had been trying to carry out "real reforms" and had not received the credit he deserved from the international community for his efforts; he went on to warn that any sort of "unilateral sanctions" against Syria were likely to do more harm than good.[63] At the same time, officials in Moscow invited a delegation of critics of the existing political order to come to Moscow for talks; the delegation was led by 'Ammar al-Qurbi of the Syrian National Council for Human Rights and included representatives of the Kurdish and tribal communities.[64]

Russia's representative to the UN Security Council put Moscow's continuing sympathy for the Ba'thi regime in Damascus on public display in early October when he joined the People's Republic of China in vetoing a proposed resolution that would have imposed "targeted measures" on Syria as a way to force President al-Asad to step down. The draft resolution grew out of a plan that had been formulated by the Arab League and was strongly supported by France, Britain, and the United States.

In late November, the day after the Arab League voted to impose economic sanctions on Syria, Foreign Minister Lavrov expressed Russia's view that Syria should not be given any more ultimatums by outside actors. He urged foreign governments and international organizations instead to engage in dialogue with Damascus and pointed out that the Syrian authorities had resorted to force only after they had been "provoked" by armed opposition groups.[65] It was simultaneously announced that the Russian aircraft-carrying heavy cruiser *Admiral Kuznetsov*, antisubmarine warfare vessel *Admiral Chabanenko*, and frigate *Ladny* were going to call at Tartus in December as part of a scheduled tour of Mediterranean ports; news of the deployment followed reports that a U.S. aircraft carrier group had just taken up positions off the Syrian coast.[66] As Western banks moved to freeze Syrian financial assets, the Commercial Bank of Syria and Real Estate Bank opened accounts denominated in euros and rubles in various Russian banks so that they could continue to operate outside the country.[67]

Reports that Russian intelligence agencies were working with Syrian security forces began to appear during the last week of 2011.[68] The Russian agencies were credited with tracking shipments of arms and fighters from Libya to southern Turkey and with monitoring the movements of the Turkish armed forces along the border. Russia meanwhile signed a contract to supply the Syrian air force with 36 YAK-130 combat training aircraft.[69] Immediately after the *Admiral Kuznetsov* and its escorts left Tartus in the first week of January 2012, a cargo ship carrying crates of ammunition from the Russian state arms agency Rosoboronexport stopped at Tartus after switching off its automatic identification system.[70] Foreign Minister Lavrov then told reporters that Russia would block any attempt to use the United Nations to exert pressure on Damascus; he went on to say that his government did not "consider it necessary to explain and justify ourselves in connection with a Russian vessel unloading at a Syrian port, as Russia does not violate any international agreements or UN Security Council resolutions."[71]

Moscow welcomed the publication of the final report submitted by the Arab League's fact-finding mission to Syria, which tended to support Damascus's claims that it had exercised restraint in dealing with the ongoing protests.[72] Syria's Minister of Agriculture and Agrarian Reform Riyad Hijab signed an agricultural assistance and trade pact with Russia at the end of January 2012. The agreement opened the door to imports of Russian veterinary medicines and animal fodder, and laid the groundwork for greater exports of citrus fruit, olive oil, potatoes, and vegetables.[73]

Russia on February 4, 2012, vetoed a draft UN Security Council resolution that would have condemned the Syrian government for using violence against its opponents and laid out a strict timetable for regime change in Damascus; Lavrov called the angry reaction that the veto elicited from Western countries "hysterical." The Russian foreign minister traveled to Damascus shortly afterwards in the company of senior intelligence officers and pointedly commended President al-Asad for taking steps to curb the "armed extremist groups" that were continuing to operate inside Syria.[74] He called on all parties to the conflict to lay down their arms and voiced support for the proposed revisions to the Syrian constitution that had been put forward by the authorities.[75]

Impatience with Syria at last bubbled to the surface in early April as the authorities in Damascus showed evident disdain for the UN mediation mission led by Kofi Annan. Standing alongside Foreign Minister Walid al-Mu'allim, Lavrov told reporters, "We told our Syrian colleague [that] we think their actions could be more active, more decisive in regard to the fulfillment of the points of the [UN peace] plan."[76] Moscow then announced that a Russian warship would be stationed on permanent patrol off the Syrian coast, remarking somewhat disingenuously that the deployment had "nothing to do" with developments in Syria.[77] When it became clear that Annan's mission had failed, Lavrov told a visiting delegation of loyal critics of the Syrian regime that outside forces had derailed the initiative "by delivering arms to the Syrian opposition and stimulating the activity of rebels who continue to attack both government facilities and civilian facilities on a daily basis."[78] Russia then circulated a proposed Security Council resolution that increased the number of UN monitors on the ground from 30 to 300 but included no punitive measures if the Syrian government rejected the demand to institute a cease-fire.[79]

News that 100 men, women, and children had been slaughtered in the region of al-Hulah in mid-May prompted Russia to vote in favor of a Security Council resolution that condemned the massacre and charged that the Syrian regime had engaged in an "outrageous use of force." Foreign Minister Lavrov unexpectedly remarked in the presence of British Foreign Secretary William Hague that "the [Syrian] government bears the main responsibility for what is going on"; he pointedly failed to rule out the possibility that President al-Asad might step down in the wake of the killings but remarked that changing the leadership in Damascus was "not the most important thing."[80] When a second massacre was uncovered a week later, officials in Moscow insisted that "it is essential to give the plan of Kofi Annan time to work" and that further action by the United Nations might "only exacerbate the situation for both Syria and the region as a whole."[81] As fighting escalated in early June, President Putin and a visiting delegation from the People's Republic of China issued a joint statement affirming that "Russia and China are decisively against attempts to regulate the Syrian crisis with outside military intervention, as well as imposing a policy of regime change."[82]

U.S. Secretary of State Hillary Clinton charged in June 2012 that Russia was shipping helicopter gunships to Syria to boost the Ba'thi regime's capacity to suppress the uprising. Russian officials denied the accusation and retorted that it was the Arab Gulf states and other strategic partners of the United States that were sending armaments into the country.[83] State Department officials quietly acknowledged a week later that the helicopters in question were actually Syrian and were being returned after undergoing routine maintenance. The head of Rosoboronexport then announced that anti-aircraft and antiship missiles, including the Pantsir S-1 system, were headed for Syria.[84] Two amphibious landing ships carrying several hundred marines set out for Tartus, tasked with protecting the Russian citizens who were working at the Syrian port.[85] And a Russian radar installation was set up adjacent to Hatay to keep track of activity around the Turkish air bases at Incirlik and Kurecik.[86]

June 2012 ended with the Russian foreign ministry issuing an official statement regarding the downing of a Turkish reconnaissance plane by Syrian forces: "We believe it is important that the incident is not viewed as a provocation or an intentional action, and that it does not lead to destabilising the situation."[87] Shortly thereafter, a Russian military source observed that "the three Mi-25 [attack] helicopters and air defense systems [that had incited Secretary of State Clinton's indignation] could easily be delivered to Syria by air. Russia has to fulfill its obligations," the source continued, "but everything will depend on if we can resist pressure from the West who want us to break military co-operation with Syria."[88]

When Annan called for an international conference in Geneva to discuss the uprising in Syria and its regional impact, Moscow insisted that the Islamic Republic of Iran be invited to the meeting. Foreign Minister Lavrov also reiterated his government's opposition to outside interference in the conflict: "Foreign players should not be dictating their solutions to the Syrians. We do not and cannot support any intervention or solutions dictated from abroad."[89] In the wake of the Geneva meeting, an unnamed Russian official speculated publicly that the destroyed Turkish reconnaissance aircraft had represented "a provocation" to the Syrians. "The crew," the source remarked, "had to have only one motive for such actions—to test the combat readiness of the Syrian air defense systems and it indeed tested them."[90]

Russian warships returned to positions off the Syrian coast in early July. A month later, a delegation headed by Deputy Prime Minister for Economic Affairs Qadri

Jamil arrived in Moscow to ask the Russian authorities to supply Syria with desper-
ately needed refined petroleum products in exchange for shipments of crude oil.[91]
When U.S. President Barack Obama warned in mid-August that the use of
chemical weapons by the Syrian armed forces constituted a "red line" that would
prompt Western military intervention, Lavrov responded immediately that
"external interference" was "hindering efforts by Syrians themselves to resolve this
problem."[92] As fighting escalated across northern Syria in late September 2012,
Foreign Minister Lavrov told the UN General Assembly that outside support for
opposition forces was "pushing Syria even deeper into internecine strife," although
he went on to observe that both government forces and rebel fighters were impli-
cated in a growing number of "war crimes."[93]

NOTES

1. Avi Shlaim, "Husni Zaim and the Plan to Resettle Palestinian Refugees in Syria," *Middle East Focus* 9 (Fall 1986).

2. Flynt Leverett, *Inheriting Syria* (Washington, DC: Brookings Institution Press, 2005), 135.

3. *New York Times* (NYT), May 11, 2004.

4. Robert G. Rabil, *Syria, the United States and the War on Terror in the Middle East* (Westport, CT: Praeger Security International, 2006), 172.

5. Ibid., 186.

6. International Crisis Group, "Engaging Syria? U.S. Constraints and Opportunities," *Middle East Report*, no. 83 (February 11, 2009): 19.

7. Ibid., 20.

8. Raymond Hinnebusch, "Syria under Bashar," in *Syrian Foreign Policy and the United States: From Bush to Obama*, eds. Raymond Hinnebusch, Marwan J. Kabalan, Bassma Kodmani, and David Lesch (Boulder, CO: Lynne Rienner, 2010), 22.

9. Ibid., 23.

10. *al-Nahar*, April 19, 2010.

11. *al-Sharq al-Awsat*, April 21, 2010.

12. British Broadcasting Corporation (BBC), April 30, 2010.

13. BBC, April 30, 2010.

14. *Middle East International* (MEI), May 14, 2010.

15. *al-Quds al-'Arabi*, June 8, 2010.

16. *al-Quds al-'Arabi*, June 21, 2010.

17. BBC, April 29, 2011.

18. BBC, September 27, 2011.

19. *Russia Today* (RT), November 25, 2011.

20. *Wall Street Journal*, January 19, 2012.

21. *Washington Post*, March 7, 2012.

22. *Wall Street Journal*, June 13, 2012; NYT, June 21, 2012.

23. Fred H. Lawson, *Constructing International Relations in the Arab World* (Stanford, CA: Stanford University Press, 2006), 47.

24. Ibid.

25. Patrick Seale, *The Struggle for Syria* (New Haven, CT: Yale University Press, 1986), 162.

26. Rami Ginat, "The Soviet Union and the Syrian Ba'th Regime: From Hesitation to Rapprochement," *Middle Eastern Studies* 26 (April 2000): 156.

27. Seale, *Struggle for Syria*, 102.

28. Ibid., 233.

29. Ibid., 219.

30. Ibid., 237.

31. Ibid., 255.

32. Ibid., 255–56.

33. Ibid., 259.

34. Karen Dawisha, "Soviet Cultural Relations with Iraq, Syria and Egypt 1955–70," *Soviet Studies* 27 (July 1975), 426.

35. Seale, *Struggle for Syria*, 261.

36. Ibid., 301.

37. Ibid., 324–25.

38. Youmna Boustany, "Soviet Policy towards Syria 1973–1980," unpublished master's thesis, American University of Beirut, February 1983, 23–24.

39. Ginat, "Soviet Union," 164–66; Boustany, "Soviet Policy," 34–35.

40. Efraim Karsh, *Soviet Policy towards Syria since 1970* (London: Macmillan, 1991), 64.

41. Ibid., 69.

42. Boustany, Soviet Policy, 42.

43. Galia Golan, "Syria and the Soviet Union since the Yom Kippur War," *Orbis* 117 (Winter 1978), 778.

44. Karsh, *Soviet Policy*, 85.

45. Golan, "Syria and the Soviet Union," 787.

46. Ibid., 791.

47. Ibid., 791–794. An alternative view, which claims that by the spring of 1975 Syria had become "the pivot of Soviet Middle Eastern policy," is offered in Karsh, *Soviet Policy*, 89.

48. Karsh, *Soviet Policy*, 111.

49. Ibid., 133.

50. Ibid., 145.

51. Ibid., 160.

52. Ibid., 170–71.

53. Robert O. Freedman, "Russian Policy toward the Middle East: The Yeltsin Legacy and the Putin Challenge," *Middle East Journal* 55 (Winter 2001).

54. Mark N. Katz, "Putin's Foreign Policy toward Syria," *Middle East Review of International Affairs* 10 (March 2006), 53–54.

55. Ibid., 55.

56. Ibid., 56.

57. Ibid., 60.

58. Robert O. Freedman, "Russia and the Middle East under Putin," *Ortadogu Etutleri* 2 (July 2010), 31.

59. Ibid., 32.

60. Ibid., 35; "Russia Still in Talks with Syria on MiG Sale," Radio Free Europe/Radio Liberty, September 3, 2009.

61. *Middle East Economic Digest*, January 20–26, 2012.

62. BBC, September 17, 2010.

63. *Voice of Russia*, September 1, 2011; BBC, September 3, 2011.

64. *al-Hayah*, September 8, 2011.
65. BBC, November 29, 2011.
66. RT, November 28, 2011.
67. *al-Watan* (Damascus), November 29, 2011.
68. *al-Quds al-'Arabi*, December 2, 2011.
69. *Christian Science Monitor*, January 23, 2012.
70. *France 24*, January 14, 2012.
71. *Los Angeles Times*, January 20, 2012.
72. *al-Quds al-'Arabi*, January 27, 2012.
73. Syrian Arab News Agency (SANA), January 26, 2012.
74. BBC, February 10, 2012.
75. NYT, February 18, 2012.
76. Reuters, April 10, 2012.
77. Reuters, April 13, 2012.
78. Reuters, April 17, 2012.
79. Associated Press (AP), April 20, 2012.
80. AP, May 28, 2012; *Guardian*, May 28, 2012.
81. Agence France Presse (AFP), May 30, 2012.
82. AFP, June 6, 2012.
83. NYT, June 13, 2012.
84. *Santa Rosa Press Democrat*, June 16, 2012.
85. AP, June 18, 2012.
86. Oytun Orhan, "What the Jet Crisis with Syria Give Rise to Thought [*sic*]," *ORSAM*, June 29, 2012.
87. AFP, June 26, 2012.
88. AFP, June 27, 2012.
89. AFP, June 28, 2012.
90. AFP, July 4, 2012.
91. Reuters, August 3, 2012; Reuters, August 21, 2012.
92. BBC, August 21, 2012.
93. AP, September 29, 2012.

FURTHER READING

Helena Cobban. *The Superpowers and the Syrian-Israeli Conflict*. New York: Praeger, 1991.
Robert O. Freedman. "Russia and the Middle East under Putin." *Ortadogu Etutleri* 2 (July 2010).
Rami Ginat. "The Soviet Union and the Syrian Ba'th Regime: From Hesitation to Rapprochement." *Middle Eastern Studies* 36 (April 2000).
Efraim Karsh. *Soviet Policy towards Syria since 1970*. London: Macmillan, 1991.
Mark N. Katz. "Putin's Foreign Policy toward Syria." *Middle East Review of International Affairs* 10 (March 2006).
David W. Lesch. *Syria and the United States: Eisenhower's Cold War in the Middle East*. Boulder, CO: Westview Press, 1992.
Neil Quilliam. *Syria and the New World Order*. Reading, UK: Ithaca Press, 1999.
Andrew Tabler. *In the Lion's Den*. Chicago: Lawrence Hill, 2011.

APPENDIX A

Chronology

1725–1757	al-'Azm family governs Damascus for Ottomans
1831–1840	Egyptian occupation of Syria
1850	Muslim-Christian riots in Aleppo
1860	Muslim-Christian riots in Damascus
1885	Chamber of Commerce set up at Aleppo
1908	Young Turk revolution restores Ottoman constitution
1909	Emergence of first Arab nationalist secret societies
1913	Syrian-Arab Congress in Paris demands Arab autonomy
1915–1916	Public executions of Arab nationalists at Damascus and Beirut
1918	British and Arab troops capture Syria
1919	French awarded control of Syria at Paris peace conference
1919–1921	Armed resistance to French occupation
1920	General Syrian Congress in Damascus declares Faisal bin Husain Al Hashim king of Syria; Faisal's troops defeated by French army at battle of Maisalun; French create states of Aleppo, Damascus, Jabal Druze, and Latakia
1924	States of Aleppo and Damascus merged to form State of Syria
1925–1927	Great Revolt against French rule
1927	Emergence of National Bloc
1930	Beginning of parliamentary politics under French auspices
1936	Jabal Druze and Latakia incorporated into State of Syria
1940–1941	Vichy French administration
1941	British and Free French troops defeat Vichy forces in Syria
1943	Emergence of Ba'th Party
1945	Syria admitted to United Nations and Arab League; emergence of Arab Socialist Party
1946	Withdrawal of all French forces from Syria; emergence of Syrian Muslim Brothers
1947	Emergence of People's Party
1948	First Arab-Israeli war
1949–1954	Succession of military seizures of power
1953	Merger of Ba'th Party and Arab Socialist Party
1954	Restoration of parliamentary politics
1955	Soviet diplomatic mission upgraded to embassy
1958	Syria merges with Egypt to form United Arab Republic
1961	Syria secedes from United Arab Republic
1963	Seizure of power by officers associated with Ba'th Party
1964	Israel bombs water project north of Sea of Galilee
1966	Seizure of power by radical Ba'thi military officers; Israel bombs water project north of Sea of Galilee

1967	Second Arab-Israeli war results in loss of Golan
1970	Syrian military intervention in Jordanian civil war; seizure of power by pragmatic Ba'thi military officers
1971	Hafiz al-Asad elected president
1973	Third Arab-Israeli war
1974	Syria-Israel disengagement agreement; U.S. President Richard Nixon visits Damascus and restores diplomatic relations
1976	Syrian military intervention in Lebanese civil war
1980	Treaty of Friendship and Cooperation with Soviet Union
1980–1982	Islamist uprising against Ba'thi regime
1982	Syria accepts principle of negotiating directly with Israel
1990	Syria joins alliance against Iraq
1991	U.S.-sponsored Arab-Israeli peace initiative
1994	Syria-U.S. summit in Geneva; Syria-Israel talks begin in Washington, DC
1998	Crisis with Turkey; Syria renounces radical Kurdistan Workers' Party (PKK)
2000	Collapse of U.S.-sponsored Syria-Israel negotiations; death of Hafiz al-Asad; Bashshar al-Asad elected president
2003	U.S. military intervention in Iraq; Israeli air strike on Palestinian camp outside Damascus; U.S. adopts Syria Accountability and Lebanese Sovereignty Restoration Act
2004	United States imposes economic sanctions on Syria
2005	Syrian troops withdraw from Lebanon; United States renews economic sanctions on Syria
2006	Israel-Hizbullah war in Lebanon
2007	Israeli air strike on alleged Syrian nuclear facility
2007–2008	Syria-Israel talks mediated by Turkey
2008	Israel-HAMAS war in Gaza; U.S. raid on Al Bu Kamal
2009	United States renews economic sanctions on Syria
2011–2012	Popular uprising sweeps across Syria

Documents

DOCUMENT 1

The Damascus Declaration for Democratic National Change, October 16, 2005

As published in English by *Syria Comment* (http://faculty-staff.ou.edu/L/ Joshua.M.Landis-1/syriablog/2005/11/damascus-declaration-in-english.htm). Used by permission.

Today Syria stands at a crossroad and needs to engage in self-appraisal and benefit from its historical experience more than at any time in the past. The authorities' monopoly of everything for more than thirty years has established an authoritarian, totalitarian and cliquish regime that has led to a lack of politics in society, with people losing interest in public affairs. That has brought upon the country such destruction as that represented by the rending of the national social fabric of the Syrian people, an economic collapse that poses a threat to the country and exacerbating crises of every kind . . .

. . . In view of the signatories' feeling that the present moment calls for a courageous and responsible national stand, . . . they have reached an accord on the following bases: Establishment of a democratic national regime is the basic approach to the plan for change and political reform. It must be peaceful, gradual, founded on accord and based on dialogue and recognition of the other. . . . Adoption of democracy as a modern system that has universal values and bases, based on the principles of liberty, sovereignty of the people, a State of institutions and the transfer of power through free and periodic elections that enable the people to hold those in power accountable and change them.

... Guarantee the freedom of individuals, groups and national minorities to express themselves, and safeguard their role and cultural and linguistic rights, with the State respecting and caring for those rights, within the framework of the Constitution and under the law.

... Abolish all forms of exclusion in public life, by suspending the emergency law; and abolish martial law and extraordinary courts ... ; release all political prisoners; allow the safe and honorable return of all those wanted and those who have been voluntarily and involuntarily exiled with legal guarantees; and ending all forms of political persecution, by settling grievances and turning a new leaf in the history of the country.

... [W]e call on the Ba'thi citizens of our homeland and citizens from various political, cultural, religious and confessional groups to participate with us and not to hesitate or be apprehensive, because the desired change is in everyone's interest and is feared only by those involved in crimes and corruption.

The process of change can be organized as follows: 1. Opening the channels for a comprehensive and equitable national dialogue among all the components and social, political and economic groups of the Syrian people ... 3. Form various committees, salons, forums and bodies locally and throughout the country to organize the general cultural, social, political and economic activity and to help it in playing an important role in advancing the national consciousness, giving vent to frustrations, and uniting the people behind the goals of change ... 6. Call for the election of a Constituent Assembly to draw up a new Constitution for the country that foils adventurers and extremists, and that guarantees the separation of powers, safeguards the independence of the judiciary and achieves national integration by consolidating the principle of citizenship.

DOCUMENT 2

President Bashshar al-Asad's Televised Address to the People's Assembly, March 30, 2011

As translated by Syrian Arab News Agency.

You are fully aware of the great shifts and changes happening in our region for the past few months. They are important changes, which will have repercussions throughout the region without exception ... This obviously concerns Syria, because Syria is part of this region.

But if we want to consider what concerns us in Syria in what has happened so far on the larger Arab scene, we can say that what happened vindicates the Syrian perspective, in the sense that it expresses a popular consensus. When there is such a consensus we should be assured, whether we agree or disagree on a number of points. What this means is that this popular Arab condition, which has been marginalized for three or four decades, is now at the heart of developments in our region. This Arab condition has not changed. They tried to domesticate it, but it has not yielded.

. . . Today, there is a new fashion which they call "revolutions". We do not call them so, because we think this is mostly a popular condition. . . . Consequently, if there are calls for reform—and I believe we all call for reform—we go along with them without knowing what is really happening. That is why they mixed up, in a very clever manner, three elements: . . . sedition, reform and daily needs. Most of the Syrian people call for reform, and you are all reformers. Most of the Syrian people have unmet needs; and we all discuss, criticize and have our disagreements because we have not met many of the needs of the Syrian people. But sedition has become part of the issue and started to lead the other two factors and take cover under them. That is why it was easy to mislead many people who demonstrated in the beginning with good intentions. We cannot say that all those who demonstrated are conspirators. This is not true, and we want to be clear and realistic.

The conspirators are few in number; this is natural. Even we in the government did not know, like everybody else, and did not understand what was happening until acts of sabotage started to emerge. . . . They will say that we believe in the conspiracy theory. In fact, there is not conspiracy theory. There is a conspiracy.

. . . We have not yet discovered the whole structure of this conspiracy. We have discovered part of it, but it is highly organized. There are support groups in more than one governorate linked to some countries abroad. There are media groups, forgery groups and groups of "eyewitnesses".

. . . In any case, the blood that was spilled on the streets is Syrian blood, and we are all concerned because the victims are our brothers and their families are our families. It is important to look for the causes and those behind these events. We need to investigate and bring the people responsible to account. . . . Let us act as quickly as possible to heal our wounds and restore harmony to our larger family and maintain love as our united bond.

DOCUMENT 3

Pledge and Covenant of the Syrian Muslim Brothers, March 25, 2012

As published online in English by the Middle East Media Research Institute (http://www.memri.org/report/en/print6250.htm#_ednref1). Used by permission.

The Muslim Brotherhood pledges to strive for a future Syria that will be:

1. A modern, civil state with a civil constitution rooted in the will of the Syrian people and based on national consensus. [The constitution] will be drafted by a founding assembly

that will be chosen in free and fair elections. It will protect basic individual and collective rights from any exploitation or violation, and will ensure just representation for all elements of society.

2. A democratic, pluralistic state [that operates on the principle of] transition of power, based on the loftiest [ideals] that modern human thought has achieved. [A state] with a parliamentary republican regime, in which the people elects its representatives and rulers in free, fair, and transparent elections.

3. A state [based on] citizenship and equality, in which all citizens are equal regardless of their ethnicity, faith, school of thought, or [political] orientation. [A state] based on the principle of citizenship, which is the basis for rights and duties, and in which every citizen can attain the highest positions based on [one of] two principles: elections or [personal] qualifications. Furthermore, [a state in which] men and women are equal in human dignity and legal capacity, and [in which] the woman enjoys her full rights.

4. A state committed to human rights as dictated by divine law and international conventions, [namely the rights to] dignity, equality, freedom of thought and expression, freedom of religion and worship, freedom of the media, political partnership, equal opportunities, social justice, and the provision of basic needs for a dignified life. A citizen shall not be discriminated against due to his faith or [religious] practices, and shall not be restricted in his private or public life. A state that rejects discrimination and forbids torture, seeing it as a crime.

5. A state based on dialogue and participation rather than monopoly, exclusion, and domination. [A state] in which all [citizens] take an equal part in construction, defense, and the enjoyment of wealth and resources, and undertake to respect the rights of [fellow citizens, regardless of] their ethnicity, religion, or school of thought, and [to respect] the cultural and social uniqueness of these [groups] and their freedom to express that uniqueness. Acknowledging this diversity is enriching, and is the continuation of a long history of coexistence, as part of dignified human tolerance.

6. A state in which the people is the sovereign and decision-maker, and chooses its own way and future without the guardianship of a tyrannical ruler, or of a single party or ruling group.

7. A state that respects institutions and is based on the separation of the legislative, judicial, and executive branches, whose officials are at the service of the people, and whose constitution defines [officials'] authority and the mechanisms that hold them to account. [A state] whose armed forces and security apparatuses [operate] to defend the homeland and the people, rather than the authority or the regime, and do not interfere in the political contest between the parties and national forces.

8. A state that purges terrorism and combats it; respects international contracts, conventions, alliances, and agreements; and is a [source] of security and stability in its regional and international environment. [A state] that maintains the best equal relations with its [Arab] brethren, chiefly with neighboring Lebanon, whose people, like the Syrian people, has suffered under the rule of corruption and tyranny. [A state] that works to realize the strategic interests of its people and to restore its occupied land by all legal means, and which supports the legal rights of the brethren Palestinian people.

9. A state of justice and rule of law, where there is no room for grudges, blood feuds, or [other forms of] vengeance. Even those whose hands are stained with the blood of the

people, from any group, should have the right to receive a fair trial at the hands of a fair, free, and independent judiciary.

10. A state of cooperation, camaraderie, and love among members of the greater Syrian family, under the auspices of a complete national reconciliation, which eliminates all the false excuses that the regime of corruption and tyranny used to scare the sons of the homeland from one another, with the aim of extending its rule and control over all.

These are our views and ambitions for the future we long for, and this is our pledge and charter before Allah, our people, and all. This is the view we stress today, after a decades-long history of national activity, since the movement was founded by the late Dr. Mustafa Al-Siba'i in 1945. We have [already] presented [this view] openly in the 2001 Charter of National Honor, in our 2004 political platform, and in official documents approved by the [Muslim Brothers] on various social and national issues.

Our hearts are open and our hands reach out to all our brethren and partners in our beloved homeland, so that [Syria] can occupy a proper place among the civilized human societies. [As Allah said in the Koran:] "And cooperate in righteousness and piety, but do not cooperate in sin and aggression. And fear Allah; indeed, Allah is severe in penalty." [Koran 5:2].

Bibliography

Ababsa, Myriam. "Agrarian Counter-Reform in Syria (2000–2010)." In *Agriculture and Reform in Syria*, edited by Raymond Hinnebusch, Atieh El Hindi, Mounzer Khaddam, and Myriam Ababsa. Boulder, CO: Lynne Rienner, 2011.

Ababsa, Myriam. "The Shi'i Mausoleums of Raqqa." In *Demystifying Syria*, edited by Fred H. Lawson. London: Saqi Books, 2009.

Abboud, Samer. "The Transition Paradigm and the Case of Syria." In *Syria's Economy and the Transition Paradigm*, edited by Samer Abboud and Ferdinand Arslanian. Boulder, CO: Lynne Rienner, 2009.

Abboud, Samer N., and Fred H. Lawson. "Antinomies of Economic Governance in Contemporary Syria." In *Governance in the Middle East and North Africa*, edited by Abbas Kadhim. London: Routledge, 2012.

Abd-Allah, Umar. *The Islamic Struggle in Syria*. Berkeley, CA: Mizan Press, 1983.

al-Ahsan, Syed Aziz. "Economic Policy and Class Structure in Syria: 1958–1980." *International Journal of Middle East Studies* 16 (August 1984).

Alantar, O. Zeynep Oktav. "The October 1998 Crisis: A Change of Turkish Foreign Policy toward Syria?" *Cahiers d'etudes sur la Mediterranee Orientale et le monde Turco-Iranien* no. 31 (2001).

Alhaj, Abdulrahman. *State and Community: The Political Aspirations of Religious Groups in Syria 2000–2010*. London: Strategic Research and Communication Centre, n.d.

Altunisik, Meliha Benli, and Ozlem Tur. "From Distant Neighbors to Partners? Changing Syrian-Turkish Relations." *Security Dialogue* 37 (June 2006).

Armanazi, Ghayth N. "Syrian Foreign Policy at the Crossroads." In *State and Society in Syria and Lebanon*, edited by Youssef M. Choueiri. New York: St. Martin's Press, 1993.

Arslanian, Ferdinand. "Growth in Transition and Syria's Economic Performance." In *Syria's Economy and the Transition Paradigm*, edited by Samer Abboud and Ferdinand Arslanian. Boulder, CO: Lynne Rienner, 2009.

Aykan, Mahmut Bali. "The Turkish-Syrian Crisis of October 1998: A Turkish View." *Middle East Policy* 6 (June 1999).

Balanche, Fabrice. *La Region Alaouite et le Pouvoir Syrien*. Paris: Editions Karthala, 2006.

Baram, Amazia. "Ideology and Power Politics in Syrian-Turkish Relations 1968–1984." In *Syria under Assad*, edited by Moshe Ma'oz and Avner Yaniv. New York: St. Martin's Press, 1986.

Batatu, Hanna. "Some Observations on the Social Roots of Syria's Ruling, Military Group and the Causes for Its Dominance." *Middle East Journal* 35 (Summer 1981).

Batatu, Hanna. "Syria's Muslim Brethren." *MERIP Reports* no. 110 (November–December 1982).

Batatu, Hanna. *Syria's Peasantry, the Descendants of Its Lesser Rural Notables and Their Politics.* Princeton, NJ: Princeton University Press, 1999.

Bolukbasi, Suha. "Ankara, Damascus, Baghdad and the Regionalization of Turkey's Kurdish Secessionism." *Journal of South Asian and Middle Eastern Studies* 14 (Summer 1991).

Böttcher, Annabelle. *Syrische Religionspolitik unter Asad.* Freiburg, Germany: Arnold Bergsträsser Institut, 1998.

Carr, David W. "Capital Flows and Development in Syria." *Middle East Journal* 34 (Autumn 1980).

Drysdale, Alasdair. "The Regional Equalization of Health Care and Education in Syria since the Ba'thi Revolution." *International Journal of Middle East Studies* 13 (February 1981).

Drysdale, Alasdair. "The Succession Question in Syria." *Middle East Journal* 39 (Spring 1985).

Drysdale, Alasdair. "The Syrian Armed Forces in National Politics: The Role of the Geographic and Ethnic Periphery." In *Soldiers, Peasants and Bureaucrats,* edited by Roman Kolkowicz and Andrzej Korbonski. London: George Allen and Unwin, 1982.

Ehteshami, Anoushiravan, and Raymond A. Hinnebusch. *Iran and Syria.* London: Routledge, 1997.

Freedman, Robert O. "Russia and the Middle East under Putin." *Ortadogu Etutleri* 2 (July 2010).

Freedman, Robert O. "Russian Policy toward the Middle East: The Yeltsin Legacy and the Putin Challenge." *Middle East Journal* 55 (Winter 2001).

Gauthier, Julie. "The 2004 Events in al-Qamishli: Has the Kurdish Question Erupted in Syria?" In *Demystifying Syria*, edited by Fred H. Lawson. London: Saqi Books, 2009.

George, Alan. *Syria: Neither Bread nor Freedom.* London: Zed Books, 2003.

Ginat, Rami. "The Soviet Union and the Syrian Ba'th Regime: From Hesitation to Rapprochement." *Middle Eastern Studies* 26 (April 2000).

Golan, Galia. "Syria and the Soviet Union since the Yom Kippur War." *Orbis* 117 (Winter 1978).

Goodarzi, Jubin M. *Syria and Iran.* London: Tauris Academic, 2006.

Gottheil, Fred. "Iraqi and Syrian Socialism: An Economic Appraisal." *World Development* 9 (September–October 1981).

Haddad, Bassam. "The Political Economy of Syria: Realities and Challenges." *Middle East Policy* 18 (Summer 2011).

Haddad, Bassam. "Syria's Curious Dilemma." *Middle East Report* no. 236 (Fall 2005).

al-Hardan, Anaheed. "A Year On: The Palestinians in Syria." *Syrian Studies Association Newsletter* 17 (2012).

Haugbolle, Sune. *The Alliance between Iran, Syria and Hizbollah.* DIIS Report No. 2006:10. Copenhagen: Danish Institute for International Studies, November 2006.

Hersh, Seymour M. "Syria Calling." *The New Yorker*, April 6, 2009.

Heydemann, Steven. "Taxation without Representation." In *Rules and Rights in the Middle East*, edited by Ellis Goldberg, Resat Kasaba, and Joel S. Migdal. Seattle: University of Washington Press, 1993.

Hinnebusch, Raymond A. "The Political Economy of Economic Liberalization in Syria." *International Journal of Middle East Studies* 27 (August 1995).

Hinnebusch, Raymond. "Syria under Bashar." In *Syrian Foreign Policy and the United States: From Bush to Obama*, edited by Raymond Hinnebusch, Marwan J. Kabalan, Bassma Kodmani, and David Lesch. Boulder, CO: Lynne Rienner, 2010.

Hirschfeld, Yair. "The Odd Couple: Ba'athist Syria and Khomaini's Iran." In *Syria under Assad*, edited by Moshe Ma'oz and Avner Yaniv. New York: St. Martin's Press, 1986.

Holliday, Joseph. *Syria's Armed Opposition*. Middle East Security Report No. 3. Washington, DC: Institute for the Study of War, March 2012.

Husaini, Ishak Musa. *The Moslem Brethren*. Beirut: Khayat's, 1956.

International Crisis Group. "Engaging Syria? U.S. Constraints and Opportunities." *Middle East Report* no. 83 (February 11, 2009).

International Crisis Group. "Restarting Israeli-Syrian Negotiations." *Middle East Report* no. 63 (April 10, 2007).

International Crisis Group. "Syria after Lebanon, Lebanon after Syria." *Middle East Report* no. 39 (April 12, 2005).

International Crisis Group. "Uncharted Waters: Thinking through Syria's Dynamics." *Middle East Briefing* no. 31 (November 24, 2011).

Ismail, Salwa. "Changing Social Structure, Shifting Alliances and Authoritarianism in Syria." In *Demystifying Syria*, edited by Fred H. Lawson. London: Saqi Books, 2009.

Kanovsky, E. *Economic Development of Syria*. Tel Aviv: University Publishing Projects, 1977.

Karsh, Efraim. *Soviet Policy towards Syria since 1970*. London: Macmillan, 1991.

Katz, Mark N. "Putin's Foreign Policy toward Syria." *Middle East Review of International Affairs* 10 (March 2006).

Kaufman, Asher. " 'Let Sleeping Dogs Lie': On Ghajar and Other Anomalies in the Syria-Lebanon-Israel Tri-Border Region." *Middle East Journal* 63 (Autumn 2009).

Kaufman, Asher. "Who Owns the Shebaa Farms? Chronicle of a Territorial Dispute." *Middle East Journal* 56 (Autumn 2002).

Keilany, Ziad. "Land Reform in Syria." *Middle Eastern Studies* 16 (October 1980).

Keilany, Ziad. "Socialism and Economic Change in Syria." *Middle Eastern Studies* 9 (January 1973).

Khader, Bichara. "Propriete agricole et reform agraire en Syrie." *Civilisations* 25 (1975).

Kienle, Eberhard. *Ba'th v. Ba'th: The Conflict between Syria and Iraq 1968–1989*. London: I. B. Tauris, 1990.

Kota, Suechika. "The Syrian Muslim Brotherhood and Mustafa al-Siba'i." *Asian and African Area Studies* 2 (2002).

Kushner, David. "Conflict and Accommodation in Turkish-Syrian Relations." In *Syria under Assad*, edited by Moshe Ma'oz and Avner Yaniv. New York: St. Martin's Press, 1986.

Lawson, Fred H. *Constructing International Relations in the Arab World*. Stanford, CA: Stanford University Press, 2006.

Lawson, Fred H. *Why Syria Goes to War*. Ithaca, NY: Cornell University Press, 1996.

Leenders, Reinoud. " 'Regional Conflict Formations': Is the Middle East Next?" *Third World Quarterly* 28 (May 2007).

Lesch, Ann Mosely. "Contrasting Reactions to the Persian Gulf Crisis." *Middle East Journal* 45 (Winter 1991).

Lesch, David W., Syria: *The Fall of the House of Assad*. New Haven: Yale University Press, 2012.

Leverett, Flynt. *Inheriting Syria*. Washington, DC: Brookings Institution Press, 2005.

Lobmeyer, Hans Günter. "Al-dimuqratiyya hiyya al-Hall? The Syrian Opposition at the End of the Asad Era." In *Contemporary Syria*, edited by Eberhard Kienle. London: British Academic Press, 1994.

Lobmeyer, Hans Günter. "Islamic Ideology and Secular Discourse: The Islamists of Syria." *Orient* 32 (September 1991).

Longuenesse, Elisabeth. "The Class Nature of the State in Syria." *MERIP Reports* no. 77 (May 1979).

Lund, Aron. *Divided They Stand: An Overview of Syria's Political Opposition Factions*. Uppsala, Sweden: Foundation for European Progressive Studies, May 2012.

Marschall, Christin. "Syria-Iran: A Strategic Alliance, 1979–1991." *Orient* 33 (September 1992).

Mayer, Thomas. "The Islamic Opposition in Syria, 1961–1982." *Orient* 32 (December 1983).

Metral, Francoise. "Le monde rural syrien a l'ere des reformes." In *La Syrie d-Aujourd'hui*, edited by André Raymond. Paris: CNRS, 1980.

Middle East Watch. *Syria Unmasked*. New Haven, CT: Yale University Press, 1991.

Moussalli, Ahmad S. "The Geopolitics of Syrian-Iraqi Relations." *Middle East Policy* 7 (October 2000).

Muslih, Muhammad. "Syria and Turkey: Uneasy Relations." In *Reluctant Neighbor: Turkey's Role in the Middle East*, edited by Henri J. Barkey. Washington, DC: United States Institute of Peace Press, 1996.

Olson, Robert. *Turkey-Iran Relations, 1979–2004*. Costa Mesa, CA: Mazda, 2005.

Olson, Robert. "Turkey-Iran Relations, 2000–2001." *Middle East Policy* 9 (June 2002).

Olson, Robert. "Turkey-Syria Relations, 1997 to 2000." *Orient* 42 (March 2001).

Olson, Robert. "Turkey-Syria Relations since the Gulf War: Kurds and Water." *Middle East Policy* 5 (May 1997).

Olson, Robert. *Turkey's Relations with Iran, Syria, Israel and Russia, 1991–2000*. Costa Mesa, CA: Mazda, 2001.

Pace, Joe, and Joshua Landis. "The Syrian Opposition." In *Demystifying Syria*, edited by Fred H. Lawson. London: Saqi Books, 2009.

Perthes, Volker. "The Syrian Private Industrial and Commercial Sectors and the State." *International Journal of Middle East Studies* 24 (May 1992).

Petran, Tabitha. *Syria*. New York: Praeger, 1972.

Pierret, Thomas. "Sunni Clergy Politics in the Cities of Ba'thi Syria." In *Demystifying Syria*, edited by Fred H. Lawson. London: Saqi Books, 2009.

Pierret, Thomas. *Baas et Islam en Syrie*. Paris: Presses Universitaires de France, 2011.

Pierret, Thomas, and Kjetil Selvik. "Limits of Authoritarian Upgrading in Syria." *International Journal of Middle East Studies* 41 (November 2009).

Rabil, Robert G. *Syria, the United States and the War on Terror in the Middle East*. Westport, CT: Praeger Security International, 2006.

Rabinovich, Itamar. *Syria under the Ba'th 1963–66: The Army-Party Symbiosis*. New York: Halsted Press, 1972.

Reissner, Johannes. *Ideologie und Politik der Muslimbrüder Syriens*. Freiburg, Germany: Klaus Schwarz Verlag, 1980.

Robins, Philip. "Turkish Foreign Policy since 2002." *International Affairs* 83 (March 2007).

Seale, Patrick. *The Struggle for Syria*. New Haven, CT: Yale University Press, 1986.

Shlaim, Avi. "Husni Zaim and the Plan to Resettle Palestinian Refugees in Syria." *Middle East Focus* 9 (Fall 1986).

Springborg, Robert. "Baathism in Practice: Agriculture, Politics and Political Culture in Syria and Iraq." *Middle Eastern Studies* 17 (April 1981).

Spyer, Jonathan. "The Syrian Opposition before and after the Outbreak of the 2011 Uprising." *Middle East Review of International Affairs* 15 (September 2011).

Stanley, Bruce. "Drawing from the Well: Syria in the Persian Gulf." *Journal of South Asian and Middle Eastern Studies* 14 (Winter 1990).

Stenberg, Leif. "Naqshbandiyya in Damascus: Strategies to Establish and Strengthen the Order in a Changing Society." In *Naqshbandis in Western and Central Asia*, edited by Elisabeth Ozdalga. Istanbul: Swedish Research Institute, 1999.

Tabler, Andrew. *In the Lion's Den*. Chicago: Lawrence Hill, 2011.

Teitelbaum, Joshua. "The Muslim Brotherhood and the 'Struggle for Syria', 1947–1958." *Middle Eastern Studies* 40 (May 2004).

van Dam, Nikolaos. "Middle Eastern Political Clichés: 'Takriti' and 'Sunni Rule' in Iraq; 'Alawi Rule' in Syria—A Critical Appraisal." *Orient* 21 (January 1980).

van Dam, Nikolaos. *The Struggle for Power in Syria*. 4th ed. London: I. B. Tauris, 2011.

Vavilov, V. V. "The Nature of the Socioeconomic Changes in Syria." In *Problems of the Economy and History of the Countries of the Near and Middle East*, edited by E. S. Tefimov et al. Washington, DC: Joint Publications Research Service, 1967.

Weismann, Itzchak. "Sa'id Hawwa: The Making of a Radical Muslim Thinker in Modern Syria." *Middle Eastern Studies* 29 (October 1993).

Wieland, Carsten. *A Decade of Lost Chances*. Seattle: Cune Press, 2012.

Winder, R. Bayly. "Islam as the State Religion: A Muslim Brotherhood in Syria." *Muslim World* 44 (July 1954).

Zambelis, Chris. "The Turn to Armed Rebellion in Syria: The Rise of the Free Syrian Army." *Terrorism Monitor* 9 (December 16, 2011).

Zisser, Eyal. *Commanding Syria: Bashar al-Asad and the First Years in Power*. London: I. B. Tauris, 2007.

Zisser, Eyal. "Syria, the Ba'th Regime and the Islamic Movement." *Muslim World* 95 (January 2005).

Zisser, Eyal. "Syria and the Gulf Crisis." *Orient* 34 (December 1993).

Index

About the Author

FRED H. LAWSON is Lynn T. White, Jr. professor of government at Mills College. He is author of *Constructing International Relations in the Arab World* (Stanford University Press, 2006) and *Why Syria Goes to War* (Cornell University Press, 1996), and editor of *Demystifying Syria* (London: Saqi Books, 2009). He was Fulbright lecturer in international relations at the University of Aleppo in 1992–1993 and visiting fellow at the Georgetown University School of Foreign Service in Qatar in 2009–2010. From 2009 to 2011, he served as president of the Syrian Studies Association.